In Search of Wholeness

African American Teachers and Their Culturally Specific Classroom Practices

Edited by Jacqueline Jordan Irvine

palgrave

First published 2002 by PALGRAVE™
175 Fifth Avenue, New York, N.Y.10010 and
Houndmills, Basingstoke, Hampshire RG21 6XS.
Companies and representatives throughout the world.

PALGRAVE is the new global publishing imprint of St. Martin's Press LLC Scholarly and Reference Division and Palgrave Publishers Ltd. (formerly Macmillan Press LTD).

ISBN 0–312–29462–X hardback
ISBN 0–312–29561–8 paperback

Library of Congress Cataloging-in-Publication Data
In search of wholeness : African American teachers and their culturally specific classroom practices / edited by Jacqueline Jordan Irvine.
    p. cm.
    Includes bibliographical references and index.
    ISBN 0–312–29462–X (hard)—ISBN 0–312–29561–8 (pbk.)
    1. African American teachers—Attitudes—Case studies. 2. Teacher effectiveness—United States—Case studies. 3. Race awareness—United States—Case studies. I. Irvine, Jacqueline Jordan.

LC2731.I5 2002
371.1'0089'96073—dc21
                                                            2001057532

A catalogue record for this book is available from the British Library.

Design by Letra Libre, Inc.

First edition: May 2002
10 9 8 7 6 5 4 3 2 1

Printed in the United States of America.

Dedication
To my Emory University students
whose brilliance, hard work, enthusiasm,
and commitment to children whom schools have failed
continue to inspire and motivate me.

CONTENTS

FOREWORD

James W. Fraser

There are no more urgent educational issues before us today than those discussed in this book. Anyone who talks about improving student achievement and fails to attend to the issues addressed here is simply fooling themselves. If we (perhaps especially those of us who are European Americans) want to get serious about improving the educational success of students in today's schools, *In Search of Wholeness: African American Teachers and Their Culturally Specific Classroom Practices* offers a good place to start.

The very important current national attention on high standards for all students will only make a difference if we who are educators find the ways to actually help our students reach the standards. And so the focus must properly move from the instruction we offer to the student learning we actually secure. We will only succeed at this latter venture if we can effectively connect with our students. *In Search of Wholeness* is about making that connection. It describes ways in which teachers can take seriously their own cultural backgrounds and then find ways to connect with students of similar and of quite different cultural traditions. Culturally responsive pedagogy is pedagogy that takes students seriously. Teachers who implement what can be learned from these pages will be teachers who succeed at the most basic educational goal—ensuring academic success on the part of all of their students.

The title of this volume, *In Search of Wholeness,* tells a great deal about its focus. We live in a society that is fractured in so many different ways. And too often we have schools that replicate the divisions of the larger society. But if we are to improve our schools, if we are to offer our young people the kind of education that they need to successfully participate in the nation's economy and in our democracy, then we need schools that find ways to heal the divides that permeate our society.

Some of the first healing that needs to take place is in teachers themselves. Indeed, if I were to summarize the chapters that are offered here it might be to say that they lead to an important conclusion: we need whole/healthy urban teachers far more than we have understood. In describing the work of Emory University's Center for Urban Learning/Teaching and Urban Research in Education and Schools (CULTURES) that motivated the studies reported here, Jacqueline Jordan Irvine notes how the authors were motivated to "investigate and reflect upon how teachers' cultural experience and prior socialization affect the manner in which they view their profession and practice their craft." What could be more obvious?—the culture of the teacher, as much as her or his psychological make up, prior experiences in school, and educational attainment, help shape their future teaching. And a teacher, of any culture, who cannot reflect carefully on their own cultural experiences is not going to have the cultural and emotional health to create a healthy classroom.

So, what is a healthy/whole urban teacher? One who knows her/himself. One who has taken the time, energy, discipline to examine her/himself—especially in relationship to their own race and racial identity and in relationship to the race and racial identity of their students. In other words, a healthy and whole teacher is a culturally responsive teacher.

Each of the chapters describe this wholeness and this self-examination in slightly different words. Gretchen McAllister speaks of "self-acceptance," and the development of "non-racist attitudes." Franita Ware describes teacher's beliefs about themselves and their ethic of caring. Patricia M. Cooper talks about "authority and its meaning across cultures." For Gloria Harper Lee the emphasis is on "efficacy." Kim Nesta Archung looks at the need for teachers who are pioneers, learners, and risk-takers throughout their careers. Maria Leonora Lockaby Karunuñgan offers a sobering reflection on the importance of community support for any teacher. Finally Jacqueline Jordan Irvine reminds us of the African American tradition of "other mothering," in which demanding the best is an honored calling.

Each of these authors brings a slightly different emphasis to the conversation. But all of them are united in their concern with the needs for teacher health and teacher wholeness before healthy and whole schools can be created. This is not, "I'm OK, You're OK." This is not a "feel good" approach to teaching. It is something much tougher. And its primary focus is always student learning and effective classroom practice. A whole teacher is an effective teacher. The chapters offered here call on all of us who are teachers to strive for what is ultimately a hard won sense of self and self-acceptance in terms of race, culture, class, and gender. And they make it exceedingly clear that this kind of healthy self acceptance can only come after a teacher has offered the same level of respect and acceptance to her or his students through taking the time and intellectual effort for a deep immersion in the culture of the students whether or not that culture matches the culture of the teacher.

It is this sort of self-examination that will allow what Paulo Freire called dialogue. Dialogue is not chat. It is certainly not teacher silence, though it has sometimes been misunderstood in that way. Dialogue, for Paulo Freire, is a carefully disciplined ability to speak with confidence and listen and engage with students with respect; respect for who the student is and for who the teacher is and for the unique gifts that each brings to the conversation. A respectful teacher must, therefore, know subject matter for it is not respectful to students to fail to teach what the students need to know. But a respectful teacher must know more than subject matter. They must also know their students and the cultural setting in which a specific group of young people have been learning prior to their arrival in a specific classroom. So, Ware speaks specifically of "mutual respect" as the goal. And mutual respect demands the creation of a classroom with high standards for student and teacher.

As I have read these chapters I have become more and more convinced that one should never trust a teacher who is not self-accepting, no matter how dedicated they may be. A teacher who does not accept themselves is sure to fail at accepting their students, especially if their students are from a different culture than they are. They may fail to hold the students to sufficiently high standards. They may fall into the trap of "understanding their students to death," rather than developing the skills in students that will allow them to succeed in multiple cultural contexts. But it is only through the kind of healthy respect within and across cultures that is illustrated in these pages that successful teaching will take place.

In reading the wonderful essays in this volume I would urge readers to keep a couple of important things in mind. First, culturally responsive pedagogy is a different thing from multicultural education. Both are very important, but I think we mix them at our peril. Multicultural education, which has received far more attention, focuses primarily on the curriculum; on the what is to be taught question. At minimum, multicultural education focuses on a commitment to have a curriculum that reflects the diversity of students in a classroom and the diversity of students in the nation and world, even if the classroom is far from being diverse. For some of us, multicultural education goes beyond diversity to reflect a specifically anti-racist stance and a consideration of the issues of power and oppression that always accompany diversity, however much we might hide them.

Culturally responsive pedagogy, on the other hand, as its name implies, focuses much more on the issue of pedagogy. Instead of the curriculum, this movement looks at teachers and teaching. Culturally responsive pedagogy is concerned with issues of sensibility and style; on how one teaches and moves beyond teacher knowledge to focus on teacher practice. Ultimately it focuses on the teacher's soul, the health and hard won integrated wholeness that is essential if one is to understand oneself and one's relation to students, some of whom will be similar and some of whom will be quite different from any individual teacher.

As one begins reading *In Search of Wholeness*, it is also useful to remember that this book offers the reader a very different dialogue from the dominant dialogue of educational reform in this country today. In the course of my professional work I spend a great deal of time in state and national meetings focused on questions of school reform and improving student achievement. I am quite certain that the words "culturally responsive pedagogy" have not been uttered at very many of them. In fact, I am fairly certain that the words "culture" or "responsive pedagogy," have not been uttered with any noticeable frequency. I suspect I am not alone in this experience.

The current focus seems to be: Teach the subjects to the kids. Test them. Teach them some more until they learn enough to pass the test. Now I am in favor of teaching. And I am in favor of high standards. But I am deeply worried about a moment when attention to diversity and respect—for culture or for students or for teachers—is far back on the agenda. Until that changes, too many students are going to be seen as having failed to meet the standards because their schools and teachers failed to engage them in a culturally appropriate and respectful way.

The notion of cultural synchronization, which the authors of these pages offer us, is a very hopeful approach to this sad state of affairs. It is hopeful because it allows for change. It allows for change in teachers who could be written off as hopeless by some of our progressive, anti-racist colleagues. It allows the hope that people who are unresponsive do not have to stay that way. And it focuses our attention on changes at the grass roots, where all real change must come about.

The current state of American education is not going to change because scholars decry it, however important good scholarship may be. It is going to change because small clusters of academics and teachers and parents, and community-based organizations simply start to change, and as they change demand more and more from the institutions nearby. It is going to change because of a new movement of people who care about this nation's children, all of the nation's children. It is going to change because groups of teachers in schools across the country find the ways to develop culturally responsive approaches to student success. This volume, if it is read and considered carefully, represents a very important step in building that new movement. I hope it will receive the widespread attention that it deserves.

In Search of Wholeness

Introduction

THE COMMON EXPERIENCE

Jacqueline Jordan Irvine

THE CULTURES EXPERIENCE:
A PROFESSIONAL DEVELOPMENT PROGRAM
FOR EXPLORING CULTURAL DIVERSITY IN SCHOOLS

T he ways in which African American teachers think about their practice became clear to me over a four-year period (1994–98) in which
I directed a professional development center I founded at Emory
University called the Center for Urban Learning/Teaching and Urban Research in Education and Schools (CULTURES). The chapters in this book
all share a common setting and background. The teachers who are the
focus of the case studies were participants in the CULTURES program,
and most of the chapter authors assisted in the planning and implementing of the professional development curriculum.

CULTURES was designed as a response to the demographic challenges associated with the increasingly culturally diverse public school systems. The
program assisted practicing elementary and middle school teachers to work
effectively with culturally diverse students and to enhance the quality of
teaching and learning in their urban schools. CULTURES provided a supportive, nonevaluative, and nonthreatening environment in which teachers
learned to transform their classrooms and schools into learning communities
for students of color who have heretofore experienced only school failure.

Unlike traditional teacher education and inservice staff development
programs, which are often short term and decontextualized, the professional development activities in CULTURES centered around the estab-
lishment and maintenance of ongoing teacher cohort groups that involved

a combination of theoretical knowledge, demonstration, and practice of skills in actual classrooms. The professional development curriculum connected teachers' classroom experiences with current research and knowledge. CULTURES provided teachers with knowledge of and experience in five reconceptualized roles based on the National Board for Professional Teaching Standards (NBTPS): teachers as culturally responsive pedagogists, school systemic reformers, community members, reflective practitioners, and pedagogical content specialists.

Teachers as Culturally Responsive Pedagogists

NBTPS core principle: Teachers are committed to students and their learning and are aware of the influence of context and culture on students' behavior.

The term "culturally responsive pedagogy" is used interchangeably with several terms, like "culturally responsible," "culturally appropriate," "culturally congruent," "culturally compatible," and "culturally relevant," to describe a variety of effective teaching approaches in culturally diverse classrooms. These terms all imply that teachers should be responsive to their students by incorporating elements of the students' cultures in their teaching. The teaching effectiveness research literature informs us that a responsive teacher is sensitive to the needs, interests, and abilities of *all* students, their parents, and communities.

The tenets of a culturally responsive pedagogy[1] suggest that teachers should: (1) have an attitude of respect for cultural differences, a belief that all students are capable of learning, and a sense of efficacy; (2) know the cultural resources that their students bring to class and be aware of the culture of their classroom; (3) implement an enriched curriculum for all students; (4) build bridges between the instructional content, materials, and methods, and the cultural background of their students; and (5) be aware of cultural differences when evaluating students. CULTURES incorporated the principles of culturally responsive pedagogy in its curriculum by recognizing that the purpose of culturally responsive pedagogy is the maximization of learning for culturally diverse students.

Teachers as Systemic Reformers

NBPTS core principle: Teachers are members of learning communities. They are knowledgeable about specialized school and community resources that can be engaged for their students' benefit and are skilled at employing such resources as needed.

Calls for school improvement increasingly speak of the need for systemic reform. Systemic reform involves a comprehensive approach to restructuring schools and is often referred to by such loosely-defined terms as "school-based management," "site-based governance," "shared decision making," and "teacher empowerment." Initial results from these types of promising systemic change programs indicate that teachers are unfamiliar with the role of systemic reformer and need professional development in the area of organizational theory, diagnosis, and change. Excessive isolation, lack of experience in collegial inquiry, inadequate pre and inservice preparation, and inherent role conflicts have left teachers unprepared to assume a leadership role in the systemic reform movement.

CULTURES' systemic reform module noted the importance of developing teacher readiness for school change. Readiness involves acquiring knowledge of the change literature, building networks of colleagues that support change and assist in the resolution of anxiety that accompany it, planning for change, developing vision, identifying resources, and becoming comfortable with new roles.

Teachers as Members of Caring Communities

NBTPS core principle: Teachers are members of learning communities.

Teaching is about caring relationships. The professional development needs of teachers of culturally diverse students must involve and incorporate personalized and caring instructional strategies such as cooperative learning, whole-class discussions, debates, and group projects. More importantly, teachers need assistance with authentic instruction that helps students construct meaning and produce knowledge that has value and meaning beyond simply passing a test in the classroom.

In addition to becoming vital members of caring school communities, teachers of diverse urban students must reach out to the home community of their students. Unfortunately, some teachers believe that culturally diverse parents and their children's communities are hostile, confrontational, and the causes of their children's lack of achievement.

CULTURES' professional development activities enabled teachers to embrace their roles as members of caring communities. Activities related to this module included visiting homes, exploring the communities of diverse students, interviewing residents and community leaders, and researching the community's history. This module built on the work of the Experiential Curricular Project at Stanford, in which teachers were trained in community-building pedagogical strategies.[2]

Teachers as Reflective Practitioners

NBPTS core principle: Teachers think systematically about their practice and learn from experience.

Because there are no quick and simple solutions, no single program or packaged professional development program, no "one best way" to prepare teachers of culturally diverse students, the issue of reflection becomes critically important. Teachers must be reflective practitioners[3] with attitudes of open-mindedness and observational, communication, empirical, analytical, and problem-solving skills necessary to continually monitor, evaluate, and revise their own teaching practices.[4] Reflection enables teachers to probe the school, community, and home environments, searching for insights into the culturally diverse students' abilities, preferences, and motivations.

Teachers as Pedagogical Content Specialists

NBPTS core principles: Teachers know the subjects they teach and how to teach those subjects to students.
Teachers are responsible for managing and monitoring students' learning.

Previous attempts to develop teachers professionally have naively separated pedagogy from the content or subject to be taught. Shulman[5] has stressed the importance of pedagogical content knowledge defined as "that special amalgam of content and pedagogy that is uniquely the province of teachers."[6] This curriculum module of CULTURES attends to the presentation of subject matter content in culturally responsive ways and acquaints teachers with discipline-specific standards such as the standards outlined by National Council of Teachers of Mathematics (NCTM), Standards Project for English Language Arts, Geography Standards Project, and the content specific standards developed by the National Board for Professional Teaching Standards. The use of these content standards will assist teachers in answering critical questions like: What should students know and be able to do? What are teachers expected to teach?

A CULTURES training notebook was given to each teacher who participated in the program. This notebook contained the required readings as well as supplemental materials that might assist the participants in implementing the activities when they returned to their schools. There were ten four-hour sessions. The brief framework for the 40-hour curriculum included: readings, discussion of local and national demographic trends, local and national achievement data, cultural self-awareness activities, visits and interviews with teachers and students at culturally diverse schools, visits to Hispanic, Vietnamese, and African American communities, training in cooperative learning, learning styles and instructional strategies, sessions with content specialists on designing culturally responsive lessons, individual project presentations, and microteaching.

In summary, the chapters that are included in this edited volume evolved from the CULTURES professional development experiences. The work of the center motivated the authors to investigate and reflect upon how teachers' cultural experiences and prior socialization affect the manner in which they view their profession and practice their craft. Although it would be unfair to imply that teachers are solely a product of their cultural experiences, it would be equally naive to assume that their instructional behaviors and attitudes are uncontaminated by cultural variables and their ethnic and racial backgrounds. There is some evidence[7] to support the findings that teaching styles and teacher thinking are influenced by personal traits and characteristics like general intelligence, sense of efficacy, locus of control, cognitive style, gender, and social class. Consequently, the authors of this edited volume believe that it is important to discuss the implications associated with the supposition that teachers' race and culture are critical components of their conscious and subconscious selves and hence are manifest in the teaching act.

Research on African American teachers and other teachers of color is noted by its absence. Although the demographic data predict that educational researchers will increasingly study teachers and students of color, too few researchers understand "situated" pedagogy and how teachers, particularly African American teachers, "make meaning" within their classrooms and how they describe their teaching roles. African American teachers bring to their work values, opinions, and beliefs; their prior socialization and present experiences; and their race, gender, ethnicity, and social class.

These cultural attributes shape the ways African American teachers view their profession and practice their craft.

In calling for research in this area, Foster states, "Black teachers' unique historical experiences are either completely overlooked or amalgamated with those of white teachers. In those few instances where black teachers are visible, their cultural representations are biased by society's overarching racism. For the most part, these cultural representations continue to render black teachers invisible to students of their own or other ethnic backgrounds, while casting white females of other ethnic backgrounds as heroic figures."[8]

Most of the studies of teacher thinking, including the most recent "wisdom of practice" studies (Shulman, 1987), do not consider the influence of the racial identity of teachers on their belief systems. This is so despite the fact that the previous life experiences of teachers—their backgrounds, identities, cultures, and the critical incidents in their lives—help shape their view of teaching as well as essential elements of their practice.

The significance of this topic is related to researchers[9] who suggest that individuals do not become sensitive and open to different ethnic groups until and unless they develop a positive sense of self, including an awareness and acceptance of their own ethnic group. Cultural self-awareness—the recognition and enhancement of the cultural self—must become part of the professional development agenda of preservice and inservice teachers if issues of tolerance and sensitivity toward others are to be realized. More importantly, tolerance and sensitivity toward the cultural "other" are a necessary condition to the implementation of instructional programs aimed at increasing the achievement of students of color.

This edited volume, *In Search of Wholeness: African American Teachers and Their Culturally Specific Classroom Practices,* is a theoretical and practice-oriented treatment of how culture and race influence African American teachers. The book assumes that teachers cannot become fully functional persons and competent (whole) professionals if their cultural selves remained denied, hidden, and unexplored.

The book is divided into two parts. Part one, "The Salience of Race and Culture on Teachers and Teaching: Research and Theory," presents three chapters that review the literature related to teachers' race and culture. Part two, "The Stories of Culturally Responsive Teachers," includes five chapters that combine research studies about the integration of culture and race in teachers' lives, as well as the voices of the teachers whose stories are portrayed in the previous chapters.

Chapter one, "Multicultural Professional Development for African American Teachers: The Role of Process-Oriented Models," by Gretchen McAllister, examines and critiques stage-based models that have been used to describe the development of individual's racial and cultural selves. The three models include racial identity models, typologies of ethnicity models, and models of intercultural sensitivity. The chapter concludes with a discussion of how African American teachers' different levels of multicultural awareness are associated with cultural self-awareness, nonracist attitudes, and teaching effectiveness.

Chapter two, "Black Teachers' Perceptions of Their Professional Roles and Practices," by Franita Ware, reports and analyzes the existing research about African American teachers, particularly describing their ethic of caring and its influence on their teaching. Also discussed are the teachers' culturally specific instructional strategies and their relationship with the students' parents and community.

Chapter three, "Does Race Matter?: A Comparison of Effective Black and White Teachers of African American Students," by Patricia Cooper, discusses the implications of the decreasing number of African American teachers and the growing number of African American students in public schools. Specifically, the author compares the pedagogy and beliefs of effective white teachers with the pedagogy and beliefs of effective black teachers.

Chapter four, "The Development of Teacher Efficacy Beliefs: A Case Study of an African American Middle School Teacher," by Gloria Harper Lee, considers how teachers' perceptions of their sense of efficacy affect their general orientation toward themselves as professionals and toward their students. Teacher efficacy is a powerful construct related to student outcomes such as students' achievement and motivation. The issue of teacher efficacy is seldom looked at from the perspective of an African American teacher who teaches African American urban students. This case study focuses on this missing perspective and chronicles the teaching experiences of a documented and acknowledged efficacious teacher, Beverley Cockerham.

Chapter five, "The Influence of Professional Development on a Teacher's Changing Praxis: The Journey of an African American Teacher," by Kim Archung, centers on the professional development of a veteran African American teacher, Vivian Stephens, recording changes she adopted as well as dismissed in her classroom practice. The professional development journey of effective teachers has received some attention in the research and practice literature. However, little is known about the professional development of effective teachers of color, particularly African American teachers, and the influence of their education and training on their beliefs and instructional strategies.

Chapter six, "Chasing Hope through Culturally Responsive Praxis: One Master Teacher and her African American Eighth Grade Readers," by Maria Leonora Lockaby Karunuñgan, explores the philosophy, pedagogy, and praxis of one African American teacher, Patricia White, who teaches reading to African American eighth graders. The work illustrates how the quest for good teaching necessitates situating teachers in their milieus and reveals three major themes—adaptation, burnout, and hope. Current research indicates that in order to enhance the school achievement of culturally diverse students, teachers must organize and implement instruction that builds on their students' cultural backgrounds. However, there are few descriptions of how teachers actually use this culturally responsive principle in their classrooms. This chapter provides such a description.

Chapter seven, "African American Teachers' Culturally Specific Pedagogy: The Collective Stories," by Jacqueline Jordan Irvine, summarizes how African American teachers' ethnic identity, classroom practices, and beliefs are related to the achievement of their African American students. This chapter describes the culturally specific pedagogy of African American teachers who participated in CULTURES and the various ways they situate themselves professionally and personally to address the needs of their students. Irvine concludes that African American teachers not only viewed teaching as telling, guiding, and facilitating mastery of mandated content standards, but they also defined teaching as: caring, "other mothering," believing, disciplining, demanding the best, and as a calling.

Chapter eight, "Responses from the Teachers: Comments from Beverley Cockerham, Vivian Stephens, and Patricia White" is a response by the three teachers who were profiled in the case studies in part two of the book. The teachers report their perceptions about participating in the writing project, discuss the accuracy of the writers' work, and reflect on how their ethnic identity influences their professional roles as teachers.

Part One

THE SALIENCE OF RACE AND CULTURE
ON TEACHERS AND TEACHING:
RESEARCH AND THEORY

Chapter 1

MULTICULTURAL PROFESSIONAL DEVELOPMENT FOR AFRICAN AMERICAN TEACHERS

The Role of Process-Oriented Models

Gretchen McAllister

I t was the eighth day of the CULTURES professional development course, and I was driving four of the African American teachers to a cultural immersion experience in the Vietnamese community. As I turned into the driveway of the apartment complex, I felt excited for the teachers who had never met a Vietnamese family. We walked to the small first floor apartment where we met our interpreter, Lyn, a Vietnamese language specialist for the school district. Lyn knocked and a Vietnamese woman came to the door and invited us in. As the teachers attempted to enter the home, I noticed that the door was not completely opened because some of the family's furniture was behind the door, limiting access to the entrance. Lucinda, one of the African American teachers, was reluctant to enter and said, "I'll wait out here." It was obvious that Lucinda thought that she was too big to fit through the tiny entryway. Our Vietnamese host looked at Lucinda, pointed to the sliding glass door at the rear of the apartment, and said, "You too fat. Go around the back." Lucinda was dumbfounded, embarrassed, and appeared ready to leave the Vietnamese home; however, I encouraged her to enter through the sliding glass door. After about 25 minutes of eating Vietnamese snacks and learning about the culture, we left.

Lucinda did not talk about the incident publicly until I saw her a year later at a CULTURES follow-up meeting. She asked me if I remembered "that day." I knew what she was referring to—the visit to the Vietnamese home. She told me that incident was a critical point in her professional development and caused her to reflect deeply on issues of culture and ethnicity.

As an African American teacher working in a predominately low-income, African American school, the CULTURES experience generated questions for Lucinda about the role of race and culture in her classroom. She thought about issues such as: Was the Vietnamese woman who embarrassed her insensitive and racist? How do my Vietnamese students perceive me? How can I build community and connections with the increasing number of students from non-African American backgrounds? Lucinda's experience in particular, and her participation in the multicultural professional development program in general, gave her a context and a catalyst to begin rethinking about the role of race and culture in the teaching and learning processes.

For Lucinda, her African American ethnicity and culture became a salient aspect of her worldview and, more specifically, of her role as a teacher. Carter and Goodwin pointed out that the "racial identity levels of educators themselves influence how they perceive and interact with children of color."[1] Teachers' racial identities and worldviews influence their behaviors, attitudes, and cognitive frames,[2] which in turn shape their responses to and participation in professional development programs for multicultural education. When race and culture become central in a teacher's worldview, she is more apt to foster children's racial, ethnic, and cultural identities, respond proactively to crossracial and crosscultural interactions, and choose and implement curricula and pedagogy that is relevant for all students.[3]

Little is known about how teachers develop their worldviews and cross-cultural capabilities to effectively teach diverse students in their classrooms.[4] For example, what experiences in the CULTURES professional development program or the particular incident at the Vietnamese home described above caused Lucinda to think differently about race relations between herself and the Vietnamese community or about her students in her classroom?

The disciplines of counseling and intercultural relations offer some understanding about how people shift their interpretive frameworks. Stage-based models, or "process-orientated models," define a typical process that people undergo as they learn more about themselves and others as cultural beings. Little research exists that examines the use of such models in multicultural professional development or in the field of education. Examination of these models in relation to multicultural professional development may assist teachers and teacher educators to better understand the process of becoming multicultural as well as to build stronger racial, cultural, and ethnic identities for teachers and students.

This chapter will explore the development of a racial or ethnic identity, or a worldview in which race and culture are predominant lenses through which teachers understand their students. Identity and the development of a worldview is a complex process that is influenced by a variety of factors, such as prior socialization, history, family, social and political contexts, gender, race, and sexual orientation. These factors shape teachers' identities and the worldviews that subsequently inform their practice.

For example, historically, race and culture have played an important role in influencing black teachers' pedagogy, curriculum, and interactions in their classrooms and schools.[5] Historical educational researchers have documented African American teachers' strong racial identities.[6] Societal forces, such as institutionalized racism and segregation, forced African American teachers to deal with race and culture because these issues were salient in their lives. Ware in this volume describes how African American teachers acted as role models, promoted antiracist thinking, and practiced teaching in culturally relevant ways, such as developing caring, kin-like relationships and promoting high expectations. Teachers' focus on the development of a strong racial identity helped students to assess critically society and to develop proactive strategies to deal effectively with the racism in their environments. All of these factors fostered the academic and social success of their students.[7]

As we turn to the current context, we find African American teachers who are working in a variety of settings—in resegregated schools in urban communities, predominately white schools, or diverse schools with children from various linguistic, ethnic, and racial backgrounds. In addition, these African American teachers reflect their own personal histories and racial identities. What is the salience of race and culture in today's classrooms? How do teachers' worldviews shape their teaching? How can professional development assist teachers to explore issues related to their identity and other cultures? These questions have been examined mostly in the context of white teachers, predominately preservice teachers.[8] The focus on white educators is clearly related to researchers' and policy makers' concerns regarding white counselors'[9] and white teachers'[10] ability to work effectively with diverse populations. In addition, there is a common belief that people from marginalized groups may already be bicultural and have the necessary skills to interact effectively with people from diverse backgrounds. Some researchers, such as Bennett, have questioned this assumption. He argued that "marginalized people may understand and even respect differences with which they are familiar, but they may be unable to recognize or use this sensitivity as part of a generalized skill in adapting to cultural differences,"[11] such as African American teachers interacting with Vietnamese or Hispanic students and their families.

These concerns about African American teachers' sensitivities to other marginalized groups needs to be further explored in the research literature. Archung and Irvine in this volume point to the lack of work that has focused on the relevance of African American teachers' race and culture in the crosscultural learning process. Examination of the relationship between African American's worldviews and their classroom practices may expand our understanding of the role of racial, ethnic, and cultural identity in teachers' practices. For the most part African American history supports the proposition that race and culture continue to be notable elements of African American schooling experiences. What remains to be explored is how African American teachers will respond to the growing numbers of students whose cultures will be different from their own. A body of theory and research instructive in examining this issue is found in three models that look at the role of racial, ethnic, and cultural identity in the teaching and learning processes with children from diverse backgrounds. These three models are Cross' racial identity models, Banks' Typology of Ethnicity, and Bennett's developmental model of intercultural sensitivity.

RACIAL IDENTITY AND TEACHERS' PRACTICE

Research has pointed to the relationship between an increased understanding and belief in the salience of race and culture and one's practice in the classroom.[12] In order for teachers, including African American teachers, to be effective with diverse students, it is crucial that they first recognize and understand their own worldview, and then understand the worldviews of their students.[13] In addition, teachers must confront their own racism and biases,[14] learn about their students' cultures, and perceive the world through diverse cultural lenses.[15]

Though it is difficult to draw direct causal relationships between teachers' identities and worldviews and their practice, correlational studies have indicated that teachers who have a strong racial identity in which race and culture are salient lenses are more likely to foster effective teaching for all their students.[16] Teachers accomplish this task through fostering children's racial or cultural identity, responding proactively to crosscultural and crossracial situations, and designing and implementing pedagogy and curricula that is culturally responsive. In other words, they use "teaching that strives to maximize learning by using students' cultures as the basis for helping students to understand themselves and others, to structure social interactions and to conceptualize knowledge."[17]

Children's Identities

Teachers have been viewed as a key variable in a child's academic success. Irvine explains: "Teachers are significant others in their students' lives; as significant others, they affect the achievement and self-concept of their students, particularly Black students. Because schools are loosely coupled systems and teachers frequently operate autonomously and independently, their impact on the lives of students is perhaps greater than one might imagine."[18]

When teachers project a positive and healthy cultural and racial identity themselves, children are more likely to imitate it. A healthy ethnic identity helps those from oppressed groups deal more effectively with racism, prejudice, and discrimination. Gay points out that a positive ethnic identity can serve as protection from racist attacks. "This protection takes the form of being able to separate one's personal worth from the social problems encountered and to distinguish personal responsibilities from attempted impositions of blame by others."[19] Fostering a healthy identity helps children distinguish between a racist society and their own weaknesses and strengths. Moreover, teachers have opportunities to help children develop the ability to assess critically their world and understand oppression, such as racism and sexism.

Proactive Responses

African American teachers need a framework for understanding crossracial and crosscultural interactions in their classrooms.[20] Depending on their beliefs regarding children and learning, a teacher may misinterpret children's behaviors, their language, and their abilities. Different studies have shown that children are often placed in academic tracks and grouped based on teachers' subjective impressions of students' ability level, race, behavior, and even appearance.[21]

One important aspect of developing the skills, attitudes, and behaviors that are effective with children from various cultural backgrounds is knowledge of how teachers themselves have been socialized into a specific culture. Once teachers understand their own cultural socialization, they can address similarities and differences they share with their students' values, communication styles, and worldviews.[22] When teachers have some understanding of these interactions, they may be more comfortable in fostering discussions about race and diversity rather than shying away from controversial topics.[23] In addition, teachers may be more likely to address racist acts in their schools and classrooms and become advocates for students, particularly their students of color.[24]

Curriculum and Pedagogy

Research regarding effective teachers of diverse children has pointed to the importance of fostering curriculum and pedagogy that is culturally responsive.[25] For teachers to connect academic content to children's experiences, teachers need to understand multiple worldviews, especially when they may not share the children's experiences. Cross, Strauss, and Fhagen-Smith have described such awareness as "bridging."[26] This occurs when a Black person is able to immerse him or herself in another cultural or racial group's experiences without needing to give up or suppress his or her own identity. In other words, the African American teachers' self concept and racial identity are not threatened by their involvement, connection, or increased understanding of another racial or cultural group.

In addition, teachers need to recognize and choose materials that foster the healthy racial, ethnic, and cultural identities of their students. Tomlinson has found that when teachers choose literature that addresses different stages of children's ethnic identity development, children grow in their understanding of themselves as racial and cultural beings, as well as in their understanding of the societal dynamics of race relations.[27]

Relationship to Teacher Education

Although the factors described above are frequently espoused in teacher education, there is little empirical research about the process by which teachers, particularly African American teachers, develop their cultural, racial, and ethnic identities to effectively teach diverse students in their classrooms.[28] Cochran-Smith confirmed the importance of understanding teachers' beliefs about culture. She pointed out that, "it is less important for the successful teaching of diverse learners what the teacher's actual racial, cultural, or ethnic identity is and more important how she constructs knowledge of *self, other,* and *otherness.*"[29]

Inconsistent findings in the research have hindered the field of teacher education in developing effective strategies that produce desired changes in teachers' beliefs, attitudes, and behaviors that result in school success for culturally diverse students. Some educational researchers and practitioners have suggested helpful strategies that describe how a person can alter their beliefs regarding the saliency of race, ethnicity, or culture.[30] These strategies assist educators to construct learning experiences that foster more complex beliefs about the role of race, culture, and ethnicity in their lives, as well as beliefs, attitudes, and behaviors that foster effective teaching. However, more work is needed in this area of research.

PROCESS FRAMEWORKS

One conceptual framework that has not been thoroughly examined in multicultural teacher education research is process-oriented models. These type of models assist teacher educators and professional developers to better understand the change processes and assist teachers in becoming more effective with their diverse learners. Process-oriented models, which describe how people grow in terms of their cultural identities or worldviews, can assist educators in three areas: understanding teachers' behaviors (including resistance), sequencing course content, and creating conducive learning environments.

First, process-oriented models help situate teachers' behaviors, attitudes, and interactions with their students. They will interact with their students according to their understanding and beliefs regarding the salience of race and culture in the teaching and learning process. The models inform teacher educators about issues of resistance to multicultural education, as well as the persistence of a "colorblind" belief in which teachers claim that they do not see the relevance of race or culture in their classrooms.

A second advantage of process models is their structure for designing and sequencing effective course and program interventions. Researchers of multicultural education have noticed that most teachers, teacher educators, and crosscultural consultants do not connect topics and course purposes to an overall theory or some predefined structure.[31] Courses are often arranged in a topical or chronological order that may not support crosscultural development. For example, teachers may be plunged into a new cultural community before they have gained the ability to recognize their own or others' cultural views, norms, values, and biases. The structuring of topics and learning experiences along a process framework fosters environmental congruence[32] between students' levels of understanding and the course content and pedagogy. Some believe that such congruence can foster the development of crosscultural beliefs, attitudes, and behaviors.[33]

The third advantage of process models is that they provide instructional and pedagogical strategies to create conducive learning environments for students. In the case of the CULTURES professional development experience, teachers were provided opportunities to experience diversity, either indirectly, through reading or watching videos, or directly, by interacting with people from other cultures. Other learning strategies include reflection,[34] role playing,[35] consciousness-raising groups that promote self-awareness and self-assessment,[36] and community inquiry into questions concerning race, class, and culture.[37] Some researchers and educators nurture crosscultural growth by creating a balance between experiential learning and reflection,[38] and between support and challenge,[39] and by making sure that adequate time is given for the learning experience.[40]

Framework

In this section three different models of crosscultural development will be explored. They include Cross' racial identity development model, Banks' typology of ethnicity, and Bennett's developmental model of intercultural sensitivity. These models describe a process (often referred to in "stages") that is helpful in understanding how African American teachers change their behavior and attitudes about themselves and others as cultural beings.

Despite the fact that the models emanated from different disciplines, they share several characteristics, such as their structure. The structure of the models are similar in that they are all process-oriented cognitive models in which individuals move through a set of stages or statuses.[41] The stages progress from little differentiation or conception of complexity to higher levels of abstraction and differentiation.[42] According to the models, people move from a self-centered state to identification with society and eventually with the larger global community, thusly improving their ability to place their identities or those of others within an increasingly larger perspective. As people mature or move through the models they become increasingly "inclusive, discriminating and more integrative of experience"[43] until they approach a common end. The telos or end stage of each model contains capacities desired for teaching in a culturally diverse classroom, such as perspective-taking and reflection skills, but does not mean that learning stops. Rather, people recycle through parts of the learning process[44] as they experience new contexts, situations, or people that may cause them to reflect on the saliency of race and culture in their worldview. These later stages are considered desirable because ostensibly teachers have gained skills and understanding that facilitate the achievement of their culturally diverse students.[45]

Process models have their critics. These models have been accused of lacking empirical evidence, oversimplifying a complex problem,[46] generalizing across race and gender, and diminishing personal agency.[47] Some researchers believe that identity development is a complex process that involves many factors and needs to be viewed within the context of those factors, rather than through a single lens such as race.[48] Questions also have been raised regarding the broad application of ethnic identity and cultural awareness models to both majority and minority populations.[49] Another area of contention regarding these models concerns the lack of personal agency that Meyers et al. contend ignores the individual's ability to control their responses to the environment.[50] Despite these limitations, the process models should not be dismissed summarily and should be reviewed for their applicability and utility in teacher education research and practice in the area of cultural diversity.

THREE PROCESS MODELS OF ETHNIC AND RACIAL IDENTITY

Three process models, the racial identity development model, Banks' typology of ethnicity, and Bennett's developmental model of intercultural sensitivity, were selected because of their use in and application to the field of education. Each of the models will be described as well as the related empirical research regarding the relationship between development within the model and the manifestation of desired attitudes, behaviors, and skills for working with diverse children.

Racial Identity Model

Racial identity development models, predominately used in the counseling field, focus on how people develop their racial and ethnic identity. More recently, racial identity theory has been suggested as a tool for examining racial identity development and facilitating meaningful interactions and instruction in classrooms.[51] Racial identity development models have been used by researchers and teacher educators to foster antiracist thinking and behavior[52] and to encourage teachers to examine institutional, individual, and cultural racism that exist in schools and society.[53] Educators adhering to this approach believe that societal structures as well as racist attitudes and behaviors support the academic failure of poor urban children.[54]

Specifically, "racial identity development models" refer to a "sense of group or collective identity based on one's perception that he or she shares a common racial heritage with a particular racial group."[55] Racial identity development models address the psychological implications of racial group membership, "that is, belief systems that evolve in reaction to perceived differential racial-group membership."[56]

Several process models have been developed for specific racial groups, such as white,[57] black,[58] and Asian,[59] while others include several races in one multiracial model.[60] In each of these racial identity development models the individual moves and changes toward a greater progression of salience of race and culture in one's life.[61]

Racial identity development models, in general, grew out of black racial identity models that emerged in the 1970s in response to the Civil Rights movement.[62] William Cross' model, which consists of four stages (pre-encounter, encounter, immersion/emersion, internalization), was one of the predominant and most popular of the black racial identity development models that appeared during this era.[63] Cross, Strauss, and Fhagen-Smith, in their most recent work, have expanded on some of the complexities within the racial identity development process, which has accentuated the diversity of experiences and identities within the African American community.[64] The following description of Cross' black racial identity model is not meant to simplify the identity process within the African American community, but rather to focus on the model's use as a heuristic tool for teacher educators.

The first stage of his model is pre-encounter, in which the salience of race is minimized. In the active phase of this stage, some black people may seek to meet and accept the standards of the white culture and/or to denigrate black culture. They may recognize they are black but do not see it as an important aspect of their identity. For example, an African American teacher in CULTURES talks about how she does not focus on the racial aspect of herself: "Teachers think I lie when I say this. But I don't see myself as a minority, majority, being Black or this. It's just that I accept people for that person, not because of the color of their skin. I don't look at color."

Teachers in this stage do not believe that race, culture, or ethnicity influences the teaching and learning process. They often articulate a colorblind stance. When teachers in the pre-encounter stage address culture in their classrooms, they usually focus on exotic artifacts of a culture, such as foods, festivals, and celebrations.[65] Teachers may exhibit versions of low salience through the next stage, encounter.

During the encounter stage, people have an encounter or series of events that shake their current worldview or perception of themselves. Often this brings about black people's awareness that the white cultural worldview is not compatible or supportive of black people's identities. In this stage people may experience confusion, disappointment, anger, and depression as they realize that their worldview has not been "right." Another African American CULTURES teacher illustrates her new understanding of the role of the majority culture: "I used to think that we all need to try as much as possible to become a part of this, the majority, culture, meaning the White majority culture. Now I feel [after participating in CULTURES] that there's room for all of our cultures."

In the immersion/emersion stage people absorb themselves in the black culture, learning and exploring as much as they can. The black reference group becomes the standard by which people judge themselves and others. Some of these standards may be based on stereotypical behavior. Often at this stage, black people manifest anger toward the white culture. Though this point may seem a goal in and of itself, it can become dangerous if people remain at this point as they "get stuck in a never-ending state of militancy and hatred."[66] At some point people transition to the emergence aspect of this stage. As they move out of a rigid conceptualization of blackness, they begin to see the black culture as more diverse and complex. For example, a CULTURES teacher discusses the diversity of her African American children: "I can see that there really is a difference. And I guess in some aspects, I really did know that there was a difference. But when teaching children of the same ethnic background that I am from, I really didn't see that until I took the [CULTURES] class. So it helped me to see that even though we're both from the same ethnic background, I need to be aware of the differences."

Teachers during this transition may focus more of their attention and curricula on their black students. Hollins[67] suggests that teachers may also send mixed messages, one day encouraging their students' African American identity while on other days encouraging them to assimilate more. This comes out of the emotional ups and downs as people at this stage wrestle with the salience of race and culture in their lives.

As black people gain a stronger identity, they move into the internalization stage, where they develop a positive racial identity in which they have blended their own personal identity with other roles of their identity, although blacks are their primary reference group. At this point black people recognize racism and other forms of oppression. They are, however, able to establish relationships with whites and evaluate the strengths and weaknesses of white culture. In addition, some people will actively work to dismantle oppression. Cross has suggested that there are at least three different manifestations at this point, focusing on nationalism, biculturalism, and multiculturalism.[68] Hollins posits that teachers need to develop a more multicultural identity with which they can relate to children of all backgrounds.[69] An African American teacher in CULTURES talks about how she has shifted from a focus on black culture to a more multicultural perspective: "Prior to the CULTURES program, I was more Black-oriented than culturally oriented. So now I think I'm more culturally oriented as to all the cultures and my emphasis is not so much on helping my . . . you know, my thing was to help my race of people, help the Black people. But now my thing is just to help everybody understand each other's cultures and stuff; and I think that way the Blacks will fall into place, Hispanics, Caucasians, everybody. At first I think I was probably just one-culture-oriented and now I think I'm multi-cultured."

Hollins has correlated her typology of multicultural teaching methods with stages in the racial identity development model.[70] She suggests that the relationship illustrates that the later stages reflect more culturally relevant practices, as well as attitudes, behaviors, and thinking that counter racist behavior in the school context. Most of the empirical research regarding racial identity development has been in the context of counseling and psychology. There are few educational studies that examine the correlation between teachers' practices and beliefs and the stages on the racial identity development model.

Research does reveal that as people progress through the steps in racial identity development they become open to other cultures,[71] they appreciate the influence of racial attitudes on people of color, and they exhibit less racist behaviors.[72] In addition, they promote social justice and equality,[73] recognize racism,[74] and accept racial differences.[75] A study of teachers involved in an antiracist professional development program found that as race become more salient in teachers' worldviews, teachers interrupted racist practices in their schools and other aspects of their professional life, integrated the topic of racism into the curriculum and classroom discourse, increased interactions with parents and students of color, and raised expectations of students in their classrooms.[76]

Despite the positive relationship between people's racial identities and behaviors and attitudes that promote diversity, tolerance, and positive interaction, fostering such growth can be challenging. Sleeter found in her multicultural professional development program that teachers reported changes, but that the actual changes observed in the classroom were much more subtle and usually consisted of extensions on current practices rather than paradigmatic shifts in beliefs, thinking, or worldviews.[77] For example, teachers expanded their pedagogy to include cooperative learning and to pay more attention to their African American students.

Banks' Typology of Ethnic Identity

Banks' typology of ethnic identity, though similar to racial identity development models, is distinctive in its inclusion of multiple ethnicities and its focus on education.[78] Banks' typology is not race specific and can be used with individuals of any ethnic or racial group. Banks has further distinguished his model by aligning his work with schools and curriculum in multicultural education.

Banks' model involves six stages: ethnic psychological captivity, ethnic encapsulation, ethnic identity clarification, bi-ethnicity, multi-ethnicity and reflective nationalism, and global competency and globalism.[79] These stages exist as points along a dynamic and multidimensional typology, or "ideal-type construct."[80] He states that each stage is a "gradual and developmental process. . . . The stages should not be viewed as strictly sequential and linear. I am hypothesizing that some individuals may never experience a particular stage."[81] He further states that every ethnic group is highly diverse and dynamic and that each person within a single ethnic group may not begin at the same stage in the cultural learning process. Persons from marginalized ethnic groups will have a different identity development journey than those from the dominant culture. But he does hypothesize that "once an individual experiences a particular stage, he or she is likely to experience the stages above it sequentially and developmentally."[82]

Stage one, ethnic psychological captivity, demonstrates the sociohistorical nature of Banks' model. Members of the dominant culture will most likely not experience this stage as strongly as some people from marginalized groups, if at all. During the stage of ethnic psychological captivity, people internalize negative messages from the past regarding race and ethnicity. The greater the stigmatization, the more people internalize the oppression. As with Cross' first stage, preencounter, the teacher does not believe that race and culture are important factors in the teaching and learning process. An African American teacher in CULTURES explains, "I can keep myself in the mind frame that they [parents and children from other cultural backgrounds] are actually just like me. There are certain goals that they want. They want a certain quality of life. They want a good education for their children. They want happy lives and that's what we all want. And if we can remember that, then it wouldn't matter what color we are or where we are from. Because we're all striving for the same thing—you know food, clothing, shelter, and happiness."

Continuing with Banks' positional framework, in stage two, ethnic encapsulation, the dominant culture internalizes the myth about their superiority and the inferiority of other groups, while marginalized groups become insular either out of fear or strong ethnic identity. The stronger the experiences in stage one, the higher the level of ethnocentrism in the second stage. Gradually people begin to resolve the conflict around their ethnic identity, which leads them into the next stage.

In stage three, ethnic identity clarification, all ethnic groups begin to see both the positive and negative aspects of their own groups. Racial identity development in one's own group is not based on hate or fear of other groups. An important aspect of this stage revolves around self-acceptance. Banks stated that "self-acceptance is a prerequisite to accepting and responding positively to other people. Individuals are more likely to gain self-acceptance when they have experienced positive contact with other groups as well as achieved some measure of economic and psychological security."[83]

An African American teacher in CULTURES confirms the importance of learning about one's self as a prerequisite to connecting with others from different cultures: "Yes it's [CULTURES] making me want to travel more, and be a lot more understanding. It's helped me to learn and want to learn more about myself, my background, and my heritage. Because, although I'm a Black American, most Black Americans have so many cultures within. So I do want to explore and learn more about me. And then I'll be—I think better with other people too."

Learning about one's self at this stage is key to self-acceptance.

In stage four, bi-ethnicity, individuals have the skills and the desire to function in two cultures. They learn how to do this in different ways, depending on their social location in society. In order to gain economic mobility, some groups, such as African Americans and Hispanics, must learn to function in the dominant culture as well as their own. Certain groups living in homogeneous environments may not achieve this stage quickly; it seems that this stage necessitates certain experiences, such as contact with other groups.

Stage five, multi-ethnicity and reflective nationalism, includes individuals who have developed their crosscultural competency so that they are moving beyond the obvious aspects of a culture, such as the holidays and food, to understanding and appreciating the values, symbols, and institutions of other cultures. People at this point along the continuum should be able to switch comfortably between cultures and become responsible, reflective, and active citizens. A CULTURES teacher who is at this stage discusses how she approaches one aspect of her curriculum: "When I teach about explorers, we talk about Cortez and how he treated Montezuma. I mean I have made it my business to know these things now and to get materials to support my learning and the students' learning so they won't view history the same way and they won't view other cultures the same way, I think as their parents would."

The sixth and final stage, globalism and global competency, is an extension of the fifth in that people learn increasingly how to balance their three identities: ethnic, national, and global. Throughout this stage people learn when to use which identity and in which context.[84] A CULTURES teacher points to the importance of using her curriculum to foster this level of ethnicity.

I have realized that education is developing more and more as a global study. I think that it is important for students to know more about the world around them. It is not possible (in my way of thinking) for anyone to learn about the earth and not read about the people within the earth. I feel that it is important for students to learn about other people because it makes them more accepting and better exposed. This type of thinking is the beginning of the process to end racism, ignorance and poverty. I believe that it also increases an appreciation for life when cultural studies are done. Students can learn that all societies have something to offer; all cultural heritages are rich in knowledge and background. Students who know more about themselves can appreciate greatly learning about the background of someone else.

Research involving Banks' typology has highlighted the important point that people have different levels of ethnic awareness and identity development, as shown by the varying placements on Banks' typology of ethnicity,[85] and that placement at the higher stages is generally associated with multicultural competencies[86] and greater interest in multicultural courses.[87] In addition, Tomlinson's work has pointed to the importance of using Banks' typology as a curriculum guide that can inform how you can use literature in a purposeful way to foster children's identity growth within Banks' typology.[88]

Bennett's Developmental Model of Intercultural Sensitivity

Bennett's developmental model of intercultural sensitivity (DMIS) suggests a significant departure from Cross and Banks.[89] However, the DMIS describes similar changes in a person's behavior, cognition, and affect and deals with the learner's subjective experience in understanding how different cultures "create and maintain world views."[90] The difference is the organizing key to Bennett's model, in that each stage represents a new way of experiencing cultural differences. The model has two aspects; the first part of the continuum has three stages of decreasing levels of ethnocentrism (denial, defense, and minimization) and the second has three stages of increasing ethnorelativism (acceptance, adaptation, integration).

The first stage of the model, denial, represents the lack of knowledge of difference. People assume that their worldviews are the only worldviews and behave accordingly. One does not often find such a perspective among teachers, except among those who might have been very isolated. Teachers in this category may base their understanding of other cultures on stereotypes, such as assuming all people from Africa still live in huts. Unfortunately, such misinformation can be passed on to students.

In the second stage, defense, people realize differences exist, but, in an ethnocentric fashion, they strive to preserve their own cultural view. People may do this in one of three ways: (1) they may put down or denigrate another culture; (2) they may uplift their own as superior; or (3) if living in another community outside their own, they may uplift that particular community as superior. Bennett noted that elevating another's community as superior is often misinterpreted as cultural sensitivity, but the uplifting of the other culture is, in this case, done in an egotistical fashion by "presenting one's self as more culturally sensitive."[91] Teachers in the first example of this stage may ask questions such as, "Why do some non-English speaking students and parents not learn English? Didn't they know that they were coming to an English speaking country?"

The third stage of the ethnocentric half of the continuum, minimization, represents people who claim they are "colorblind." People at this level minimize cultural differences and continue to interact from their own cultural paradigms. There is an assumption that others share their behaviors and perceptions. No awareness of their own cultures has occurred yet. An African American teacher in CULTURES captures a typical response of an individual in this stage. She stated, "I've taught many types of cultures and experienced many types of cultural experiences with kids and I find them to be basically the same. They have the same needs and wants and desires." Usually teachers who profess such beliefs do not acknowledge the cultural influence on the learning process.

Movement to stage four, acceptance, represents a critical change from ethnocentrism to the first stage of ethnorelativism. At this stage people recognize that others have different values and worldviews, and people begin to accept and respect different behaviors and communication styles. People move away from a reactive mode of always seeing the "other" to one of interaction, where the individual and the other become a "we-creating reality."[92] Ideally, at this stage a teacher will be interested in learning about effective instructional approaches with her students, such as the following African American elementary teacher in CULTURES. She stated: "I have a number of students who come from a diverse variety of backgrounds. I have taught here for a number of years and I am interested in gaining more insight into their lives, educational strategies, enhancing my teaching to assist these students better whether they are African American, Korean, or Ethiopian. I want to know more about their learning styles. I have students who speak very little English—I'm very interested in what types of techniques I could use with these students. And are there different types of materials that would be successful for these students?"

Stage five, adaptation, reflects the behavioral changes in individuals when they are more able to act in an ethnorelative fashion. Bennett views this stage as a crucial point.[93] People are finally able to (1) change their processing of reality; (2) modify their behaviors so that they are more appropriate; and (3) think and/or act from another cultural perspective—or, as Bennett says—to exhibit empathy.[94]

In the sixth and last stage, integration, people are not simply sensitive to other cultures, but rather they are in the process of becoming a part of and apart from a given cultural context.[95] This stage has two subphases. One is the contextual evaluation, in which people evaluate a phenomenon from another perspective, for example, a teacher who evaluates her African American-focused curriculum from other cultural perspectives. The second is constructive marginality, in which people stand outside of all cultural frameworks.

The DMIS works within a paradigm that focuses on cultural differences between the school and children's cultures.[96] While cultural difference theory shifts the responsibility for children's academic success to schools and teachers, this approach encourages teachers to learn continuously about their children's culture, as well as adapt their classrooms, pedagogy, and personal behaviors and thinking to meet the needs of the children and their cultures.[97] The DMIS supports the desired goals of this approach because of its focus on cultural differences and increased understanding of cultural nuances. It also provides a useful framework for understanding teachers' crosscultural growth. The DMIS has been used in training[98] and found to be helpful in identifying and assessing people at different stages of development. Initial empirical research using Bennett's DMIS model has found that that in order for people to achieve greater levels of crosscultural interaction and to interact in different cultural contexts, more ethnorelative levels of intercultural sensitivity are needed.[99]

SUMMARY AND IMPLICATIONS

Having presented and reviewed three process-oriented models, how do these models contribute to our understanding of multicultural professional development for teachers, particularly African American teachers who work with students who do not share their ethnicity and cultural experiences? How can these models help teachers, like Lucinda, the African American CULTURES teacher described in the beginning of this chapter, connect their own development to their practice with their students?

Despite the limited number of empirical studies pertaining to the process models, the studies' findings shed light on the importance of the salience of race and culture in teachers' worldviews and the importance of fostering growth in this area. From these studies we learned that people tend to be at different levels of multicultural awareness[100] and that higher levels are positively associated with multicultural competency,[101] nonracist behavior[102] and knowledge about other cultures and races.[103] The studies revealed that levels of racial, cultural, and ethnic identity vary,[104] and that teachers do not start with the same type of crosscultural understanding, skills, or attitudes. Process models can help to identify and differentiate racial attitudes,[105] understandings of cultural difference,[106] and acceptance and understanding of one's own ethnicity and others.[107] These findings have implications for assessing readiness to learn, designing effective learning opportunities, and providing appropriate support and challenges for teachers.

First, concerning learner readiness, the research suggested that teachers in the ethnocentric stage of any of the models will be more hesitant, more vulnerable, and less open.[108] Those in the higher ethnorelative stages will be more interested in learning about other cultures and in taking risks.[109] Knowledge of the general level of readiness of pre and inservice teachers in a multicultural professional development courses, like CULTURES, can facilitate the development of appropriate course and field work. As diagnostic tools the models inform teacher educators of possible stages and readiness levels of their students. For example, when would have been the best time for Lucinda to visit the Vietnamese family and did the CULTURES program provide enough preparation for the immersion trip?

Second, the structure of the intervention can provide support and challenges when designed in ways that reflect the process—and not just the content—of crosscultural learning. Sequencing topics in a process framework provide more support for the learner and fosters greater development.[110] For example, self-awareness regarding one's culture has been identified as a key prerequisite and a first step for learners in multicultural programs.[111] When participants explore their own culture in the early stages of an intervention, they are more likely to move toward a multicultural frame of reference. Before embarking on the cultural immersion trip to the Vietnamese home, should the CULTURES curriculum have allotted more time for teachers, like Lucinda, to reflect on their own cultural and racial identity?

Third, there are implications for both support and challenges for teacher education students. Personal reflections on the self and discussions on issues of racism can be difficult for pre and inservice teachers as well as teacher educators.[112] There is a need to encourage risktaking to foster crosscultural growth,[113] but too much risk discourages learners from engaging in the process and encourages resistance.[114] The intentional use of groups is one source of support as well as a challenge for learners and provides opportunities for learners to interact with people of diverse backgrounds, experiences, and beliefs.[115] For example, after Lucinda's experience with the Vietnamese family, she was able to go back to the classroom and share what happened with her cohort colleagues. Group support, however, must be well-designed and as authentic as possible. Merely plunging teachers into a new setting with little support or at the inappropriate time according to their developmental level may increase stereotyping and produce negative feelings on the part of the learner.[116]

Recommendations

Process frameworks, specifically the models discussed in this review, may provide a systematic map for teacher education researchers to design and evaluate interventions aimed at increasing the crosscultural competence of their students. The process models support Grant and Secada's recommendation that more research focus on how teacher cognition and beliefs develop. As Grant and Secada stated, "If we could map how teachers move from the former to the latter, we might be able to plan teacher education programs to help teachers develop these skills."[117] However, more research must be conducted regarding these models' effectiveness in teacher education, particularly well-designed observational studies in naturalistic classroom settings.

Although much of the research on process models had only small groups of African American participants, the models can be useful guides for examining African American teachers' professional growth. More research must be conducted with African American and other nonwhite teachers who work with students who share their racial and cultural backgrounds, as well as those who do not. Further research in this area will expand our understanding of effective pedagogy, beliefs, and skills that foster the education of all children. Moreover, understanding how teachers understand their own identity may assist us in finding better ways to stem the high attrition rate among all teachers and increase retention among teachers of color.

Chapter 2

BLACK TEACHERS' PERCEPTIONS OF THEIR PROFESSIONAL ROLES AND PRACTICES

Franita Ware

INTRODUCTION

There are few academic writings that provide insights about black teachers' perceptions of their professional roles and practices as teachers. However, in recent years, an increasing number of researchers have focused on this segment of the education community, and the research on black teachers has become an emergent field of literature offering links between teachers' perceptions of their roles as teachers and their cultural background.

This chapter raises three critical questions. Specifically,

1. How does the ethic of caring of black teachers influence how they teach black students?
2. What are their beliefs regarding themselves as teachers, their students, and the parents and communities in which they teach?
3. What are the instructional strategies and practices that have been found successful in teaching black students?

Why is there a need to document the similarities and differences among exemplary black teachers? As noted in the chapter by Patricia Cooper in this book, the number of teachers of color is decreasing as the number of students of color is increasing. In addition, and more problematic, black students' test scores are significantly lower than their white counterparts. Does the recruitment of more black teachers offer a solution to black students' school failure? Are there lessons to be learned from the pedagogy and beliefs of black teachers?

Contrary to the assumption that black teachers are only important as role models for black students, Irvine's research indicated that students identified teachers as mentors who helped them manipulate the school's culture.[1] These mentors, according to Irvine, frequently supported students as cultural communicators and assisted students who lacked the savvy to succeed in mainstream school culture. Further, students who were identified as having low socioeconomic status and those identified as low achievers were frequently more dependent on black teachers because those teachers helped their students to develop their self-concept.[2]

Black teachers have contributed to the academic achievement of black students with their unique pedagogy that "affirm[s] the importance of education and the relationship of education to academic, political, social, economic success and advancement of African Americans."[3] This chapter identifies culturally specific ways black teachers instruct and nurture black students to academic success as a result of their ethic of caring, their beliefs, and teaching strategies. Most importantly, Meier, Stewart, and England concluded that the higher the percentage of black teachers in schools the lower the numbers of black student placed in special education or subjected to expulsion or suspension.[4] Meier, Stewart, and England also indicated that the presence of black teachers was associated with more black students being placed in gifted classes and graduating from high schools.

ETHIC OF CARING

The literature reveals that caring is a characteristic that undergirds and explains many of the actions of dedicated and committed black teachers. Caring, as demonstrated by black teachers, exceeded the mere declaration that "teachers should care for students." In Toliver's work, she stated, "Caring is the foundation of good teaching. In my classes, caring can and does take many forms."[5] She described caring as (1) giving time to students outside of the classroom; (2) listening to her students' problems; and (3) encouraging problem students to grow academically. Toliver wrote, "If students perceive that their teachers are there to help them and willing to assist them in getting through difficulties, it is then impossible not to teach them."[6] Although caring is a very important characteristic that defines black teachers, Toliver revealed the complexity of the issue when she identified the various forms of caring she demonstrated in her classes.

Similar to Toliver's description of caring, Foster defined black teachers' caring as "a kinship, connectedness and solidarity."[7] Furthermore, Cochran-Smith reviewed the work of Ladson-Billings and Collins and concluded that the ethic of caring is consistent with the work on successful teaching of all students of color.[8]

Collins situated the ethic of caring as a critical element of the black community when she described African American women who felt a sense of accountability to all of the black community's children.[9] Collins extended the ethic of caring to a wider and more inclusive cultural phenomenon. She employed the slogan "lifting as we climb" to describe the sense of responsibility demonstrated by educated black women when they used their professional position to improve their community.[10] Black teachers used an assortment of caring behaviors for the benefit of their students by addressing the specific needs of their students and responding to those needs out of a sense of accountability to the black children and their community.

Black teachers' caring was also demonstrated in more subtle ways, like creating and maintaining a caring physical classroom environment. For example, Lipman wrote about an urban black teacher's classroom that was in contrast to the classrooms of other teachers in his school.[11] The teacher's room was attractive and decorated with students' work and plants. The teacher kept the room immaculate and he swept the room and hallway many times during the day. He even had a rug at the door so students could wipe their feet before entering. The students' saw this teacher's room as a type of "home base" where they could drop by during lunch hour and before and after school, as well as a place to work on special projects or finish assignments. Similar to Toliver's explanation of caring,[12] this teacher was available to his students beyond the regular school hours. In response to his demonstration of caring, the teacher thought his students were more involved and committed to academic achievement.

Dedication to Students' Needs

Dedication to students' needs is another aspect of caring. Foster's works on exemplary black teachers provide insight into this area.[13] Everett Dawson, for example, was one of the teachers that Foster described in her work.[14] Dawson recognized his students' needs and demonstrated a dedication to those needs. Foster documented Dawson's description of a math class he taught for students who "weren't supposed to be good in academics." He made the coursework consistent with real world applications and the students' fields of interest, such as masonry, carpentry, and computers. Dawson's adaptation of the curriculum to ensure the students' success is an example of his caring. This teacher's efforts resulted in a class of students who, through success and discipline, contradicted the school administration's negative assumptions about their capabilities.

Further, Foster supported Toliver's identification of the complexity of caring and Collins' idea of "lifting as we climb" through her description of Mr. Dawson, who saw himself as connected to his students by a "Black umbilical cord."[15] Despite obvious class differences between Mr. Dawson and his students, he understood that he and his students had a shared destiny, and he remained committed to their school achievement despite oppressive forces outside of the school. These students' low socioeconomic status could have easily led this teacher to assume his students could not achieve and were therefore undeserving of his care. Instead, Mr. Dawson chose to care for his students.

Other-mothers

Collins documented the historical and cultural context of the term, "other-mothers."[16] In West African traditions, women care for the children of other women who, for a multiplicity of reasons, are unable to provide for their children. Communal care of children strengthened families and communities and prevented the abandonment of neglected children. Although Collins used the term "other-mothers," it must be noted that historically African American male teachers also assumed the role of parent surrogate.

Foster's research also contained an example of another teacher, Mrs. Forsythe, who created a familial relationship with her students.[17] This teacher found that relating to students as relatives helped to establish an affectionate bond with the students and foster discipline. Mrs. Forsythe outlined how she related to her students: "The first thing I do is try to become a mother to all of them. I tell them, as long as you are here with me, I'm your mama until you go back home, and when you go back home, you go to your other mother."[18] She stated that only after this maternal level of affection had been established could she address discipline issues.

This concept of other-mother was also found in the work of Henry and Lipman.[19] Lipman's ethnographic study identified other-mothers whose classroom behaviors were consistent with this ethic of caring. The teachers in Lipman's work were school mothers and advocates for students who were identified as at risk, but whom black teachers chose to define as "their kids." The other-mothers were typically African American teachers who demonstrated caring by showing affection, being problem solvers, and listening to their students so they could be successful in a school climate that often did not support them.

Similar to the teachers in Lipman's study in American schools, Henry's research of black women in Canada supported the concept of other-mothering.[20] Like their American counterparts, these teachers acted as parent surrogates to Canadian children of African heritage. Through their activism and service, they believed and practiced their craft as a member of the students' extended family and challenged Eurocentric concepts of the superiority of patriarchal, nuclear families. For example, Henry described women who were supportive of the needs of children and parents in their own community, who shared their own limited resources, and, through membership in professional organizations, found other ways to help parents.

Therefore, black teachers who chose to become other-mothers to their students were found in America and Canada. The frequent occurrence of other-mothering lends credibility to a conclusion that black teachers' caring, regardless of their location in the world, is a cultural response to black children who need support. By acting as other-mothers, black teachers demonstrated a historic and cultural aspect of what has been described in the moral development literature as an ethic of caring.

Anti-Racism Teachings

Embedded in the ethic of caring is a unique variable that is shared by people who share a history of oppression and racism. Specifically, many of the black teachers identified the importance of preparing black students to challenge and resist racism. Because teachers shared their students' culture, they recognized the impact of racism on these students' lives and were determined to support their students' achievement in spite of racism.

Examples of this type of care as demonstrated by black teachers was found in Foster, who identified teachers who helped black students deal with the realities of racism and challenge the limitations that racism imposed on their achievements.[21] Foster's work on black teachers focused "on the various individual and collective means that Black teachers used to resist racism and thereby challenged the status quo."[22] One of the ways these teachers resisted racism was to discuss openly the realities of racism with their students and to prepare them to overcome these socially imposed barriers.

One of Foster's teachers explained the importance of identifying and overcoming racism: "There's always been a lot of prejudice against black people. Today there is still a lot of prejudice and racism, and it's gonna be here a long time. . . . I try to teach my children that they can't let that get in the way. We have to forget about those who try to keep us down, we have to protect ourselves, and we have to keep going on."[23]

Similar observations were made in the early work of Baker, whose research examined the characteristics of effective urban teachers of language arts.[24] Baker documented the teaching career of Mary Jane Wingfield Payne, who expected her students to read newspapers and other published works in order to be aware of current events that were "openly hostile to blacks . . . biased and unflattering stories regarding black citizens."[25]

The literature on black teachers examined a unique teaching style that acknowledged and taught resistance to racism. This pedagogy, often called "liberatory" or "emancipatory," pitted black teachers against the dominant practices and policies of the districts where they were employed. The teachers, however, responded with a common, culturally derived solution—teach students about the existence of racism and prepare them to overcome it.

In summary, black teachers were more than educators whose only concern was effective delivery of their subject area. Rather, these teachers possessed culturally specific pedagogies that helped them address the needs of their black students. These teachers, through the creation of other-mother relationships and a desire to "lift as they climbed," formed bonds with their students that are consistent with African cultural paradigms.

The next section of this chapter examines the beliefs of black teachers about themselves, their students, and the parents and communities in which they taught.

BELIEFS

Beliefs of Black Teachers about Themselves as Professionals

Teachers have a unique professional perspective on teaching because they were once students. As students, they watched teachers throughout their numerous years of schooling. During their years as students in black teachers' classrooms, the students decided to become teachers themselves and modeled their former black teachers' methods in their own classes. Although the teachers in this literature frequently stated their beliefs about numerous subjects, it was interesting to note the frequency with which they indicated who influenced them to become exemplary teachers. These teachers identified their own former teachers, frequently in segregated schools, who challenged them to become successful students and citizens. It was the memories of these experiences that influenced their current beliefs.

Stanford's study documented how black teachers remembered their own teachers who recognized their potential.[26] The beliefs of contemporary black teachers were not created in historical isolation and were influenced by strong memories of the black teachers who had taught them in the past. It appears that the exemplary teachers relied upon remembered teachers and the educational experiences those teachers provided to instill in them a sense of mission and purpose for their communities as black teachers. As such, many of these teachers believed they were giving back to the community, fulfilling a valuable service, and carrying on a cultural tradition.[27]

Beliefs about Students

Within the literature on black teachers, there was an overwhelming consensus on teachers' beliefs about being responsible for black students. These teachers believed their students could learn, achieve, and be successful in school and life.[28] Moreover, they maintained these beliefs while simultaneously understanding the realities of racism, poverty, and schools that alienated students and labeled them as "at risk."[29] The teachers in the literature observed the dangers of urban communities, gangs, violence, increasing drop-out rates, and decreasing test scores, but were not deterred or discouraged.[30] In fact, many of these teachers believed that school systems did not attempt to educated black students[31] and too often identified them as uneducable and culturally deprived.[32] In contrast to the school's perception, black teachers believed in their students' potential, and remarked that "Black kids are creative, inquisitive, and bright."[33]

Similar to the connections that the teachers felt to their remembered teachers, another frequently stated belief of black teachers was that they saw themselves when they looked at their students.[34] The reflection of their own life experiences in their students' faces strengthened their beliefs in their students' abilities. Thus, despite the apparent disadvantages of single parent households, low socioeconomic status, and urban school conditions, black teachers had empathy for their students. Because of a shared background, they chose not to pity or victimize their students[35]; instead they used their shared ethnic identity and experiences to challenge them.

Regardless of the expectations of black teachers for their students' success, there were obstacles within the confines of the school. Racism was not the only barrier students had to overcome. Additional barriers for academically inclined black students were teachers who did not want them in their classes. In these instances, white teachers were more critical of black students' behavior, found ways to have them removed from the classes, and displayed other negative attitudes about the students.

Therefore, despite the many positive beliefs black teachers had about their students and the frequency with which they expressed these beliefs, they believed their black students faced opposition from white teachers and administrators that prevented their success in schools.

Teachers' Beliefs about Parents and Communities

Teachers in the Henry, Lipman, Toliver, and Walker studies expressed the belief that they were connected to the communities where they taught and that they worked to insure that parents were involved and welcomed in classrooms.[36] Many of the black teachers remembered the involvement of their own parents in segregated schools and attempted to replicate that relationship. Similar to the productive relationship of parents, teachers, and students that was noted in Walker's historical research, many of these teachers knew that the impact of a close working relationship with parents and community could have a positive impact on black students' success.

Ladson-Billings remembered the historical context of parent and teacher relationships from her own segregated education experiences.[37] Similar to statements made by Irvine and Irvine and Walker, teachers, parents, and students were members of a community where there was significant overlap in the relationships and places where teachers and parents met and talked.[38]

Ladson-Billings did not remember her parents being active in the school; however, if a teacher called her parents would comply.[39] Walker explained that during the school day parents generally were not present unless invited.[40] She quoted a parent who explained, "You didn't go to the school during the day or after school to talk about your children. . . . Parents just didn't go in the school and disturb a teacher."[41] Further, Walker explained that parents were expected to attend PTA and to teach their children to respect the teacher. What is historically significant about these accounts is the level of shared understanding displayed by all members of community regarding the importance of education.

Teachers in Foster's and Toliver's works realized schools could be uncomfortable for parents who themselves had not been successful in school.[42] Yet, they knew the importance of parental involvement and assumed the responsibility to create conditions where parents could support their children's academic achievement. Thus, research in this area noted teachers who worked to build relationships with the parents and community.

Toliver used a strategy to help her parents support their children in mathematics, a subject that had been difficult for many of the parents of her middle school students.[43] She implemented family math nights so the parents could participate in nonthreatening math activities with their children. Family math helped her build supportive and productive relationships with the parents, and this strategy helped the parents overcome some of their fears of mathematics.

Many of the black teachers in this research literature described how they welcomed parents in the class and prevented adversarial relationships with them.[44] Foster noted a teacher who began the school year by sending notes, making positive phone calls, and sending her phone number home so parents could reach her.[45] Teachers in Ladson-Billings' research documented similar behaviors.

BLACK TEACHERS' INSTRUCTIONAL STRATEGIES AND PRACTICES

Similar to notions that an ethic of caring and beliefs affect teachers' actions, this literature suggested that there were instructional strategies and practices that contributed to the success of black teachers. These strategies included cooperative learning, values and character education, performance—high involvement and active learning, use of community language and dialect, and discipline.

Cooperative Learning

Through her observation of a television documentary and attendance at a lecture, Hollins reviewed the work of noted educator Marva Collins to determine what strategies contributed to her success with black students who frequently were identified as at-risk by the public schools they once attended.[46] One of the practices that Hollins found was the use of cooperative learning.

Research supporting teachers' use of cooperative learning has been identified in the work of Slavin.[47] This author's research noted that cooperative learning is a successful strategy for urban schools for two reasons. First, it builds upon a cultural value of black people and other students of color, who often prefer cooperation instead of competition as a modality of learning. Second, as noted by the teachers in Ladson-Billings and Foster, cooperative learning builds positive students' relationships, particularly as noted by Slavin in multicultural and economically diverse classrooms.[48]

Values and Character Education

Teachers taught values and character development as part of their curriculum. Teachers who taught respect for others were identified in the works of Foster, Henry, King, and Stanford.[49] In the work of Stanford, a science teacher identified only as Ed explained the importance of respect: "When we provide an environment where learning can happen, children learn. To create such an environment, respect and trust were the essential ingredients."[50] Thus, this teacher's behavior was clearly an extension of his ethic of caring for students. He used his classroom as an environment to teach mutual respect.

Additionally, teachers in King's research found it important not only to teach the value of respect for others but also personal values and friendship.[51] King wrote, "They accomplish this by structuring classroom social relations to support certain values that are consistent with their notion of responsible learning."[52] The author described learning that was not simply knowledge attainment but that taught students how to treat each other as humans. These teachers saw character education as an "essential foundation for learning."[53]

Performance, High Involvement, and Active Learning

Additional instructional strategies used by some of the teachers in this research were performance, active learning, and high involvement. The works of Noblit and Toliver provided interesting examples of ways teachers implemented these strategies. In the previous section on the ethic of caring, Toliver identified building on her students' interests as a way to teach her students.[54] Students became interested, according to Toliver, through the skillful use of performance and high involvement. Tolliver described how she would dress as Zorra (the female version of Zorro) in a costume made for her by students. When she drew a big "Z" on the board to teach angles, the students were fascinated by the angles found in the letter. This was just one of the ways Toliver ensured her students were actively engaged in the lesson.

Another way she facilitated engagement was through a project called the Math Trail. To counter the many negative comments her students had about their community and school, Toliver developed a lesson to teach the students an appreciation for the community.[55] Students were expected to plot a course from the school, through the community, and back to the school. Along the course, the students created math problems about various real-life situations. Finally, the students prepared a book with problems, illustrations, or photographs. At the completion of their Math Trail book, a group of students wrote, "the purpose of this experience is to prove that the classroom is NOT the only place to learn Math."[56] Toliver was ultimately successful in engaging her students and improving their academic skills.

Noblit documented the teaching strategy of Pamela Knight in his ethnographic study of a black teacher.[57] The teacher often called on students to answer questions. Noblit described a process that he called "public testing." However, it was the way the teacher interacted with the students, took the time to make kind or encouraging comments, acknowledged students who were eager for attention, or engaged students who tried to disappear that made this ritual a special moment in the class day. Noblit recalled that for the students it was a "moment in the sun" and that "the students loved it."[58]

Use of Community Language and Dialect

In addition to structuring lessons to engage and connect students to their communities and classroom, black teachers created classroom environments based on mutual respect as a way to acknowledge and validate their students. For example, some black educators accepted students' use of black dialect. Other teachers insisted on standard English or taught students when it was appropriate to use standard English[59] and when it was appropriate to use black dialect.

Hollins wrote that Marva Collins made use of the home language and the verbal style of the community in her school.[60] Students were allowed to use familiar language patterns that were consistent with black students' culture. Although the teacher occasionally corrected the students' spoken grammar, students used analogies and "jive talk" in their class communications.[61]

Lipman noted the behavior of a teacher in her research, Samuel Thompson, who validated his students' home language but also taught them the language and discourse style of standard English.[62] He would, "in an expression of cultural solidarity . . . sometimes switch to Black vernacular, but in class he was a stickler for Standard English discourse, correcting his students' oral and written grammar and pushing them with a weekly list of challenging vocabulary words."[63]

Similarly, Ladson-Billings quoted a teacher who discussed the issue of appropriate language usage for students: "I get so sick and tired of people trying to tell me that my children don't need to use any language other than the one they come to school with. Then those same people turn around and judge the children negatively because of the way they express themselves. My job is to make sure that they can use both languages, that they understand that their language is valid but that the demands placed upon them by others mean that they will constantly have to prove their worth. We spend a lot of time talking about language, what it means, how to use it, and how it can be used against you."[64]

These quotes are significant for several reasons. Teachers acknowledged the students' home language as well as standard English and made sure that their black students knew how to "code switch"[65] so they could be successful in society.

Discipline

Maintaining discipline, a classroom management strategy, was an important part of the instructional tactics of black teachers reviewed in the literature about black teachers. They noted the importance of consistent discipline for class management, but it appeared that once their procedures were established early in the school year, they were not overbearing with the issue of discipline.[66] Accordingly, a teacher in Ladson-Billings' work indicated that she established the rules in a loving way.[67] Likewise, Baker concurred that it was possible to be firm without being mean or insensitive.[68]

The teachers thought that once students understood their expectations, the instructional content of the class occurred without disruption. It should be noted that teachers assumed that their students were capable of managing their own behavior and therefore did not need excessive or demeaning classroom management policies.

Discipline also was maintained because black teachers understood that their students needed classrooms that were safe and secure. A class climate was considered safe and secure when students felt they could speak and even make mistakes without fear of retribution from peers. This sense of safety and security was extremely important to black teachers who taught in urban settings.

Hollins' article about Marva Collins described how this master teacher used the "latent functions of the Black church" to provide discipline and security to her class.[69] In particular, the school provided a "place where individuals could participate, be accepted and be valued by standards established within their own environment."[70] Like the culture of the black church, Marva Collins encouraged performances with high levels of participation and the achievement of high standards.

CONCLUSIONS

This chapter documents a specific culturally based practice of black teachers who have been successful with black students. Although the research base is new and limited in size, some clear themes surfaced regarding black teachers and their ways of caring, their particular beliefs about themselves and their students, and their teaching strategies. The beliefs and instructional practices of black teachers have much to offer researchers and policy makers as they attempt to find solutions to the problems of schools and teachers who have failed to educate black students.

Chapter 3

DOES RACE MATTER?

A Comparison of Effective Black and White Teachers of African American Students

Patricia M. Cooper

INTRODUCTION AND SIGNIFICANCE

A National Education Association survey[1] found that approximately nine out of ten teachers in America are white, confirming numerous reports in recent years documenting the decreasing number of minority teachers in American public schools.[2] Of the remaining 10 percent, black teachers represent less than 7 percent, and Asian and others less than 3. At the same time, students of color comprise 30 percent of the students nationally and 76 percent of the students in America's 20 central cities.[3] It is widely expected that this number will increase well into the next century.[4] One clear implication of these statistics is that children of color are very likely to be taught by white teachers. This has particular relevance for black children for whom, traditionally, black teachers have figured prominently in their development beyond the classroom, often serving as role models, community leaders, activists, and substitute mothers.[5] To what extent this important teacher-student relationship changes when the teacher is white is a question that in light of current and projected demographics cannot be ignored. How and when is it effective? How does it compare to that of black teacher-black students? The problem is exacerbated by the fact that discussion of race as a determinant in children's personal and academic success is still an emotionally charged and often misunderstood issue that is an impediment to effective teacher education and teaching across racial lines.[6]

Acknowledging King's call for further research comparing the experiences and methods of African American teachers to those of Euro Americans,[7] this chapter compares selected white teachers whose work on behalf of African American children challenged the status quo of underachievement to the growing body of research on effective black teachers of black children. The seven white teachers highlighted here were chosen for their influence on the academy's or the public's view of black children and urban education. An overview of Irvine's concept of "cultural synchronization"[8] provides a frame of reference for interpreting the research.

CULTURAL SYNCHRONIZATION

Irvine described the black child's experience in the classroom through the concepts of "cultural synchronization" or "lack of cultural synchronization," which refer to the quality of fit between the teachers' and students' primary cultures.[9] This concept appeared highly relevant to the findings on effective black teachers. According to Irvine, cultural synchronization for black children is "rooted in the concepts of Afrocentricity and the cultural distinctiveness of Afro-American life."[10] The importance of this concept can be felt at the school level (though it is not limited to schools) when the combination of black children's African ancestry and the influence of prevailing community norms becomes manifested in a certain learning style. This learning style can leave children at odds with white teachers and schools since both traditional practice and institutions most often reflect Eurocentric worldviews, customs, teaching styles, and expectations for student behavior. As Irvine wrote:

> This lack of cultural sync becomes evident in instructional situations in which teachers misinterpret, denigrate, and dismiss black students' language, nonverbal cues, physical movements, learning styles, cognitive approaches, and worldviews. When teachers and students are out of sync, they clash and confront each other, both consciously and unconsciously, in matters concerning proxemics (use of interpersonal distance), paralanguage (behaviors accompanying speech, such as voice tone and pitch and speech rate and length), and coverbal behavior (gesture, facial expression, eye gaze).[11]

Irvine placed cultural synchronization at the center of a process model for black student achievement. She argued that its presence accounts for teacher beliefs, school policies, for whether communication and instruction are effective, and for whether teachers hold high expectations of black children. In an earlier review of the research on teacher expectations, Irvine found that white teachers had "more negative expectations for black students than for White students."[12] Since it is widely acknowledged that negative expectations of students are directly tied to underachievement, it follows that the greater the cultural synchronization between teacher and student, the greater the expectations of the student's academic achievement. Teacher expectations also appeared key to helping students bridge the gap between culturally synchronized and nonsynchronized school environments. Black educators and scholars, including Irvine, Foster, and Hilliard, allowed that historically, and in light of social and economic realities, success in standard educational venues has always been a priority of the black community.[13] By way of example, Bryk, Lee, and Holland's extensive study of Catholic schools, which included a focus on minority student achievement, supported this claim.[14] York's review of the research on African American students in Catholic schools reinforced this view.[15]

Teacher expectations were also tied to the teacher's willingness to teach information that black children may not be exposed to in their primary culture. This was considered essential to their success in schools that were not culturally congruent.[16] Common to the literature on effective black teachers was the fact that although culturally synchronistic teaching strives to connect with the students' home and community culture and promotes active resistance to curriculum subordination, it is not an automatic rejection of the standard curriculum. Again, almost without exception, black teachers in the literature articulated the need to expect black students to excel in traditional subjects and by traditional measures. Central to this was the ability to read and use standard English, despite how much black vernacular English was valued in the community. Delpit is closely associated with this view.[17]

In sum, the concept of culturally synchronistic schooling involves the twin foci of working within the norms of the black culture while at the same time helping black children succeed in traditional venues. At first, these goals may appear paradoxical, but they are, in fact, complimentary, though they may be manifested in varying proportions to each other and with varying degrees of interdependence. The first goal supports the idea that culturally synchronistic teaching accounts for what the black community generates in style, language, behavior, tradition. The second ensures that black children are not excluded from access to the greater society by virtue of a teacher's lack of expectations or failure to provide information or training not common to their backgrounds, even if this information or training requires some temporary suppression of a primary cultural characteristic (such as the use of nonstandard English). The research also suggested, however, that the potential for cultural synchronization at this fully realized level in mainstream schools is rare, thus reinforcing the role that the family, churches, and social groups also play in black children's education.[18] Individual teachers, though, may be expected to embody what the setting or institution as a whole cannot.[19] It is important to note that culturally synchronized teaching does not depend on what Ladson-Billings[20] referred to as the "cult-of-personality," which explains good teaching by virtue of singular, idiosyncratic, teaching styles.

EFFECTIVE BLACK TEACHERS

Any comparison of white teachers of black students to effective black teachers necessitates a review of the definition of effectiveness and a summary of some major perspectives. For the purposes of this chapter and in keeping with a cultural synchronization approach, effective teaching is defined from an emic perspective.[21] As interpreted by black scholars, including Banks, Boykin, Delpit, Dyson, Foster, Irvine, Ladson-Billings, and Siddle Walker, an emic perspective captures the values and norms of the community with regard to a particular condition or situation.[22] According to Siddle Walker, an effective teacher of black children is one who knows her subject matter, sees herself as the authority in the classroom, and holds high expectations for all children.[23] In practice this is called "being hard on them" and involves a willingness to use power or authority judiciously but unsparingly. At the same time, Siddle Walker found that an effective teacher is a caring, involved member of the community who treats all children like members of her own family, employing a relational versus analytical method of interaction.

Ladson-Billings, along with Foster, employed a method called "community nomination" to identify effective black teachers.[24] Results from Ladson-Billings' interviews and observations with the nominated teachers showed that, by and large, effective black teachers have many characteristics in common. The author essentialized the effective black teacher as one who practices "culturally relevant teaching," that is, the promotion of academic achievement without sacrificing the students' African and African American identity. According to Ladson-Billings, the most important function of such teaching is to cultivate a "relevant Black personality" through incorporating "cultural referents" into practice and the curriculum.[25]

Pedagogically, Ladson-Billings wrote that culturally relevant teaching exemplified certain "principles at work" in the classroom.[26] These included the personal attributes of high self-esteem and a high regard for others as well as a resistance to the status quo for African Americans. These qualities were accompanied by the teacher's identification with and obligation to the African American community, with students seen as part of the teacher's extended family. Principles at work meant making connections between students' communities, the nation, and the world. Principles at work also incorporated a belief that all children could succeed if they were helped accordingly and that teaching was an art and that teachers were artists. The principles further required the utilization of students' prior knowledge, an emphasis on the classroom as community, a willingness to subject all knowledge to analysis and revision, faith in literacy and math as the foundations of academic achievement, and, finally, a commitment to providing the necessary authority and structure that students required.

Foster, as noted, also employed the "community nomination" method for selecting effective black teachers and identified similar themes in her qualitative study of effective black teachers.[27] In the collective opinion of the teachers in Foster's study, the findings of which echoed Ladson-Billings', effective black teachers of black children act cognizant of their obligation to the next generation; do not allow racism to get in the way of their teaching a demanding curriculum; promote a family model of teaching, including caring, empathy, and respect for the black community; hold high expectations for black children; embrace performance behavior, reading aloud, and rhythmic responses; and demonstrate model authoritative behavior.

Other researchers who conducted studies of effective black teachers of black children include Stanford, who looked at six African American teachers who received teaching awards between 1986 and 1993.[28] Her results fell in line with Foster's and Ladson-Billings'.[29] Lipman's three-year study[30] of two junior high schools in the process of restructuring also offered a parallel picture to Foster's and Ladson-Billings' of the effective black teacher. Lipman, a white researcher, also argued that the common tenets of school restructuring—that is, teacher participation and initiative, teacher collaboration and dialogue, and smaller, more supportive organizational structures—do little to advance the academic and social needs of the black students because they either reinforce racist policies or dismiss successful teachers of black students (who are almost all black) as idiosyncratic or, ironically, culturally based. It is worth noting that the black teachers in this study did not believe that the failure of restructuring to advance black students precluded their individual ability to do so. Noblit[31] conducted a case study of a black teacher investigating the concept of caring as described by Noddings.[32] He concluded that black teachers demonstrate caring through a selective use of power in the classroom that exemplifies and promotes their centrality to black children's learning (recalling Siddle Walker's description of black teachers "being hard on them"[33]). This power is not to be confused with oppression or authoritarianism, which has been associated with black teachers.[34] Rather, it is to be seen as a positive means to increase student achievement, self-respect, and group membership, which, in turn, can be seen as a defense against an oppressive educational system.

In all, the research on effective black teachers appears dominated by several key findings. Effective teachers of black children (1) are committed to the black community and provide a sense of family, (2) promote positive racial identity, (3) help students to succeed in school endeavors, despite the racist nature of both the institution and society in general, by using alternative instructional methods when necessary, (4) take personal responsibility for their students learning, (5) know their subject matter, and, (6) are demanding of students in all areas, including curriculum and discipline.

WHITE TEACHERS OF BLACK CHILDREN: DOES RACE MATTER?

Aside from the question of what makes an effective teacher of black children, many researchers have inquired whether white teachers are de facto inappropriate and ineffective teachers of black children. In other words, are white teachers, by virtue of their race, unable to teach and serve black children well? Some scholars have suggested that a deficit view of black children's abilities, and other like models, is rooted within white teachers' hegemonic, Western epistemological framework, which is often unconscious and almost always unstated.[35] Basically, this framework prohibits white teachers from taking a black child's point of view and thus insidiously reduces the possibility of effective teaching. These scholars also suggested that this negative orientation toward black students may account, at least in part, for the fact that, historically, black children have fared less well than whites on such measures as standardized test scores, graduation rates, and college admissions rates.

Other scholars generally agreed on the complexity of white teachers adopting an equitable, crosscultural perspective, but they did not view the problem as insurmountable, especially in terms of individual classrooms.[36] Others suggested that teacher education was the key to adopting a crosscultural perspective.[37] In keeping with a culturally synchronistic approach, Hilliard said that black students could learn from teaching that was not culturally sensitive if teachers' expectations of student performance were high enough.[38] He wrote that black children were failing not because they could not learn from white teachers or even a different pedagogical style, but because of "systematic inequities in the delivery" tied to negative teacher expectations. (Even black teachers can fall prey to the trap of negative expectations. Rist's classic study that found that teachers' expectations for students' achievement were tied to teachers' perceptions of student social class.[39] The teachers in that study were all black.) Kleinfeld et al.,[40] echoing Delpit[41] and others who found that cultural synchronization did not mean the community wanted to dispense with the standard curriculum, wrote that teachers from inside the community were not viewed as more effective than teachers outside of it by either the parents or the educational community. Effective teachers in this study were seen as those who could teach the standard curriculum well.

Given the theoretical possibility, then, that within certain parameters white teachers can be effective teachers of black children, traditional research on effective inservice white teachers comparable to those of inservice black teachers are few. (It should be noted that there is a growing body of studies of preservice white teachers,[42] particularly concentrated around racial beliefs.) The lack of empirical data, however, is boosted by a number of "critical personal narrative and autoethnograph(ies)"[43] by white teachers on teaching black and diverse children. These teachers are called "independent" teachers by virtue of their nontraditional career paths and educational vision. They were selected for consideration in light of their clear dedication to equal educational opportunity for black students and, in some cases, for their influence on the public's perception of teaching black children. Kohl's *36 Children,* for example, has been credited with starting the urban education reform movement.[44]

INDEPENDENT WHITE TEACHERS

The narratives of the white teachers are chiefly characterized by a highly individualistic teaching style, educational philosophy, and career path.[45] These works, spanning the three decades since the Civil Rights movement, revealed the individual authors' beliefs and methods about teaching black and diverse students. It is interesting to consider that, in contrast to Foster's[46] and Ladson-Billings'[47] studies of black teachers, the white teachers named above would not be considered "community nominated." In a sense, they must be considered "self-nominated" in that the description of their successful work with black children and the black community is based on self-report. Furthermore, while they possess many of the characteristics of "star teachers"[48] of children in poverty, their strengths may be attributed, at least in part, to the "cult-of-personality" that Ladson-Billings aimed to avoid in her study.[49] Nonetheless, it is important to acknowledge that despite their self-selection, the "narrative rendering"[50] of these white teachers' histories bears a resemblance to those found in both Foster and Ladson-Billings. This is to say, they are teachers speaking from their beliefs and experiences about the education of black students. Similar to Baldwin's[51] *A Talk to Teachers* and Delpit's *Other People's Children,*[52] these teachers have influenced teacher education and the public's perception of urban or minority education. Even more importantly, white education students in particular are drawn to their stories.[53] Interestingly, no review of this type of work in light of what is known about effective black teachers has been conducted.

Jonathan Kozol and Herbert Kohl set the stage for white teachers talking about black children with the 1967 publication of Kozol's *Death at an Early Age* and Kohl's *36 Children.* Kozol described his teaching experiences in the Boston schools prior to enforced desegregation. Kohl wrote about teaching junior high school in Harlem in the early 60s. Arriving at the height of the Civil Rights movement, these two works of young white teachers shocked the nation with their descriptions of the systemic negation of learning opportunities and subpar physical conditions in schools for black children. White teachers who wrote later of their experiences or educational philosophy on behalf of black children are Ayers, Hoffman, Meier, O'Connor, and Paley.[54] Their accounts of working with black students differed in key respects. Rough divisions are as follows: First are the teachers who advocated a pedagogy of resistance to the educational inequities that black children endure.[55] Second are the teachers who also aimed to be "transformative pedagogists"[56] but who did not engage in extensive critiques of the system at large.[57] The third are the teachers who worked and advocated for organizational and structural changes in the education of black children.[58]

Resistance took many forms in the white teachers' stories. The first was anger with coworkers who did not act as advocates of black children. Kohl and Kozol were particularly outspoken on this issue.[59] High expectations were another form of resistance in the teachers' rejection of the standard belief that black children would fail. Kohl said, "The question that never was raised within our small community of educators was whether the children could learn."[60] He even locked away children's records from past years so as not to be influenced by their past failures. Hoffman said, "I in turn rely on them [the children] to remind me daily of our responsibility to close the senseless gap between those who are tracked for success and those who are heading nowhere."[61] Paley wrote that each teacher "must figure out, each in her own way, how to care for whatever group of children enters our classroom."[62] Ayers characterized good schools as places where teachers don't consider the conditions students live with as an excuse for failure. Meier challenged the profession and asked, "The question is not, Is it possible to educate all children well? but rather, Do we want it badly enough?"[63] It is not surprising, therefore, that these teachers uniformly eschewed mainstream tracking practices.

Also related to resistance was the teachers' oppositional stance toward the mandated curriculum, which, in some cases, was deemed irrelevant to black children's lives. Standardized tests were seen as especially onerous specifically because the results were generally seen as nonrepresentative of black children's abilities. Ayers called them "malevolent."[64] Kohl taught the children "how to get around them."[65] This is not to say the teachers refused to teach the given curriculum, though this did occur at times, as they actively searched for or created an alternative curriculum in a concerted effort to acknowledge black children's personal and cultural histories. Ayers, for instance, wrote of "liberating the curriculum" to find something about which kids really cared.[66] Both Kohl and Kozol dispensed of textbooks assessed to be written from a white perspective. Kohl allowed the children to "lead him" where they needed to go. The teachers steeped their curriculum with black children's concerns. Examples are O'Connor's writing assignments featuring the racially-charged Bensonhurst and Crown Heights incidents,[67] Hoffman's use of such works as the *Autobiography of Miss Jane Pittman* in his English class,[68] and Paley's self-written fairy tale, which had a black princess at the center.[69] Kozol was eventually fired for teaching the poetry of Langston Hughes.

Linked to resistance, high expectations, and a nonstandard curriculum, and reminiscent of effective black teachers, was the independent white teachers' sense of responsibility for the children's learning. This included the obligations of teachers to listen well, observe sharply, learn about African American history, know and participate in the school community, commit to political action in favor of black children, and believe that all black children can learn. Kohl claimed: "Every teacher has a responsibility, as a craftsperson, to hone her or his skills and refuse to believe there is one child destined to failure. Similarly, every teacher has a responsibility, as a citizen, to act politically in the name of his or her students for the creation of a just world where children can do rewarding work and live happy lives. If that means being criticized by administrators, becoming involuntarily transferred or even fired, one should be proud of being a troublemaker in a troubled world."[70]

These independent white teachers also practiced a pedagogy that sought meaningful relations with students beyond mere academic goals. "Teaching is relational and interactive," Ayers wrote. "It requires dialogue, give and take, back and forth."[71] It also included affirming the children's families through conversations, assignments, and, in some cases, personal visits and long-term friendships. Kohl regularly dined with his students and tutored family members.[72] Paley gave credit to a black parent for helping her talk openly about race.[73] "What you value, you talk about," she was told, and so she did.[74] Ayers commented, "Parents are a powerful, usually underutilized source of knowledge about youngsters."[75] Those white teachers in traditional public school settings, such as Kohl, Kozol, Hoffman, and O'Connor, also expressed a personal outrage at the dilapidated school environment and believed it spoke to who and what is valued in the system. Looking beyond the subjective, several of the teachers, most notably Kohl, Meier, and Ayers, located their teaching within the democratic ideal and upheld black children's inalienable right to an equal education and the country's need for an educated citizenry.[76]

For all of these white teachers, the issue of race was as personalized as recognizing one's own skin color in relation to the children's. Kohl spoke of the "weight of Harlem and his whiteness,"[77] and Hoffman noted that "every face but mine in this sophomore English class is black or brown."[78] Paley noted the different shades of black and white in her classrooms. This is not to say that the teachers reported they were always able to talk freely about their own or the children's race. Kohl acknowledged that at first he "tried to give a color blind education."[79] Paley discussed that at first it was easier to pretend the black child was white, another colorblind approach. She later admitted she was unable to mention color in her classroom at first, no matter how much she thought about it.[80] Her "journey into black and white,"[81] to where private talk about race and her own limitations as a white teacher of black children became public, is described in two books, *White Teacher* and *Kwanzaa and Me: A Teacher's Story*, written almost 20 years apart. O'Connor wrote about his fears of being a white teacher in a black world, describing his shame in feeling afraid for himself and his baby daughter while visiting the projects where his black students lived.[82]

A final characteristic that these white teachers shared was the belief that white teachers could make a difference in black children's lives. This belief in their contribution to black children's education, however, was also tempered by an awareness on the part of some that they were not only outsiders in the black community, but were potentially be perceived as untrustworthy. Meier wrote: "We can't do away with the likelihood that some of our students' families see white teachers as inherently suspect, but white teachers can listen, we can reconsider our own reactions, offer alternative possibilities, and challenge implicit assumptions."[83]

In summary, overlapping themes emerged from the different types of white teacher narratives. All of the white teachers' narratives examined for this chapter possessed a deep respect for the black community. They actively resisted the status quo for black children and their families, acted from sense of responsibility to teach children well, and believed that white teachers could make a difference in black children's lives pedagogically, these teachers had uniform high expectations of black children. Their teaching style could be characterized as personalized and subjective, and they practiced active listening. Also, they held, for the most part, an oppositional view of the standard curriculum. Finally, these teachers had a developed racial and political consciousness that resulted in outrage at inadequate environmental conditions in schools for black children and believed that an educated citizenry was good for democracy.

COMPARISON OF EFFECTIVE BLACK
AND INDEPENDENT WHITE TEACHERS

In many and important ways, all of the white teachers in this chapter have much in common with their effective black counterparts. High expectations were common to all. Interpersonal relationships were stressed, as was involvement with families and the community. In individual ways, the white teachers called their students' attention to black history and affairs. Curriculum was recreated to appeal to the strengths and interests of black children. Two teachers, Marvin Hoffman and Deborah Meier, worked and advocated for a restructuring of schools to benefit the education of black children. However, others, William Ayers, Herb Kohl, Jonathan Kozol, and Stephen O'Connor, echoed Lipman's findings about black teachers in restructured schools: that most school reform efforts were not likely to benefit black children; instead most problems needed individualized solutions.[84] Finally, and most significantly, the white teachers developed a hyperconsciousness about race in the classroom that generated discussions of school-related race and racial issues. This occurred most notably in an effort to address inequities in the system, curriculum, and society at large. An open acknowledgement of race also gave way to a greater tolerance of, if not appreciation for, black children's learning styles.

Despite the similarities between the effective black and the independent white teachers discussed here, however, there appeared to be significant differences as well. Distinctions were found in several areas, particularly the use of authority, the role of curriculum and testing, and the purpose of schooling. Also, effective black teachers tended to discuss the role of and insist on standard English in schools when necessary and employed familial or "kin" terms in talking with children.[85]

Regarding the use of authority in the classroom, some plain disagreement stood out. Consider the following statements from six teachers:

> Listening to students' voices and responding to their interests meant giving up the authoritarian role of the teacher. I found myself much more at ease in dialogue with my students than in telling them what to do all the time.

When at last I was left alone again with the class, I had to spend a good two or three more minutes summoning people back from the water fountain, interrupting conversations, telling students that, no, they couldn't go to the bathroom; no, the checkerboards and Monopoly games had to stay in the closet. . . . The class was a shambles.

I have almost always begun the year by asking students to think about their own learning agendas: What do you want to do this year?

I know it seems old-fashioned but I believe the students benefit from the structure. It's as if it were important for them to know what comes next. I have children in here who other teachers told me couldn't read. Heck, *they* told me they couldn't read. But I look them squarely in the eye in the beginning of the school year and tell them, you *will* read, and you will read *soon*.

Some of the kids have problems and some of them don't. But the majority of students want discipline, guidance, and adults who will steer them and give them some direction. I know this is what they want because many will come back later and tell you that you were one of the few adults that made them do what they were supposed to do. They are thankful you made them do the correct thing or that you didn't take no for an answer. They may stick their tongues out when you do but we adults and teachers can't let that bother us.

Those black teachers just made us do things that they thought were good for us.

The first three statements came from white teachers Kohl, O'Connor, and Ayers. The last three came from black teachers in either Ladson-Billings' or Foster's study.[86] The difference in approach to authority and discipline is clear and fairly representative of the two groups across the board. This is not to say the black teachers saw themselves as authoritarians or that white teachers saw themselves as abdicating all control. This would be an exaggeration of the data. Still, it seems significant that most of the independent white teachers either did not address the question of teacher-as-authority figure directly or did not emphasize authority in conjunction with good teaching. Kohl was steadfast in this view even while describing uncooperative and disobedient children.[87] Paley was specific about her role as the moral center in a classroom[88] and Meier wrote of the need for leaders in school, but neither highlighted the issue of authority in their work.[89] Effective black teachers, however, consistently, pointedly, and with tradition on their side, expressed their beliefs that black children learned best when the teacher's style was not only firm, but demanding and authority-based (Irvine and Fraser called teachers who taught like this "warm demanders."[90]) As the above examples from the texts attest, the use of authority in the classroom appears to be a nonnegotiable value in the black community. It is not a matter of personal style or timeliness; it is a community-commanded demonstration of caring.[91]

It should be noted that effective black teachers did not appear to be interested in authority for authority's sake, calling to mind Whitehead's distinction between authoritarianism and authoritativeness in *The Aims of Education*.[92] Authoritative teachers have their children's best interests at heart; authoritarians have their own. In fairness, the testimonies of the white teachers make it probable that they, too, would agree to this nuanced view of authority in the classroom. The fact remains, however, that these white teachers (less so Paley and Meier) were much less willing to exercise authority *directly* than were black teachers.

Curriculum and testing comprise the second area in which effective black teachers differed from the independent white teachers. It has been shown that effective black and white teachers were committed to a curriculum that emphasized the strengths, interests, and contributions of the black community, all part of what Ladson-Billings (1994a) referred to as cultivating "a relevant Black personality." The two groups diverged sharply, however, in that the white teachers spoke certainly and often about the issue of finding, creating, and teaching an alternative curriculum. By contrast, black teachers spent comparatively little time on the topic of alternative curriculum except in so far as they adapted the standard fare to suit black history and a black perspective. Black and white teachers were also united in their belief that standardized tests failed to capture the true abilities of black children. Success in usual venues such as standardized tests, though, was of paramount importance to black teachers. Kohl was the only white teacher who claimed that he taught to the test, but he did so in the spirit of "how to get around them" and not as an educational challenge.[93] In general, the independent white teachers did not address the issue of testing except to disparage its meaningfulness.

Another distinction between the two groups was how they used language to convey cultural messages. Paley,[94] and occasionally Ayers,[95] was the only white teacher to consistently employ "kin" terms or metaphors, which imply a familial relationship with students; black teachers did so frequently. This may or may not be related to the fact that Paley (and Ayers) was a teacher of very young children. In that situation, descriptions of oneself as a substitute mother or of a class as a large family are more common in some, but by no means all, white teachers' classrooms. In general, however, the independent white teachers appeared less likely to use familial language with their black students than black teachers did. With regard to standard English, none of the independent white teachers spoke to the necessity of black children learning, speaking, and writing standard English. Many of the effective black teachers and educators, however, were very concerned that black children be taught all aspects of standard English, both as an expectation they were capable of meeting and as a buffer against discrimination in the work force and society at large. This speaks to a powerful theme in the literature on black teachers: that standard English most represents the "culture of power,"[96] a fact that cannot be ignored in black students' education.

A more subtle distinction between effective black and independent white teachers that was also suggested by the literature centered on the perceived purpose of schooling. The independent white teachers directly and indirectly veered from the black teachers' vision on what role schools serve in black children's lives. White teachers, especially Kohl, Kozol, and O'Connor, tended to see and describe the schools for black children in near conspiratorial terms. In other words, they described schools as places that consciously and deliberately operated to deprive black children of educational opportunities. Even Paley and Meier, who described their classrooms and schools as safe places, did not write as if individual schools or classrooms were connected to a *network* of safety. The white teachers also voiced shock and outrage at the subpar physical conditions, low expectations for students by fellow teachers, and institutional and individual racism. Many feared the neighborhoods where black children went to school and they went to work. In contrast, Mrs. Valentine, Mrs. Deveraux, and Mrs. Harris, three teachers from the Ladson-Billings study, all spoke of schools in general as something like warrens for black children, as places where black culture could be celebrated and transmitted and where survival in the dominant culture could be learned. This is not to say black teachers ignored the realities for black children in schools. Yet they appeared to see potential in their own teaching, and even in the system (when manipulated successfully), that would help children rise above racism and neglect.[97] They voiced the belief that black children could learn despite inadequate material resources and social hostilities, claiming DuBois' vision of schools as liberating forces for black children.

The final and telling difference between effective black teachers and independent white teachers was in regard to the role of the outsider in the education of black children. In general, the independent white teachers wrote confidently of how the black children in their classes developed and learned under their tutelage. Only Paley questioned whether a black teacher would have better served the children.[98] (The idea was actually introduced by a black former student and not directly endorsed by Paley herself.) Many black teachers, though, questioned whether white teachers could ever be full-fledged advocates of black children. A sample of teachers in Foster's study said:

> Black kids need teachers who can understand and appreciate something about black communities. Too many white teachers don't understand blacks and don't want to understand us.[99]
> White teachers give up too easily on the kids.[100]
> We have some white teachers—a few—who are concerned about the development of black students as well as the whites. But most white teachers fear that if that black child uses his ability he might override the white.[101]

This is not to say that white teachers were never appreciated by black teachers or thought to be acceptable pedagogues. The inclusion of the three white teachers in Ladson-Billings' study attested to this possibility.[102] There did seem to be, however, a general sense that white teachers as a group were less likely to act in black children's best interests than black teachers.

DISCUSSION AND CONCLUSION

This chapter asks if race matters in the effective education of black children through a comparison of effective black and independent white teachers of black children. It appears that independent white teachers share some of the significant characteristics associated with effective black teachers, but do not share others. Similarities center on the need for identification with black community norms, including high expectations for student achievement. In this sense, race does not seem to matter, and culturally synchronistic teaching prevails. Differences center on the perception of the teacher as an authority figure and the mandate for success in the standard curriculum. Differences also appear around the purpose of schooling in general. These differences present a possible threat to culturally synchronistic teaching.

These findings further suggest that there remains a great need for empirical studies of not the independent but the usual white public school teachers of black children, teachers with typical gifts and limitations, in typical schools with typical children and families. Not only would data of this kind come closer to approximating the data on effective black teachers, thus ensuring a more fair comparison, but it would generate information that could be far more valuable to teacher educators of preservice teachers than anything available today.

Part Two

THE STORIES OF
CULTURALLY RESPONSIVE TEACHERS

Chapter 4

THE DEVELOPMENT OF
TEACHER EFFICACY BELIEFS

A Case Study of an African American
Middle School Teacher

Gloria Harper Lee

I n a speech to the Texas Middle Schools Association, Hayes Mizell, director of the Program for Student Achievement at the Edna McConnell Clark Foundation, underscored the impact of the beliefs and subsequent actions of educators on the success of students by stating, "If teachers and administrators and schools want students to succeed, they have to believe that all students can and should succeed. More importantly, they have to act to make it happen, they have to do almost anything to make it happen. The practices for student success are not a mystery; they are well known. They are not, however, self-implementing."[1] Perhaps the implicit meaning of Mizell's remarks provides critical insight into the timeless question presented to educators: "What must be done if schools are to become places in which all students and staff members are successful?" Mizell suggested that teachers' beliefs and practices are ultimately at the heart of student success. By focusing on what teachers believe and how these beliefs develop, researchers and educators may explore areas that influence educational practice in very unique ways. The research literature suggests that what teachers believe about their abilities to instruct students as well as about their abilities to affect student learning and achievement may be related to individual differences in teaching effectiveness.[2] Educational inquiry in this area could bring educators to "the very heart of teaching."[3]

Notable among studies that link teachers' beliefs to teaching practices is the construct of teacher efficacy. Teacher efficacy refers to a "teacher's belief in his or her capability to organize and execute courses of action required to accomplish successfully a specific teaching task in a particular context."[4] As a belief construct, teacher efficacy has been identified as a variable accounting for individual differences in teaching effectiveness.[5]

This chapter examines one successful African American teacher's personal story to gain a clearer understanding of the ways in which teachers with a strong, positive sense of teacher efficacy develop confidence in their teaching competence. This perceived confidence judgment concerning teaching competence is a reflection of teacher efficacy beliefs. Therefore, this chapter seeks to discover the role of teacher efficacy beliefs in the success of one African American teacher's career and to better understand the factors that contributed to the development of her teacher efficacy beliefs.

The discussion in this chapter presents a timely treatment of this topic, particularly for urban schools with African American students. The creation of learning environments that encourage and support the development of the intellectual capabilities of students is linked in large part to the talents and sense of efficacy of teachers. Teachers with a high sense of efficacy expend extra effort to create successful learning experiences for all students, including the most difficult. In contrast, teachers with a low sense of efficacy believe home and community environments may limit the teacher's capacity to influence effectively the intellectual development of the unmotivated student.[6] Exploration of the ways in which teachers discuss the development of their teacher efficacy beliefs should contribute to a clearer understanding of the factors that influence the development of teachers' efficacy beliefs across stages of their careers

SOURCES OF EFFICACY INFORMATION

Bandura's work on self-efficacy provides the most useful foundation on which to build an understanding of how teacher efficacy beliefs develop and what factors contribute to the development of these beliefs.[7] Perceived self-efficacy evolves as an individual formulates beliefs of personal competence. These beliefs in turn affect behavior. An individual's self-efficacy expectations for performing tasks are constructed from the interpretation of information received from four primary sources: mastery experiences, vicarious experiences, verbal persuasions, and physiological and emotional states.[8]

Bandura argued that *mastery experiences* are the most important source of efficacy information.[9] Based on past performance accomplishments, information from mastery experiences provides the individual with the most authentic evidence of whether one can successfully execute similar tasks in the future. Mastery experiences provide the most reliable foundation on which to assess self-efficacy. Typically, perceived successes raise self-efficacy. Perceptions of repeated failure tend to lower mastery expectations and thus lower efficacy beliefs. However, resilient efficacy develops when the individual exhibits persistent effort and achieves success on difficult tasks. Once a strong sense of efficacy is developed, an occasional failure will probably not have a profound effect.[10]

Applying Bandura's theory[11] to teacher efficacy, Tschannen-Moran et al. suggested that actual teaching experiences have the most powerful influence on self-perception of teaching competence.[12] While working in classrooms, teachers gain information about their teaching effectiveness and experience the consequences of their efforts. Self-assessment of one's capabilities in an actual teaching situation provides a very influential source of efficacy information.

Individuals also obtain efficacy information from *vicarious experience*. They receive information about their own capabilities through knowledge of others. Observing similar peers successfully perform a task can convey to the observers that their skills will improve if they intensify and persist in their efforts. The individuals persuade themselves that if others are successful, then certainly they can work hard to achieve some improvement in their own performances. Individuals formulate ideas about teaching through teacher education programs, from the professional literature, in classroom observations, via images portrayed in the media, and even from "teacher talk" around school. The behavior of skillful and admired role models provides an especially important source of information for an individual efficacy appraisal.[13]

Individuals may receive information about their self-efficacy via *verbal persuasions*. The simple suggestion that an individual has the capacity to perform a task may not lead to enduring changes in self-efficacy. However, encouragement received through positive verbal messages or social persuasion can influence an individual to exert the extra effort and maintain the persistent behavior necessary to succeed when faced with a difficult task. Likewise, verbal persuasions can also undermine efficacy beliefs when the individual receives critical feedback or when the individual is encouraged to perform a task but lacks the skills for successful completion.[14]

Verbal persuasions influence teacher efficacy beliefs. Teachers receive positive persuasive messages from sources that include coursework and professional development workshops; focused and constructive performance feedback from administrators, peer teachers, and students; and pep talks and notes from colleagues. If teachers use the information to acquire and employ new skills to improve student learning, perceptions of their teaching competence may be enhanced.

A fourth source of efficacy information comes from the *physiological and emotional states* of the individual. When confronted with stressful or taxing circumstances, one may experience an emotional arousal such as exhilaration or despondency, or a physical symptom such as increased heart rate or sweaty palms that could have an impact on personal efficacy. A teacher's physical or emotional state during a teaching task influences perceptions of teaching competence and may have an impact on efficacy beliefs. Positive emotions signal feelings of confidence and the anticipation of future success, which can enhance teacher efficacy beliefs. High levels of stress and anxiety can debilitate performance and create an expectation of failure, which can diminish teacher efficacy beliefs.[15]

In summary, Bandura suggested that an individual's efficacy expectations for performing tasks are based on four primary sources of information: mastery experiences, vicarious experiences, verbal persuasions, and physiological and emotional states.[16] Individuals integrate efficacy information from these four sources into their personal belief and motivational systems. These efficacy beliefs influence the amount of effort one is willing to put forth, the level of perseverance obtained when obstacles arise, the resiliency factor when faced with adverse situations, and the level of stress or depression experienced in coping with demanding situations.

EFFICACY BELIEFS AND TEACHER EFFECTIVENESS

Researchers have explored with increasing interest the concept that teachers' beliefs about their own capabilities as teachers may actually influence instructional effectiveness. Studies have associated teacher efficacy with student achievement,[17] student motivation,[18] teachers' adoption of innovation,[19] superintendents' ratings of teachers,[20] and teachers' classroom management strategies.[21] Research findings support the view that attention to teacher efficacy as an educational variable offers an important contribution to the design of enhanced school experiences for teachers and students.[22]

Research studies suggest a strong link between teachers' perceived efficacy and their attitudes and behaviors in the classroom. Bandura concluded that high efficacy teachers strongly believe in their ability to promote learning and consequently create mastery experiences for their students.[23]

Findings indicate that teachers' efficacy beliefs influence the way they structure learning activities for students,[24] how they involve parents and community in the learning experience,[25] and what they do to create a positive school climate.[26] A strong, positive sense of teacher efficacy has been associated with teachers' classroom behaviors, including willingness to try a variety of materials and approaches,[27] increased lesson planning and organization,[28] and reduced referrals of students to special education.[29] Researchers have shown that the positive qualities of enthusiasm for teaching,[30] commitment to teaching,[31] and retention of teachers[32] are related to teachers' sense of efficacy.

In addition to linking teacher efficacy to teacher behaviors, research findings also indicate that teacher efficacy appears to positively influence student achievement, attitude, and affective growth. Researchers have found teacher efficacy to be a powerful construct related to academic student outcomes such as achievement in reading, language arts, social studies, and math.[33] Teacher efficacy has also been linked to student motivation,[34] students' positive attitudes toward school,[35] optimistic perspectives about the subject matter taught,[36] and improved self-direction.[37]

BEVERLEY COCKERHAM

The participant in this study was one African American teacher, Beverley Cockerham, selected from the faculty of a middle school (grades 6–8). In 1997–98, the school faculty included a high percentage of veteran teachers (average of 12 years' teaching experience) with advanced degrees (79 percent held a master's degree or higher) who worked with a student population that was small and diverse, both racially and economically (630 students, 64.6 percent African American, 34.2 percent European American, 0.5 percent Asian, 54.5 percent eligible to receive free or reduced-priced lunch).

Using Bandura's Teacher Self-Efficacy Scale,[38] a pool of high efficacy
teachers was identified from the faculty of the school. From the pool of
high efficacy teachers, Beverley was selected for an in-depth case study of
the development of her teacher efficacy beliefs.

Beverley Cockerham was an active participant in the CULTURES program. At the time of this study, she was a 50-year-old African American female career teacher, married, with two grown children. Beverley is from
New York City and received a BA degree from City College of New York
in 1971. She completed her MA degree from City College of New York in
1972. Beverley has completed several inservice staff development
courses/programs during her teaching career. These programs include
teacher support specialist training (state department of education), CUL-
TURES and technology courses offered by her school district, a consortium of area public schools, and a large, public, southeastern university.

The year 2000 marked Beverley's twenty-fifth year as an educator. She
spent three years, 1972–75, teaching sixth grade in New York City before
moving to her current school district, where she began substitute teaching in 1975. Beverley assumed a full-time teaching position there in
1976. With the exception of a one-school-year leave in 1981, Beverley
has taught continuously in this school district for a total of 24 years. Beverley worked at one elementary school in the school district teaching fifth
grade for 10 years, 1976–87, and third grade for one year during the
1987–88 school year. Since 1989, she has worked at the middle school,
where she taught seventh and eighth grade social studies for seven years,
1988–95. At the time of the study, Beverley was in her fourth year as a
Title I teacher, offering math and reading support to students in grades
six, seven, and eight.

INTERVIEW WITH BEVERLEY COCKERHAM

Three major themes emerged from the data of the participant's responses to
the interview questions and to items on the Teacher Self-Efficacy Scale. First,
Beverley's self-report of her general beliefs about the educational process and
her specific teaching behaviors and characteristics matched descriptions of
the beliefs, teaching behaviors, and characteristics of high efficacy teachers
reflected in the literature on teacher efficacy. Second, mastery experiences,
vicarious experiences, verbal persuasions, and physiological and emotional
states provided important sources of information for the development of

Beverley's sense of teacher efficacy in various stages of her teaching career. Vicarious experiences and verbal persuasions were especially influential sources during Beverley's childhood and preservice education years and continued to be particularly significant sources of information for the maintenance of the veteran teacher's strong, positive teacher efficacy beliefs. Third, in addition to the influence of the four sources of information described by Bandura, Beverley identified school context variables that supported and strengthened her confident teaching behaviors and characteristics, and influenced her positive sense of teacher efficacy.

Beverley's Beliefs, Teaching Behaviors, and Characteristics

A review of the responses given by Beverley to interview questions and to items on the Teacher Self-Efficacy Scale offers a profile of Beverley's beliefs, teaching behaviors, and characteristics that is consistent with the descriptions of high efficacy teachers in research studies. Beverley's profile as a teacher with a strong, positive sense of teacher efficacy provides an excellent backdrop for the examination of the manner in which Beverley discusses the development of her teacher efficacy beliefs.

Beverley expressed confidence in her teaching competence and in her ability to have a positive effect on the academic performance of her mostly African American students. She has high expectations of all students and sets clear academic goals for her students. When asked if the high score on the Teacher Self-Efficacy Scale represented a true assessment of a strong confidence in her teaching ability, Beverley responded, "Yes, I do feel confident in my teaching ability. . . . I have confidence in my ability to work with all students. . . . I try very hard to stay focused on helping each student master the material even when they find it difficult. I am determined to show patience and understanding as students struggle with material. Students must know that they can succeed if they set their goals, and that it is my job to help them meet those goals."

Beverley's confidence in her ability to have a positive impact on student achievement is supported by her responses to items on the instructional self-efficacy subscale of the Teacher Self-Efficacy Scale. In answering such questions as "How much can you do to promote learning when there is lack of support from home?" and "How much can you do to overcome the influence of adverse community conditions on students' learning?" Beverley indicated responses of eight or nine, with nine representing "a great deal."

Her total instructional self-efficacy subscale score was 75 out of a possible total of 81.

Beverley also has confidence in her ability to motivate students. She not only sets clear academic goals but also plans and implements challenging instructional activities designed to actively engage students in the learning process. Beverley stated, "[I have] confidence in my lesson planning. I'm trying now to plan lessons around the interests of my students. . . . I'm taking, getting my lessons from them. . . . Sometimes students will say, 'Oh, this lesson is boring. This is boring. Why do we have to do this?' Well, I say, 'What can we do to make it more interesting?' [I] put it back on them and they respond with good ideas." Beverley's persistence in motivating students to achieve is evidenced by her responses of eight or nine ("a great deal") to questions on the instructional self-efficacy subscale of the Teacher Self-Efficacy Scale. Such questions included, "How much can you do to get through to the most difficult student?" and "How much can you do to motivate students who show low interest in schoolwork?" In addition, Beverley expressed her commitment to planning and implementing effective instructional experiences for her students. She shared how she worked closely with another teammate and how they frequently observed each other's teaching techniques, observed each other working with students, shared feedback, gave each other tips for improvement, planned lessons together, and developed creative instructional strategies. Beverley felt this cooperation was very helpful and very beneficial to her development as a teacher.

Beverley employs effective classroom management strategies. She not only provides clear academic expectations, but she also organizes her classroom activities to encourage self-motivation and academic responsibility in her students. The classroom in which she teaches is bright, cheerful, and well organized. Bulletin board displays, posters, and learning center activities are designed to engage students in the learning process. Materials are "hands on" and "user friendly," with the expectation that students will pursue individual interests while building academic skills.

This confidence in classroom management skills is reflected in Beverley's score on the disciplinary self-efficacy subscale of the Teacher Self-Efficacy Scale. She scored 26 out of a possible maximum score of 27 and responded eight or nine to such questions as "How much can you do to get children to follow classroom rules?" and "How much can you do to control disruptive behavior in the classroom?"

Parent involvement in the school experience is a top priority for Beverley. During the interview she stated that she worked hard to involve her parents in every aspect of the school program. In response to questions about enlisting parent involvement on the subscale of the Teacher Self-Efficacy Scale, Beverley answered eight or nine to the questions "How much can you do to get parents to become involved in school activities?," "How much can you assist parents in helping their children do well in school?," and "How much can you do to make parents feel comfortable coming to school?" Her total efficacy score in enlisting parent involvement was 25 out of a possible total of 27.

Beverley not only works well with students but also works very hard in the school to create a positive climate. She obtained a score of 66 out of a possible 81 on creating a positive school climate subscale of the Teacher Self-Efficacy Scale. Beverley responded eight or nine to such questions as "How much can you do to make students enjoy coming to school?," "How much can you help other teachers with their teaching skills?," and "How much can you do to enhance collaboration between teachers and the administration to make the school run effectively?" During the interview Beverley shared a humorous story about her positive attitude: "Some children have said to me, '[Mrs. Cockerham], you're always just so happy. Why are you so happy all the time? Why are you always so bubbly?' Well, all I can say is that it's just part of me."

In summary, Beverley's responses to interview questions and to items on the Teacher Self-Efficacy Scale reflect her confidence in her ability to have a positive effect on the academic performance of students. Her beliefs, teaching behaviors, and characteristics are consistent with the descriptions of high efficacy teachers in teacher efficacy research studies

Sources of Information for the Development of Beverley's Sense of Teacher Efficacy

Beverley indicated several events and influences to which she attributed the development of her strong sense of teacher efficacy. Throughout the interview, Beverley emphasized the development over the years of her confidence in her teaching. Therefore, the sources of information for the development of Beverley's sense of teacher efficacy are presented in a chronological order that reflects the progression of her teaching career.

Childhood/Family Influences.   Very early in life, Beverley decided to become a teacher. Interactions with and encouragement from family members (vicarious experiences and verbal persuasions) influenced this decision. Beverley recalled several episodes that had a significant impact on her decision to pursue a career as a teacher. First, Beverley reflected on her childhood play experiences. She described how much she "enjoyed playing school" with her siblings and the neighborhood children. She said, "I knew I wanted to become a teacher when I grew up. That idea just really appealed to me."

Beverley also noted limited career options for African American women when she was a child. She emphasized, however, that she did not choose to become a teacher simply because there were few career options. She had strong models within her own family that influenced her decision to pursue a teaching career. She explained, "I grew up in a 'helping family.' All of my immediate family members were in careers where they helped people in one way or another. For example, my father was a minister and my mother was a nurse. I have two sisters that are social workers, and I have a brother that is also a teacher. So, it was not a surprise that I would follow that same path. I just always knew I wanted to become a teacher and my family totally supported that idea."

These vicarious experiences and verbal persuasions during Beverley's childhood years were instrumental sources of information for the development of her teacher efficacy beliefs. Positive family role models influenced Beverley's decision to become a teacher. Family members encouraged her to pursue a teaching career.

In recalling her childhood years, Beverley discussed the influence of physiological and emotional states on her teacher efficacy beliefs. One of her most memorable experiences as a young student involved interaction with her father, who she described as "a very sharp math student." Beverley had to study very hard to grasp math concepts and her father often worked with her on math skills. This experience caused Beverley to focus on becoming a caring, nurturing, patient teacher.

In summary, during the interview, Beverley shared childhood stories about her family that illustrate the influence of vicarious experiences, verbal persuasions, and physiological and emotional states on the development of her teacher efficacy beliefs.

College/Preservice Preparation.   Vicarious experiences through interactions with strong, positive role models continued to influence the development of

Beverley's sense of teacher efficacy during the preparation phase of her teaching career. As a student teacher, she worked with a cooperating teacher who had a profound impact on her teaching development. The cooperating teacher was a strong role model who provided Beverley with positive teaching experiences. Beverley described her student teaching experience: "I think positive role models have really helped me. I had a very good experience with my student teaching. So that definitely helped. I was trained in a public elementary school in Harlem and I was trained in the open classroom setting. It was a sixth grade classroom. My cooperating teacher was an African American female teacher who had taught in Harlem for many years. She always modeled effective instructional strategies and effective classroom management techniques. I liked the way she dealt with her students. So I tried to model after that. She didn't put them down. She was a nurturer. She was firm, but friendly at the same time. She is a principal now."

Beverley's cooperating teacher not only modeled effective teaching practices, but she also encouraged Beverley by expressing confidence in Beverley's teaching abilities and providing Beverley with opportunities to engage in successful teaching experiences.

Encouragement from other student teachers, supervising or cooperating teachers, and university faculty also influenced Beverley's confidence in her teaching ability. She discussed the importance of her participation in a special support program, called Training Teachers to Teach (TTT).

When asked about other field experiences during her preservice education, Beverley recalled, "I did do some community work. I remember that. But for a very short period of time. We went to a community center and worked there for a month or two. The community center was in the South Bronx and we worked with African American children. . . . They were all ages and came to the center after school for games, sports, tutoring, and other activities. I really can't remember too much about it."

In responding to interview questions, Beverley indicated important sources of efficacy information during the college/preservice preparation phase of her teaching career. Beverley described her cooperating teacher as a very positive, nurturing role model and discussed her student teaching experience with great enthusiasm. Participation in the TTT program provided Beverley with a network of support and encouragement from university supervising teachers, school district cooperating teachers, and peer student teachers. A brief experience working in a neighborhood community center afforded Beverley some interaction with students.

These mastery experiences, vicarious experiences and verbal persuasions helped Beverley gain confidence in her teaching ability.

Induction/Early Years. Beverley's positive experiences as a student teacher were especially helpful during her induction years as a beginning teacher in another public middle school in Harlem where she received very little instructional support from peers or from administrators. When asked about specific feelings experienced as a novice teacher, Beverley responded, "Oh, it was nervousness because I always wondered how effective I was going to be. What type of teacher will I be? How will the parents respond? How will the administrators respond? What about my peers? Am I planning my lessons right? I always, always . . . I didn't have a lot of confidence back then. I was concerned with handling discipline problems and how effective I would be. I didn't receive a lot of feedback in my first years of teaching in New York."

In the interview, Beverley spoke very little of the induction/early years phase of her teaching career. Her responses to specific probe questions about this phase were short, with the explanation that she could recall few if any particular events or experiences. Beverley did, however, mention the stress and anxiety she experienced as a beginning teacher and the subsequent negative impact these physiological and emotional states had on her confidence in her teaching.

Current School District. Beverley remembered the transfer to her current school district as a turning point in the development of her confidence in teaching. Working in a smaller school district, in a smaller school, and with a principal that was more involved in the instructional program of the school had an impact. The opportunity to receive support and encouragement from others through performance feedback helped Beverley become a more confident teacher.

However, Beverley did not talk a great deal about her experience as an elementary school teacher in her current school district. She had much more to say about the relationship of her assignment to the middle school and the development of her teaching confidence. For example, Beverley emphasized the influence of role models in her current school district. When asked about people who may have helped in building her confidence as a teacher, Beverley replied, "Oh, there are certain people in this school system, in this school that have been a great help. Just watching [the principal], for example, has helped me a lot. She is very calm, very low key. She's always the same. With the students, she is fair, firm, friendly. She gets what she needs done with them. [She has] high expectations. She is very calm, very professional. I see that in her and it helps me very much. I have not always been like this. No, I have not always had this confidence or taught in this way. I was very nervous, very anxious about my teaching. I have learned a lot from [the principal and two other school district administrators]."

In addition to the support and encouragement received from positive administrator role models, feedback from students, parents, peer teachers, and administrators has had a significant impact on Beverley's sense of teacher efficacy. Verbal persuasion through positive performance feedback has been a critical source of efficacy-building information. Beverley asks her students to write her letters about what they enjoy or what they do not enjoy about her classes. She solicits feedback from her students so that she may plan more effective lessons. Beverley explained the process: "Periodically, throughout the year, I like to get feedback from the students. So I ask them to write me letters with whatever they want to say. Negatives, positive, whatever. And, yes, there are some negatives, but the positives outweigh [them] . . . and it really helps. . . . Students just tell me that they enjoy my class. I make learning fun. They like the one on one interaction. When I was teaching social studies, they said social studies was fun because I gave them passports, we went all around the world . . . tasting food. I try to make learning come alive."

Beverley also appreciates any information parents are willing to share about the progress of their children who are students in her class. Parents of her students often give her feedback in conferences or in letters they write to her. Beverley shared one example: "For instance, this year, one particular child's mother who came in for a conference wrote me a letter that said her child was very happy in my class because I was able to break down the subject for [the child]. It was math. I was able to help her understand [math]. Parents often tell me that I have helped motivate their children to complete the work for my class and that their children have not only learned so much in my class but have enjoyed the class as well. This really motivates me as a teacher."

Beverley found interactions with peer teachers to be invaluable. The teachers interact by observing each other and sharing feedback about teacher performance with each other. They work together on projects for or with the students. Teachers have given her feedback on how well her instructional strategies work and how effective her calm, patient, and caring demeanor works with students.

Beverley's selection by local school and district administrators as a teacher leader in the school has provided positive feedback about her teaching abilities. She explained, "They have selected me to serve in various positions in the school and in the school system. So I guess I am doing a good job." For example, she was especially selected for her current teaching position (reading and math support) because of her outstanding teaching skills. She is trained as a teacher support specialist to work with induction level teachers in the school district. As a participant in a university-based staff development program, Beverley conducts staff development sessions on working with culturally diverse students. She is a cofacilitator in a public schools/university consortium and works cooperatively with teachers to plan staff development activities, offer feedback on instructional strategies, and help develop plans for involving parents in the school.

Beverley mentioned the influence of mastery experiences in her current teaching position just once. When asked to make additional comments about her teaching Beverley replied, "One thing that has given me confidence in my teaching ability is knowing the instructional material, studying the material, teaching the material, and planning activities or developing materials to make sure the students really understand what's going on."

Vicarious experiences from the presence of skillful and admired positive administrative role models, and the support and encouragement received through verbal persuasions of students, parents, peers, and administrators in her current school district have been powerful sources of information that strengthened Beverley's strong, positive teacher efficacy beliefs. Specific positive performance feedback about her teaching behaviors has been an especially strong influence. Beverley briefly mentioned mastery experiences through actual teaching as a source of information in the development and strengthening of her teacher efficacy beliefs.

During the interview, Beverley indicated several events and influences to which she attributed the development of her confidence in her teaching abilities. These perceived confidence judgments represent Beverley's teacher efficacy beliefs and were influenced by mastery experiences, vicarious experiences, verbal persuasions, and physiological and emotional states.

Although Beverley noted the influence of mastery experiences in the development of her confidence in her teaching competence, these experiences did not appear to represent the most critical sources of information for the development of Beverley's teacher efficacy beliefs.

Beverley recalled the potentially negative influence of physiological and emotional states early in her teaching career. However, these stressful and taxing experiences did not appear to debilitate her teaching performance or create self-expectations of failure in future teaching experiences. Beverley's teacher efficacy beliefs were not diminished by these experiences. Instead, Beverley used the experiences to conceptualize the kind of effective teacher she wanted to become.

Another source of efficacy information is the vicarious experience gained when individuals assess their own competence in relation to the attainments of others.[39] Knowledge gained by observing models or comparing oneself to peers in similar situations can have an influence on the individual's self-perceptions of competence.[40]

Beverley discussed enthusiastically the influence of positive family, teacher, and administrator role models on the development of her confidence. When asked about events or influences that helped her become confident, Beverley named "positive role models" has having a great influence. Beverley also explained that during her preservice education, she had an excellent student teaching experience working with a "very good, very, very, very helpful" cooperating teacher. Finally, beliefs of personal competence can be strengthened or weakened through verbal persuasions received from others.

Beverley identified verbal persuasions received from family members, students, parents, peers, and supervisors as critical sources of information for the development of her strong, positive teacher efficacy beliefs. The family, teacher, and administrative role models that were so important to the development of Beverley's confidence were also effective persuaders in encouraging her growth and development as a teacher.

In summary, although Beverley identified mastery experiences, physiological and emotional states, vicarious experiences, and verbal persuasions as sources of information that influenced the development of her confidence, vicarious experiences and verbal persuasions were the most critical sources of information that shaped the development of her teacher efficacy beliefs.

The Influence of School Context Variables

Although the four sources of efficacy information described by Bandura—mastery experiences, vicarious experiences, verbal persuasions, and physiological and emotional states—were used as foundations from which to examine the development of Beverley's strong positive efficacy beliefs, the influence of school context variables cannot be ignored. Researchers argue that teacher efficacy is context specific. Teachers may feel more efficacious in certain settings and under certain conditions and less efficacious in other settings under a different set of circumstances. Context is an important consideration in making an efficacy judgment.[41]

Beverley emphasized the organization of the middle school in which she teaches as an important influence on the development of her sense of teacher efficacy. After discussing the anxiety experienced during her induction years of teaching, Beverley explained, "Then coming here [the current school district], I started getting more feedback in this system. And now [that I teach in the middle school], I started getting a lot of feedback because there's a lot of interaction now with teachers in this school. We dialogue a lot. People are not in their separate little cubbies anymore. We're all working together. That has *made* the difference. Teachers working together has really set the tone in this school. I started gaining more confidence in my teaching after moving to this smaller district, but I really feel the confidence at [the middle school]."

Working in teams has been especially helpful to Beverley in building her confidence as a teacher. She not only works with Title I teachers, but she works with other teachers, as well. According to Beverley, when teachers work together instruction improves. She states, "Interdisciplinary planning has really helped my confidence as a teacher. . . . We ask each other questions and develop really good lesson plans to teach our students."

Although the interview questions of the present study were developed using principally Bandura's hypothesized sources of efficacy information, Beverley spoke most enthusiastically during the interview about school context variables as critical sources for the development and strengthening of her teacher efficacy beliefs. Because teachers are part of an interactive social system and do not work in isolation, research concerning the development of teacher efficacy beliefs must consider the social and organizational structure of educational systems.[42]

Several researchers have examined the role that context plays in the development and maintenance of teachers' sense of efficacy and have related teacher efficacy beliefs to several school-level variables. Bandura outlined the attributes of highly efficacious schools and emphasized the importance of strong academic leadership by the school principal. In a study of teacher efficacy and commitment to teaching, Coladarci found that masterful academic leadership by the school principal builds teachers' sense of efficacy.[43]

Moore and Esselman found that teachers who participated in school-based decision making had a stronger sense of efficacy than did teachers who felt that they had little influence in the school's decisions.[44] Lee and Smith reported that a sense of community in a school was the single greatest predictor of teachers' level of efficacy.[45] Chester and Beaudin examined the efficacy beliefs of newly hired novice and experienced teachers working in an urban context.[46] They noted that teacher efficacy increased as the opportunity for collaboration with other adults and the number of classroom observations increased. Ashton and Webb investigated the relationship between the organizational structure of school and teachers' sense of efficacy.[47] The researchers reported that teachers working in a school with a collaborative middle school philosophy and structure had a higher sense of efficacy than did teachers working in a more traditional junior high structure.

Beverley explained emphatically during the interview that the instructional team concept that is the foundation of the organizational structure of the middle grades' instructional model had "made the difference" in her confidence as a competent teacher. Beverley noted several areas of the middle grades' organizational structure that positively influenced her confidence as a teacher. They included interaction among teachers, dialogue among teachers concerning effective instruction and individual student needs, and participation of teachers in classroom and school-based decisions. Beverley also noted the positive influence of the school principal on the school's culture and climate.

SUMMARY

This case study of Beverley, an African American teacher in a predominately African American middle school, supports the research on teacher efficacy but also closely parallels the research on culturally responsive pedagogy as outlined in the Cooper and Ware chapters in this volume.

Like the African American teachers in the research literature, she demonstrated care for her students and assumed a familial relationship with them. She had high expectations, set clear academic goals, and planned challenging instructional activities to motivate her students. Beverley used effective classroom management techniques and experienced few disciplinary problems with her students. She also involved her African American parents in all aspects of the educational process and worked very hard in the school to create a positive climate. Unlike the culturally responsive teachers in the literature, she seldom made explicit comments about issues of race and racism. Perhaps the mostly African American school setting in which she taught is related to this finding.

Findings from this investigation have implications for the design of preservice and inservice teacher educator programs that could support and strengthen the development of strong, positive teacher efficacy beliefs. Teacher educator programs should use an apprenticeship approach to provide mastery experiences and specific feedback to preservice teachers throughout their preservice education program. In such a program preservice teachers would instruct and manage children in a variety of contexts with increasing levels of complexity under the supervision of an experienced classroom teacher. If field experiences were included in most courses, preservice teachers would have the opportunity to observe effective models (vicarious experiences), practice their teaching skills (mastery experiences), and receive specific performance feedback (verbal persuasions) over various contexts and skills. Exposure to these experiences early in their teaching careers should have a positive effect on the development of preservice teachers' efficacy beliefs.[48] Inservice teachers could have similar efficacy building experiences by organizing staff development activities around study groups, learning circles, peer observations, and other collaborative efforts specifically designed to offer the support and encouragement needed for teachers to examine and discuss curriculum, improve teaching practices, and ensure the implementation of instructional innovations.

Beverley identified school context variables as having the most significant influence on the development and enhancement of her teacher efficacy beliefs. Schools operate as social systems and develop collective beliefs about their students' capacity to learn, about their teachers' confidence in effectively teaching each child, and about the ability of the school leadership to create positive climates focused on teaching and learning.[49] Both preservice and inservice teacher educators should encourage teachers to examine school organizational models and explore the role of school practices to understand how teachers' perceptions of their own capabilities are shaped in the midst of a particular set of contextual challenges and opportunities.

The study of teacher efficacy has become an important area of research in the field of education, and research studies have linked teacher efficacy to the improvement of various dimensions of schooling. The importance of the construct to teacher education is significant. Therefore, preservice teacher educators, inservice teacher educators, and practitioners working in the area of teacher development should continue to explore the development and malleability of teacher efficacy beliefs. Of particular interest are studies that focus on how teacher efficacy develops, what factors contribute to a strong, positive sense of teacher efficacy in various contexts, and how teacher education programs can help preservice and inservice teachers develop and strengthen high teacher efficacy beliefs.

Chapter 5

THE INFLUENCE OF PROFESSIONAL DEVELOPMENT ON A TEACHER'S CHANGING PRAXIS

The Journey of an African American Teacher

Kim Nesta Archung

A significant body of research is available on the effects of professional development in a variety of educational topics such as science,[1] mathematics,[2] reading,[3] multicultural education,[4] and other similar issues. However, much of the existing research focusing on multicultural teacher preparation centers on preservice teachers.[5]

Meager attention is directed to the professional development of inservice teachers[6] and how to prepare them adequately to rethink and reshape their praxis to address issues of cultural bias and culturally inappropriate practice. Additionally, little of the research focuses on the specific effects of professional development on changing a teacher's praxis, and even less of the research focuses specifically on urban African American teachers and their professional development experiences. This chapter addresses this void by examining the professional development journey of one African American teacher.

The chapter presents a case study of one urban African American teacher's professional development history and its relationship to her praxis, in particular the relationship between her practice and her beliefs about cultural diversity in the classroom. How does the teacher perceive that her professional development history influences her practice and beliefs about cultural diversity in the classroom? How do the teacher's career development phases and the context of her professional development experiences relate to her perceptions? What relationships do the teacher's specific cultural influences, family background, social and economic status, and gender have with her praxis?

This case study of an African American teacher's professional development journey contributes to the literature on professional development, specifically the career cycles and professional development of African American teachers in urban settings. This teacher's profile offers a unique opportunity to explore the different aims and dilemmas that arise at various moments in her professional cycle and to explore the relevance of these aims and dilemmas in her personal life history.

When there is a deeper understanding of the ways in which an African American teacher develops a perspective on teaching cultural diversity, new perspectives on African American teaching practices emerge. These new perspectives not only are academically sound but they also address the needs of an increasingly diverse student body. There are no case studies or other research studies on this topic. Researchers have done life histories of white female teachers, but no comparable studies of African American female teachers have been done.[7]

PROFESSIONAL DEVELOPMENT
AND TEACHERS' CAREER CYCLES

When we examine the facilitation of professional development in teachers' lives during their career cycles, consideration has to be given to the obstacles in this process. Olson cites that one half of undergraduates who prepare for teaching careers do not enter kindergarten through twelfth grade public school classrooms for four years after graduating.[8] Of those who do begin teaching, about one in five leave after three years in the classroom, during the orientation phase. Old models of professional development contribute to these impediments for growth because they ignore the emerging literature on teacher career cycles and stages.

Huberman writes about the professional careers of teachers and their professional development.[9] He states that the relationship between teachers' professional careers and professional development is situated within the context of the different aims and dilemmas that occur at various moments in their professional cycles. Teachers' desires to gain more information, knowledge, expertise, and technical competence vary according to their specific career stages and the aims and dilemmas associated with these stages.

Fessler, Huberman, and Vonk describe specific models in a teacher's career cycle.[10] Fessler tends to describe the phases of a teacher's career cycle in detail, while Huberman outlines phases in accordance to the corresponding number of years a teacher has been teaching. Vonk, on the other hand, describes phases succinctly. While these researchers' models are delineated and defined in somewhat different phases, their descriptions of the teacher career cycle can be similarly summarized into six general stages. These are: the preprofessional or preservice phase, induction phase, competency building phase, serene or stable phase, reorientation or experimental phase, and career wind-down phase. These six stages are summarized as follows and provide the framework for further discussion of the case subject's professional development history.

The first stage may be summarized as a preprofessional or preservice phase. This phase encompasses the period of a teacher's initial education and training. The prospective teacher prepares for the role of teacher and explores various options regarding employment and teaching positions.

The next stage includes the beginning or induction years of teaching. During this period much of a teacher's activity is centered on getting a handle on the job, including gaining acceptance by students, peers, and administrators. Fessler refers to this as a socialization period in which the new teacher strives to achieve a comfort and security level dealing with the everyday problems and issues that arise in the profession.[11]

During the competency building period a teacher demonstrates increasing abilities and competencies. Teachers at this stage in their career cycles tend to be receptive to new ideas and seek to improve their teaching skills by gaining access to new materials, methods, and strategies. As such, teachers' attendance at workshops and conferences and their self-directed initiatives to enroll in graduate programs tend to be high. Fessler remarks that teachers see the job as challenging during this phase. He sees this as a pivotal period for teachers in the early stages of their careers. "Those who are successful 'in grabbing the handles' of teaching go on to periods of positive growth and development. Those who flounder during this period (either through lack of ability or lack of support) often experience career frustration or instability."[12]

Teachers experience the mastery of an accomplished professional during the serene and stable period. At this time, teachers tend to be enthusiastic and have a high level of satisfaction with their work and their professional lives. Teachers in this phase are often supportive and play a role in helping to identify appropriate inservice education initiatives and activities for their schools.

The reorientation, experimental, or growing period is the phase explored in detail in this research study. This phase can best be described as a time when a teacher may doubt or question his or her commitment to teaching. This has often been described as teacher "burn out" and is generally associated with midlife crisis. However, Fessler points out that there is an increasing incidence of such feelings happening among teachers in the relatively early years of their careers. Teachers who have either never developed the skills to succeed, find their school climate stagnant, or face the threat of "last hired/first fired" often drop out of teaching at this point or continue with less energy and enthusiasm.[13] This period can also be marked by a teacher becoming reenergized and moving on to further professional accomplishments.

The final phase, career wind down or disengagement, generally takes place just prior to retirement. Huberman describes this as the period between the thirty-first to fortieth year of teaching.[14] This period is delineated as either a calm or a bitter period of disengagement or preparation for leaving the profession.

In a review of the stages of teacher development Fessler states that previous reviews on the notions of differentiated stages conducted by Gregorc, Katz, and Unruh and Turner "have provided valuable insight into the notion of differentiated stages of teacher development."[15] However, he also points out that there are major limitations to these early attempts in that they "lump all mature teachers together without further differentiation."[16] These early theorists have not profiled the continuous growth and development of experienced teachers.

The research of Burke, Fessler, and Christensen; Fessler; and Huberman outlines the career cycles of teachers, including perspectives on the development and changes that experienced teachers encounter.[17] This research indicates that the professional development needs of teachers in this stage of their professional journeys should be focused around individualized models and approaches that are supportive of the specific problems and needs of teachers. As Fessler points out, these teacher career cycle models suggest much in the way of reinforcing the traditional use of inservice or staff development activities that emphasize improving teacher skills, especially during the skill-building periods associated with the induction and competency-building stages and, to some extent, during the enthusiastic-and-growing stage.[18] These ideas "also suggest a broadening of the notion of staff development and professional growth to include concern for personal needs and problems of teachers."[19]

Although the individual needs and problems of teachers are mentioned as significant, what is lacking in this body of research is an explicit focus on the identity development of teachers that includes, but is not limited to, issues of ethnicity, race, and class. The existing research on career cycle models does not interface with the racial identity development of teachers, as discussed in the McAllister chapter, outside of a reference to "personal environment." Personal environment is defined by Fessler as "family support structures, positive critical incidents, life crises, individual dispositions, avocational outlets, and developmental stages experienced by teachers."[20] These elements are essential in understanding the personal nature of teachers' lives and the contexts through which their professional growth is influenced by their personal environments. However, the discussions of personal environment are limited to generic descriptions of the aforementioned facets. The relevance of culturally specific history is neither mentioned nor inferred. Consequently, the significance of context and professional development (urban, suburban, or rural environments; race, ethnicity, and social class of teachers and their students) is not discussed in the professional development literature.

THE PROFESSIONAL DEVELOPMENT OF TEACHERS IN DIVERSE URBAN CONTEXTS

The research on teachers' career cycles indicates the salience of individualized approaches to models of professional development. The research on best practices in professional development supports the notion that "professional development is critical to bringing about sustained educational improvement."[21] Additionally, there is a significant body of research available on the effects of professional development on teacher attitudes, beliefs, and changing practices.[22] However, there is little research recorded in the area of professional development that focuses on culturally relevant practice and its influence on teachers' praxis. As Irvine stated in the first chapter of this book, "there is a compelling need for research that investigates how teachers' cultural experiences and prior socialization affect the manner in which they view their profession and practice their craft."

Most of the existing research dealing with cultural issues is found in the area of multicultural teacher preparation and primarily centers on preservice teachers. This research focuses heavily on the inclusion of multicultural perspectives.[23] The dominant emphasis is on the lack of cultural synchronization between preservice teachers who are predominantly "White, middle-class, heterosexual, and monolingual in English"[24] and their diverse students of color.[25] Few professional development models exist that provide inservice teachers with skills and opportunities to address issues and concerns related to attitudes toward and beliefs about students of color and the development of culturally responsive pedagogy.

Cochran-Smith is one of the few researchers who has focused attention on practicing teachers and their professional development in an effort to address issues of diversity and cultural relevance.[26] She contends that, "A coherent framework for understanding and ultimately improving the teaching of increasingly culturally diverse student populations requires attention to issues of epistemology, ideology, practice, and professional development."[27] Cochran-Smith states that culturally unresponsive teachers will not change into responsive ones simply through a particular professional development activity. However, she outlines a framework for shaping the direction of professional development that begins to lend itself to exploring issues of culturally relevant pedagogy by addressing interpretation, ideology, and practice. Cochran-Smith indicates that issues of practice and praxis rest on issues of ideology, political frameworks, knowledge, and interpretive frameworks; these ideas in themselves lay a foundation for shaping professional development and go beyond method. Ultimately she concurs that all professional development is local at its rudimentary level. Central to the perspective that Cochran-Smith outlines are factors such as the teacher's "(1) beliefs, images, and knowledge/understandings of self, particularly the self-as-teacher; (2) belief, images, and understandings of knowledge itself—both knowledge generally and subject matter knowledge specifically; and (3) beliefs, images, and knowledge/understandings of culture, cultures, and cultural difference."[28]

Several scholars have suggested that research is underrepresented on the influence of racial identity on teachers' belief systems.[29] McAllister and Irvine state that research findings are inconsistent in defining effective teaching strategies that produce desired changes in teachers' beliefs, attitudes, and behaviors regarding culturally diverse students.[30] In this regard, Helms has suggested that the broad application of the currently researched ethnic identity and cultural awareness models to both dominant and non-dominant populations is problematic.[31]

Irvine points out that it is unfair to suggest that teachers are exclusively the products of their cultural and racial backgrounds. Additionally, other researchers have posited that crosscultural learning and identity development are complex processes that include numerous factors like age, gender, ethnicity, race, social class, and sexual orientation.[32] Therefore, omissions of the influences of cultural variables—and the ethnic and racial backgrounds of teachers' instructional behaviors and attitudes—leave the realm of research on teacher identity incomplete. In order to achieve an understanding of professional development in the context that Cochran-Smith outlines, a refocus of attention on the aforementioned factors needs to be constructed to include the context of cultural, ethnic, gender, and racial considerations.[33]

A FOCUS ON THE INDIVIDUAL PROFESSIONAL DEVELOPMENT JOURNEYS OF AFRICAN AMERICAN TEACHERS

There have been a number of studies conducted that document teachers' lives and careers.[34] However, most of these studies do not differentiate teachers by their ethnic, racial, or cultural backgrounds. The few studies that speak specifically to African American teachers' cultural and ethnic backgrounds date back to the late 1800s or early 1900s[35] or come from a Canadian[36] or British[37] context. While these studies offer a perspective on the lives and careers of teachers of African descent, they do not provide a context specific to contemporary African American teachers. Studies that focus on African American teachers do not specifically look at their professional development journeys.[38]

Siddle Walker's study provides a historical description of a successful segregated African American school and the African American teachers who provided years of teaching excellence to a community of African American students.[39] While Siddle Walker's work does not focus solely on the professional journeys of these teachers, her work provides insight into the professional lives of African American teachers situated within a historical and cultural context. Inclusion of Siddle Walker's research adds to the analysis of the teacher career cycle model. This analysis provides a context for drawing inferences and relationships between the research on successful African American teachers in segregated settings and the contemporary case that is the subject of this empirical study.

Foster provides a collection of narratives that capture the professional lives and careers of a selected group of African American teachers.[40] The cases presented in Foster's work do not tell the story of these teachers' professional lives in the context of specific professional development programs. However, these narratives do provide an example of African American teachers' life journeys and at times include some mention of their professional development experiences. These teachers' voices offer an opportunity to investigate a collage of issues arising in the professional journeys of a group of teachers whose careers span the period from school segregation to the present.

Ladson-Billings' work, although not singularly focused on examples of African American teachers, does provide an opportunity to explore the cases of five African American teachers and their praxis with regard to African American students.[41] Her work specifically focuses on culturally relevant pedagogy and practice. Ladson-Billings' work demonstrates several examples of how teachers implement specific strategies and qualities in their classrooms that are specifically relevant for teaching African American students. However, these teachers do not talk about their professional development experiences.

In summary, the literature provides an analysis of research that establishes a coherent framework for understanding issues underlying the context of this case study. The complexity of the interrelationship between the teacher's ethnicity, class, gender, career cycle, and school environment are outlined.

The Teacher

When I met Vivian Stephens in June 1994, she had been teaching for 21 years in the state of Georgia. Our first meeting took place in Cambridge, Massachusetts as she embarked on a new phase of her professional development journey. Our journey literally began when I picked her up in front of her hotel for a drive to Portland, Maine.

My first impressions of Vivian were positive. She exuded a level of professionalism coupled with an air of southern cordiality that emanated genuine warmth and charm. She seemed to be comfortable meeting a perfect stranger for a two-and-a-half-hour drive into the far reaches of an unfamiliar northern state. We introduced ourselves and chatted casually throughout the trip, and our periods of silence seemed natural and not awkward. It was not until I got to know her better that I realized Vivian was nervous and anxious about driving to Portland with a complete stranger but was willing to take the risk in spite of her initial reluctance. This initial insight was the first hint that Vivian was a person who is willing to try new things and change for the benefit of her students and her own growth.

Vivian and I were to spend the next several days in Maine engaged in a professional development offering sponsored by Expeditionary Learning Outward Bound (ELOB), a comprehensive school reform design. Vivian, a fourth-grade African American teacher from Decatur, Georgia, was one of the teachers I would be working with during the upcoming school year. My work as a school designer for ELOB had just started and my orientation to my new position began with a series of summer professional development experiences with public school teachers from around the country. These teachers and their schools were engaged in processes of whole school change, reform, and redesign. Expeditionary Learning provided a host of professional development experiences to the staffs of these schools in their efforts to support the restructuring of urban public education. Vivian was among a small group of teachers who were participating in this weeklong architecture workshop in Maine.

Vivian Stephens was selected as the focal point of this research for several reasons. She was chosen because of her willingness to work collaboratively with me and because of my prior knowledge of her continuous interest in improving her classroom practices. Her principal recognized Vivian Stephens as being dedicated, effective, and always willing to participate in improvement practices for herself and her students. Through informal interviews and conversations, Vivian indicated her dedication to the students she teaches and always spoke of her personal desire for continuous professional growth and development.

As of September 2000, Vivian had taught for more than 25 years, mostly in the school system of the small, urban city of Decatur, Georgia. Most recently she taught fourth-grade students from ethnically, culturally, and economically diverse backgrounds, although the majority of her students were white and came from middle- to upper-middle-class homes. Most of the students Vivian taught throughout her teaching career were a mixture of lower income African American children and middle-class European American children. Vivian continuously indicated an interest in increasing her abilities to work more effectively with all of her students. She stated, "I was fortunate to have teachers who saw more in me than I saw in myself. Once I decided to teach, I wanted to do the same for my own students. . . . My children keep me inspired and wanting to improve as a teacher."

Vivian always thought of herself as a learner. "If my students can do it, I can do it. . . . I can still learn. I still want to learn." Vivian described herself as willing to learn and to try new things. She said that often she learns new things for the sake of her students. She did not allow difficult or intimidating things to hold her back because she said her reluctance to learn might retard her students' progress. She described an uncomfortable incident when she first learned how to use computers. "I had to go there and put myself in a position of being very uncomfortable so that I could learn how to do that for them." She stated on many occasions, "If there is some thing new to be learned about teaching and learning then I make it my business to learn it."

My second encounter with Vivian was late August 1994, when I made an initial trip to Decatur to meet the principal and faculty of the school. Vivian showed me around the school and introduced me to others. She also extended herself beyond the workday. It was apparent that Vivian was a leader of her faculty. She helped her colleagues think about and plan professional development activities for the coming school year. Her commitment to her students was an obvious model for the other teachers in her small school, and her principal often relied on her leadership among her peers.

Throughout the 1994–95 school year I spent an average of two to three days per month at Vivian's school, facilitating professional development activities. During each of my visits to the school, Vivian spent a considerable amount of time with me outside of the professional day. It was through these occasions that I became more acquainted with Vivian as a friend and as a professional. Whenever I had the occasion to visit her classroom, she introduced me to her class as an active participant. She readily encouraged me to discuss students' projects and work. There were several opportunities when she invited me to take over the lesson. Vivian's classroom became a very comfortable and familiar environment for me, and I was always welcome to spend time there, even if it was not scheduled.

Description of the School and the Principal

Clairemont Elementary School, where Vivian currently teaches, is located in the city of Decatur, a small urban school district in the greater Atlanta,

Georgia area. Clairemont is one of seven elementary schools in a nine-school district. Like the other schools in its district, Clairemont is faced with many issues that stem from profound cultural and economic diversity. In the years 1995 to 1999, between 219 and 241 students attended the school in the kindergarten through fifth grades. Thirty-five percent of the students at this small elementary school are on free and reduced lunch. A small percentage (6 percent) live outside of the district and pay tuition in order to attend the school. Approximately 3 percent of the student body are African American. The majority of these students are low income. Less than 1 percent of the students are Asian or from other ethnic backgrounds. Twenty-three full and part-time faculty members include teachers, the principal, media specialists, and counselors. A relatively large percentage (90.5 percent) of the faculty hold a masters degree or higher. Between 1994 and 1998, there were no more than two African American full-time classroom teachers on staff at one time. Vivian has remained on the staff as the one African American teacher with the longest tenure during this period. At the time of this study, there were several African American paraprofessionals and one African American social worker serving on the school's staff.

In 1990 Clairemont was one of the first schools in its district to embrace an innovative approach to a literature-based integrated reading curriculum. During the 1992–93 school year, Clairemont was the only school within the district interested in implementing ELOB, a comprehensive school reform design. Because of Clairemont's interest and commitment to the Expeditionary Learning design, they were accepted as a "Spirit School." This meant that Clairemont did not receive any external funding, but was given the opportunity to participate in ELOB's national professional development offerings. Although the district did not provide any additional financial support for Clairemont, it allowed Clairemont to adopt the ELOB design as their primary focus for curriculum, instruction, and whole-school restructuring. During the second year of implementation of the ELOB design (1994–95), a small amount of financial support from ELOB was granted. This support permitted me to work as an on-site professional development facilitator two days per month.

It should be stated that it was the principal's enthusiasm and commitment to the ELOB design that led Vivian and her fellow faculty members into the initial exploration of the professional development offerings presented by ELOB. Vivian described how her school "went out on its own" and tried to "implement some of the ELOB principles" after the principal had returned from a trip where she was first introduced to the program.

Part of Vivian's willingness to take part in ELOB came as a direct result of the support and encouragement of her principal and the collaborative efforts of colleagues in her school. Participating in the ELOB professional development offerings required Vivian to take risks greater than she had in the past. Vivian has said that her principal "has a gift for helping others grow. She's always been able to see abilities in people they can't see in themselves. She's never been one to push, but she always encourages. She always says, 'Vivian you can do it!'"

Career Development Phases as Contexts
for the Teacher's Professional Development Journey

This case study describes Vivian's professional development journey in relationship to distinct career cycle phases based on the work of Fessler, Huberman, and Vonk.[42] A summarized framework of Vivian's career cycle based on the research of Fessler, Huberman, and Vonk is used in this case study. It includes the phases outlined in Table 5.1 and is correlated with specific dates and teaching years in Vivian's career.

Table 5.1

Preprofessional/preservice period	1967 to 1971 (undergraduate work)
Beginning/induction period	1972 to 1974
	(1st to 2nd year of teaching)
Competency building period	1974 to 1984
	(3rd to 12th year of teaching)
Serene/Staple period	1985 to 1992
	(13th to 20th year of teaching)
Reorientation/experimental and grow- ing period	1993 to 1998 (21st to 26th year of teaching)
Career wind down/disengagement pe- riod (just prior to retirement)	1998–Present (27th + year of teaching)

The earlier phases of Vivian's career cycle are included in this case study. However, the study primarily focuses on the period beginning in 1994 during the reorientation/experimental and growing period, Vivian's twenty-second year of teaching, and continues through 1999, her twenty-seventh and twenty-eighth years of teaching, the beginning of her career wind down period. The reorientation/experimental and career wind down periods are primarily juxtaposed around the two professional development programs that Vivian identified as the most influential to her praxis, ELOB and the Center for Urban Learning/Teaching and Urban Research in Education and Schools (CULTURES). The ELOB program provided ongoing professional development to Vivian beginning in 1993, her twenty-first year of teaching. The CULTURES program provided Vivian with a 40-hour professional development program in 1997, her twenty-fifth year of teaching, and a 20-hour professional development program in 1998, her twenty-sixth year of teaching. Vivian plans to retire in 2002, her thirtieth year of teaching.

Preprofessional/Preservice Period: 1967 to 1971

Vivian described herself as a "child at heart."[43] Although she was the fifth of nine children, she was the first to graduate from college. Growing up in rural Georgia with a mother who had taught in a one-room schoolhouse helped Vivian to understand the value of a good education. She knew as a youngster that going to college could open doors that were closed to generations of southern African American women like her mother. Vivian viewed going to college as a way to secure financial independence. Initially she majored in vocational home economics and wanted to be a buyer for a department store. She discovered early on, however, that "this did not fit [her] personality." As Vivian began to ponder her future, she drew on the memory of one of her teachers: "Mr. James was a mentor for me. I was his assistant, and he often trusted me by giving me what seemed to my young mind to be extremely important responsibilities, like staying after school and entering grades in his grade books. When I thought about Mr. James, my mother, and all the other teachers who had had such a big impact in my life, I knew I wanted to teach."

In summary, the preprofessional/preservice period can be described as the period influenced by *memories of past role models,* in this case Vivian's mother and her former teacher, Mr. James. Vivian's mother and Mr. James helped prepare her for a teaching career by providing her with models she could rely on during the initial years of teaching. Similar to the black teachers in the segregated school Siddle Walker describes in her book *Their Highest Potential*,[44] Vivian's teachers did not allow her to fail in school. Vivian's early school experiences in rural Georgia's segregated schools helped to set the tone for the high standards Vivian applied in her teaching practices.

Beginning/Induction Period: 1972 to 1973

Vivian started teaching elementary school in Decatur in 1972 after graduating from Spelman College. Vivian "began teaching the way that [she] was taught."[45] She described the manner that her teachers taught her in the following way:

> My elementary teachers mostly lectured to us, and we read from basal readers. We rarely did projects. Every now and then, my teachers might bring something into class—a flower cutting for instance—but we would never dissect it or learn the scientific names for the parts of the flower. . . . If you had walked into my classroom during my first few years as a teacher, you would have seen children sitting in perfect rows. There might have been one or two children stuck in a corner because of behavior problems. But other than that, you would have seen row after row. There would have been very little in the way of group activity. Instead, it was "Read chapter six, and answer questions one through five." My curriculum was organized around workbooks.

Vivian's beginning/induction period can best be summarized by the phrase "teaching as I was taught." In other words, Vivian, like many teachers, modeled her classroom instruction and practices after the teachers that taught her. Her manner was caring, strictly disciplined, and methodical.

Competency Building Period: 1974 to 1984

Vivian taught in this very structured and didactic way for the first three years of her career. She then moved to another school. In the new setting, several teachers who taught math in innovative ways influenced Vivian's teaching style. The librarian also gave essential input into her classroom practices. Vivian began to view her teaching in different ways. Working with these teachers and seeing their openness to new approaches began to influence how Vivian began to think about and approach things in her classroom. When Vivian describes herself during this period, she says,

I don't think my classroom was boring, but I was bored quite frequently. I didn't trust children to have much say in what we did in the classroom. I modeled a lot as opposed to letting them get their hands dirty. Often I would start a project but because they didn't get finished quickly, I would just stop and start something new. If there were any obstacles at all, I would just abandon the project. I often wondered if my lack of interest was causing the students to think that nothing ever had to be completed, and that that was okay. I was very attentive to standards in terms of requirements for promotion, which also added to having a boring class.

In about the sixth year of teaching, Vivian began to use literature to teach reading. She found that this method also provided a natural way to discuss character development with her students. "The prevailing culture in the school where I taught was that whenever there was a new student, he or she was forced into a fight as a part of an initiation rite." Thus, she began using stories in her classroom that had the "power to give children a different way of thinking about their behavior and the choices they make." Vivian has continued to use literature that teaches morals and values for reading instruction.

The competency building period represents the *influence of colleagues* on Vivian's classroom practices. Throughout this career phase, Vivian was particularly influenced by colleagues' ideas, as she was eager to improve her repertoire of skills. During the competency building period, Vivian's ability to learn from colleagues provided her with the opportunities to build her proficiency by grabbing "the handles of teaching" in order to progress to periods of positive growth and development."[46]

Serene/Stable Period: 1985 to 1992

Vivian continued to organize her class in structured ways; students sat in straight rows and completed assignments without interacting with each other or her. Curriculum and instruction in Vivian's class often took the form of answering questions at the end of textbook chapters. She relied heavily on workbooks and "by and large students filled out a lot of work sheets." She demonstrated the solutions to math problems, but there "was never sharing of strategies." She described her classroom in this way: "They were taught one way to do things and basically, that was the only acceptable way. I would often stand in front of the classroom and using the chalkboard and the textbook, I would teach the lesson, while getting little feedback, only from the brightest students. You used to be able to hear a pin drop in my classroom. Children had to be absolutely quiet. There was little give and take. If there was, noise meant that the children must be off-task."

Having a passion for reading and literature, Vivian always promoted reading in her classroom. However, one year her students hated writing book reports in the rigid format that she required. She went to the librarian when this problem emerged. Vivian wondered if the students might become more open to writing and reading if they could talk to the librarian about the stories they read. Her students began talking to the librarian and keeping a list of the books that they read. The list grew. Vivian described the students in her classroom at that time in the following way: "Almost 100 percent of our students were African American, and most of them were quite poor, but their reading scores began to skyrocket. Each student was reading at least one book a week, which was above the norm for his or her grade level. This was a simple idea, but it worked. It was a way of encouraging children to practice, and [the librarian] was right there to support them."

Vivian became a mentor teacher in 1983, her eleventh year of teaching, and her responsibilities included coaching new teachers. Her performance as a mentor teacher earned her recognition as a well-respected professional both within the school community and throughout her district. In 1986, Vivian's fourteenth year of teaching, the librarian of her school became the principal of another school in the district and Vivian was recruited to teach the fourth grade. In 1990, Vivian's eighteenth year of teaching, she received the prestigious Milken Teacher Award, and in 1992, her twentieth year of teaching, she was nominated teacher of the year by the district.

This phase can best be summarized as a period of *testing new strategies and coaching others*. Vivian's level of enthusiasm complimented her level of competence and in turn led to recognition from others in her district. The opportunity to mentor new teachers was highlighted by the two teacher awards. Vonk describes this period as one where the "teacher demonstrates the accomplishments, skills, and mastery of an accomplished professional."[47] Concurrently, Fessler describes the enthusiastic and growing period as a time when teachers have reached a high level of competence in their jobs but continue to progress as professionals.[48] However, unlike Fessler's description of career stability, this period for Vivian was not overshadowed by disengagement, but rather was a period of renewed enthusiasm and zest for teaching.

Reorientation/Experimental and Growing Period: 1993 to 1998

It is important that the reorientation/experimental phase be the focus of this case study because it is in this phase that Vivian identified the professional development experiences most significant to her changing praxis. Vivian consistently stated that many of the innovations she made in her teaching can be attributed to the professional development she received in her experiences with ELOB and CULTURES. These professional development experiences provided Vivian with opportunities that significantly shaped and influenced this latter part of her career cycle. Although Vivian was nearing retirement, she continued to be enthusiastic and dynamic about her teaching and indicated that both the ELOB and CULTURES professional development programs provided her with a specific set of experiences that helped to reenergize her.

Vivian can be described as a *re-energized teacher* during this phase. Her energy and outlook on teaching and learning propelled her toward continuous growth and accomplishments. Several themes emerged from the analysis of data specific to this period in Vivian's career. These themes provide a frame for viewing Vivian in the latter stages of her career.

Theme 1: Perception of Self as a Leader. Vivian's perception of herself as a leader stemmed from references, descriptions, and instances where she taught and shared information and expertise with colleagues. This can be seen in her initiative to lead or implement strategies and techniques in her school community that she learned in her professional development experiences and then mastered in her classroom practice.

Requests for Vivian to participate in and lead many of the ongoing ELOB professional development efforts became a frequent occurrence in the first year of our acquaintance. During the spring of 1995, ELOB began a project with several teachers from the national ELOB network. The project entailed helping selected teachers document aspects of their work in the classroom. Both the principal and I encouraged Vivian to participate in this project. Initially, Vivian was reticent about participating. However, with constant encouragement by her principal and myself she soon relented and agreed to participate. I recollect her telling me that she was "a pioneer" and that I was "trying to make" her a "trailblazer." When I asked her about this comment some two years later, she responded by saying, "Yes, I learned that I am a pioneer, and that [my principal] is indeed the trailblazer, in that she goes out and she finds. Just looking at myself, I realize that I am open to new ideas and therefore I can be a pioneer."

On further discussion about the difference between being a pioneer and being a trailblazer, it became clear that Vivian shied away from seeing herself as a leader. She described the difference in the following way: "I think as a trailblazer I might meet with obstacles that would cause me failure. I don't want to fail. As a pioneer, somebody else has paved the way, some way."

While Vivian did not readily admit to viewing herself as a "trailblazer," she described ways that she provided leadership in her school, including participating in conferences and workshops and sharing and receiving ideas with her colleagues. Although modest about her role as a school leader, Vivian continuously thought about the benefits of her experiences in the context of her school and the other faculty members. Vivian's perception of herself as a leader was generally considered in light of collaboration with others. The perception of Vivian as a leader was not a self-proclaimed perception; it was often reinforced by the observations and comments made by the principal and her colleagues.

Theme 2: Perceptions of Self as Advocate.   Vivian primarily saw her role as an advocate for her students. She exhibited a certain self-consciousness and discomfort about the notion of being a leader. When asked about her reasons for becoming a teacher and descriptions of her job, her responses centered on her students. She described herself as a helper, facilitator, listener, confidant, parent, and encourager. She said, "I think a lot of it is born out of the desire to do something to help somebody, a desire to be needed, and as a teacher, I'm always needed by my students, and I'm also helping."

When she spoke about her role as a teacher, Vivian consistently referred to the way she perceived her students and her beliefs about their abilities, lives, characteristics, and qualities. There is a relationship between the way Vivian taught the content and the manner in which the students performed in the classroom. Because of the professional development Vivian received during the reorientation/experimentation-growing phase, she said, "Teaching now means listening to students' ideas and helping them pursue those ideas."

Vivian also believed that there was a reciprocal relationship between her beliefs about her own abilities and her beliefs about her students' abilities. Vivian said she learned things for the sake of her students. She did not allow difficult or intimidating things to hold her back because she said that will hold her students back. Vivian described putting herself in an uncomfortable place when she talked about entering the CULTURES program:

I'm a little bit nervous about it. I know there will be a lot of good work, and even though I can facilitate and be comfortable with my fourth grade students, I don't feel comfortable in groups myself. So even though I know that's the best way to learn, from other people and share ideas, just because I'm shy, I dread actually going into the classroom again, and being put in the position of student. But I hope that it will impact my teaching in such a way that I can reach all my students, cause year after year I always feel like I've failed with at least one person, meaning that I've failed to reach them and I've failed to help them reach their greatest potential in my classroom.

Theme 3: Perception of Self as Innovator. Vivian's willingness to experiment set the stage for her practice as an innovator. The week Vivian spent in Maine with me served as a career development bookmark although she had been teaching for more than two decades and had experienced a plethora of professional development. When she spoke about her professional development experiences and her history as a teacher, she highlighted the Portland summit experience. She often spoke of entering unfamiliar territory, learning new things, and doing things that she did not think she was capable of.

Vivian attributed a great deal of the innovations she made in her teaching to the professional development experiences in ELOB. Before her professional development training, Vivian taught in very traditional ways. Afterward, she organized students' desks and chairs in clusters and moved them depending on the need. Vivian began each morning with a class meeting where students shared issues and concerns. Vivian stated, "The morning meetings are one of the most important parts of our day." Students wrote in journals and Vivian built in time for reflections throughout the day.

Vivian said that attempting to teach from a multidisciplinary, project-based approach was difficult at first, especially because of the resulting noise level. However, participating in Expeditionary Learning's professional development helped Vivian learn new strategies for constructing classroom practices that led her to move beyond what she calls " a very traditional approach." Vivian took an interdisciplinary approach to delivering curriculum and instruction throughout the daily schedule. Scheduling was flexible and dependent on the time needed to finish a particular project or aspect of learning.

Rather than "being constantly bored and looking for new ways to teach the same old same," Vivian experienced a renewed spirit. She learned to involve her students in making decisions that affect their learning.

Theme 4: Perception of Self as a Reflective Practitioner. There is a direct link between Vivian's practice as an innovator and her practice of reflection. She was stimulated by reflecting on her prior knowledge in the following ways:

- Linking new knowledge to already familiar ideas and information
- Making connections to her own and students' experiences
- Reflecting on opportunities for the testing out of ideas and materials
- Assuming responsibility for implementation of new knowledge as it applies to her particular circumstances

Throughout the reorientation/experimental phase, evidence of Vivian's reflection on her praxis is apparent. This evidence comes from the way she spoke about her practice and the way she processed professional development experiences and then implemented the strategies, theories, and ideas gleaned from these experiences. When asked about how she would deal with the information presented to her in the CULTURES professional development seminar she responded, "I think that I will process the information pretty much as anybody else would, but I also know that I will go back and try to implement those things that I've learned instead of just letting it rest on the shelf. I feel like I'm learning, I'm seeing how it applies to my situation and how I can change as a result of it."

Vivian's focus on her students' achievement facilitated reflection on her practice in such a way that she continuously sought out opportunities to learn and try new things. She was energized by opportunities that provided her with the skills, techniques, and practices that make teaching and learning exciting. Vivian's practice of reflection in the craft of her teaching was enhanced by her openness to experimenting with new things. Because she thought about and changed the things that do not work with her students, she constantly considered the process of critique and revision in her own work.

This practice of reflection was evidenced through the writing and dialogue she engaged in throughout her Expeditionary Learning professional development experience. Discussions about her practice and her students took place much of the time that I spent with her in informal settings. Vivian consistently sought assistance because she was concerned about students that she feared would fall between the cracks. Many of these students were African American and came from families that had limited financial resources. Vivian first began discussing her concerns about these students in private conversations with me in the fall of 1994, her twenty-second year of teaching. I then began to notice her articulating these concerns to colleagues, as she wrote about them in the ELOB monograph in the spring of 1995. Vivian specifically wrote about an African American student she had been working with for two years. "This is my second year with Shante because she's repeating the fourth grade this year, and I'm really concerned that she not fall between the cracks."[49] Vivian used her professional development experiences with ELOB to transform practices in her classroom, which had a direct result with students like Shante.

Vivian's experiences in CULTURES also led her to reflect on her practice, particularly with regard to what it means to be a teacher: "I've thought about my own teaching more deeply and I realized there are a lot of things that I do, intuitively, and it's not that anybody's ever taught me to do it. I just do it, and I think that is something I had to have been born with. That, you know, it's like a difference between a skill and an innate ability."

Theme 5: Perception of Self as a Learner and Risk Taker.   Vivian's response revealed her thinking about her own processes. Her willingness and ability to listen to new ideas and try new things indicates that she is both a learner and a risk taker. Throughout the reorientation/experimental period, there were abundant references to and descriptions of Vivian's perceptions of her learning, as well as instances where she was challenged to do things she did not think she was capable of doing.

Vivian was, by her own admission, shy, especially in new settings. She said she often hangs back and waits to be approached by others. However, there were times when her open and assertive responses seemed to be in direct contradiction to her reticent personality, as was the case when I initially met her in the summer of 1994. Vivian was willing to open herself to new experiences when alone in an unfamiliar situation because she had the drive and determination to learn something that may be beneficial to her students.

Throughout her experiences in the CULTURES seminar Vivian displayed patterns of behavior that indicated her willingness to try new things in spite of the discomfort she may experience. One particular instance of this occurred during a cultural simulation where teachers are given a simulated culture that they take on as their own, then they are introduced to a "foreign" culture and left to learn that foreign culture's mores and modes of communication. Vivian admitted that the experience influenced her significantly. Specifically, she was able to empathize with her African American students who often perceived their school as a "foreign" culture.

Theme 6: Perception of Self as a Culturally Relevant African American Teacher. Vivian articulated a desire to "reach out for more information, knowledge, expertise and technical competence" throughout various moments in her career cycle. However, her desire to develop more expertise and technical competence regarding cultural diversity issues became particularly acute while participating in an ELOB professional development offering that focused on the exploration of school desegregation and the history of the Civil Rights movement.

During the summer between her twenty-fourth and twenty-fifth years of teaching, following the 1995–96 school year, Vivian participated in another summit offered by ELOB, one that I codesigned and cofacilitated. The topic of this summit influenced Vivian's thinking in a number of ways. The summit focused on issues of school desegregation during the Civil Rights era. One objective was to help teachers think about developing a learning expedition that focused on the topic of civil rights, a common area of study across elementary, middle, and high school curricula. Another objective focused on providing teachers with opportunities to search within themselves and think about issues of school desegregation and its effects on students, teachers, and the dynamics taking place in contemporary urban education. Vivian was touched personally and professionally by her experiences in this summit. The experience opened up many questions and issues for Vivian as a teacher, not the least of which concerned being one of two African American teachers in a predominantly white, middle-class neighborhood school. Following the summit experience, Vivian and I spent many long hours discussing issues of race and class and the influence these issues have on schools and students, particularly the students she was teaching.

Vivian began to pursue questions and issues of race and class in her praxis. She began first by asking how she could make a significant difference in the achievement of the African American students in her classroom and school. She also began to reflect on her own schooling experiences in the segregated South. She expressed that because she was only one of two African American teachers in her school, she often felt that it was generally difficult to address issues of race. She questioned how best to deal with issues of failure among her low-income, African American students. It was also at this time that Vivian first expressed an interest in exploring the CULTURES program.

As previously mentioned, approximately 3 percent of the student body at Vivian's school was low-income African American students. Less than 1 percent of the students were Asian or from other ethnic backgrounds. In the midst of the child-centered ambiance of Vivian's school were large disparities between the achievement of the low-income, African American students and the middle-class, mostly white, students.

The subtle dissonance between the outward appearance of teachers' beliefs and practices and the lack of explicit evidence pertaining to issues of diversity bothered me throughout my tenure as school designer for Vivian's school. The faculty and school personnel were friendly and warm. The initial impression of the school and faculty indicated that respect for children was commonplace and that visitors were welcomed. One thing I always noticed, however, was that there was no outward appearance of the presence of culturally diverse materials, pictures, or artifacts. I often wondered about the imprint this left on the children, particularly the African American and Asian children. As my relationship with Vivian deepened and a bond of trust solidified between us, I was able to begin to openly address some of these observations with her.

In the 1996–97 school year, Vivian's twenty-fourth year of teaching, our conversation about race, class, and culture led me to create a study group on race and culture in her school. Parents from various class and ethnic backgrounds began to articulate their thoughts about the disparities between low-income African American student outcomes and middle-class student outcomes. Motivated by the interactions in the study groups and her increasing readiness to confront issues of race and class, in the summer of 1997, her twenty-fifth year of teaching, Vivian enrolled in the CULTURES program at Emory University.

Vivian's participation in the CULTURES professional development prompted her to more openly and freely express her beliefs about issues of race, class, and culture. After a visit to the Vietnamese community as a part of a cultural immersion trip, Vivian responded by saying, "You know, I've just been so indifferent about Vietnamese cultures and people that I had not felt any way about them, but I came away [from CULTURES] feeling like I would not mind having these children in my class. The main reason is because they hold teachers in such high esteem, that I just feel like they would be easy to work with; and because their parents do everything they possibly can, I feel, to encourage them to do well in school. So I just came away feeling like I want these people to be successful in this country."

In summary, Vivian's quest to improve and develop her praxis to include a perspective on cultural diversity was heightened by her experience in the CULTURES program. Although she readily identified instances when the CULTURES experience reinforced things that she was already doing in her classroom, she also recognized how this professional development experience opened up a new way of viewing cultural diversity in her classroom.

CONCLUSION

This case study documented how Vivian Stephens' professional development validated Fessler's career cycle profile. Her preservice phase (the undergraduate years) was dominated by "memories of past mentors," particularly her mother and her teachers in segregated schools in the South. The cycle of induction (the first and second years) was labeled "teaching as I was taught" and reflected Vivian's traditional training in her preservice program and the teaching she experienced as a child. The "influence of colleagues" during competency building (the third through twelfth years) helped Vivian to improve and broaden her repertoire of teaching skills and confidence in her teaching. The serene and stable period (the thirteenth through twentieth years) was the time in Vivian's career when she experimented with her new role as "coach and mentor of other teachers." During this phase, her work was recognized by others and, unlike Fessler's description, she was not disengaged and alienated. The primary focus of this case (the twenty-first through twenty-sixth years) was the period of reorientation or "re-energized teaching." During this cycle Vivian experienced two professional development activities that significantly impacted her career, ELOB and CULTURES.

The significance of these two professional development activities was that Vivian learned and assumed several new roles as an experienced teacher—leader, advocate, innovator, reflective practitioner, risk taker, and culturally responsive pedagogist. That the new roles related to her emergence as a culturally responsive teacher is particularly interesting.

Ladson-Billings defines the notion of cultural relevance as moving "beyond language to include other aspects of student and school culture."[50] She describes culturally relevant teaching as a pedagogy that "empowers students intellectually, socially, emotionally, and politically by using cultural referents to impart knowledge, skills, and attitudes."[51] Cochran-Smith includes a perspective on teachers as culturally responsive pedagogists that "requires attention to issues of epistemology, ideology, practice, and professional development."[52]

Vivian Stephens is not unlike many African American teachers who grew up in the rural segregated South. She was influenced by her parents and teachers. She benefited from an education that provided her with strong role models for her own teaching practices. She lived in an insulated African American community that encouraged her to get a college education. Vivian then attended one of the most prestigious historically black colleges. However, what makes Vivian Stephens a unique and gifted teacher is the combination of forces that blend and come together at crucial points in her career cycle.

Although Vivian entered teaching during the early period of school desegregation, she began teaching in a school that was predominantly populated by African American students. She taught in this setting for the first ten years of her career. In this environment, Vivian was faced with many of the issues that confront teachers in the early years of their careers. She relied on her memories of childhood role models, reached out to colleagues for support, and was challenged by the opportunities that teaching and learning presented. At the center of Vivian's pedagogy was her concern for student achievement.

In these early years of teaching, Vivian was not challenged by issues of cultural diversity in her classroom. For as she says, "Almost 100 per cent of our students were African American."[53] It was not until later in her career, when she began teaching in a predominantly white setting, that issues of cultural diversity became central to the "aims and dilemmas" she encountered. It was during this time in predominantly white schools and classrooms that she discovered her voice as a culturally responsive teacher.

Finally, this research is significant because the documented journey of Vivian Stephens, one African American urban teacher, is very much related to current efforts to recruit, retain, educate, and develop African American teachers. Continued work, like this case study, is needed so that we can understand how teaching and professional development are influenced by the complex issues of context and ethnicity.

Chapter 6

CHASING HOPE THROUGH CULTURALLY RESPONSIVE PRAXIS

One Master Teacher and Her African American
Eighth Grade Readers

Maria Leonora Lockaby Karunuñgan

This chapter tells how an African American literacy teacher viewed her profession and practiced her craft with her students, who in this case were 100 percent African American. The literacy research focuses often on the debate between whole language or phonics[1] but very few studies address the teacher's perspective or place the literacy teacher within her cultural context. Indeed, some scholars argue that whether a teacher employs whole language or phonics may be entirely irrelevant to the culturally specific context surrounding African American students' achievement.[2] Other factors not considered in traditional literacy debates may be more important to African American students' success.

That African American students' literacy test scores have remained consistently lower than the test scores of white students,[3] and that alarming numbers of African American students confront failure in school[4] and drop out,[5] are facts that challenge the attainment of literacy and functional literacy. The African American community has historically valued literacy as a symbol of freedom and communal improvement.[6] In other words, because slaves were traditionally not allowed to read, literacy was concomitantly associated with freedom and the opportunity to be more aware and weigh decisions. In current times, low achievement scores and school dropout continue to be associated with less freedom because these educational outcomes result in fewer employment and lifestyle options.

Although today's African American students remain convinced that literacy is essential to their well-being, they frequently find the manner in which it is taught to be culturally out of sync with their lives.[7] The institution of schooling often presents literacy as "white" literacy, problematizing students' struggles to preserve their own cultural heritage. For example, European modes of communication, canonicized European texts, and Western frames of reference continue to dominate everyday classrooms. Yet, as Lisa Delpit[8] has stressed, there are ways to teach students so that becoming literate is not the equivalent of "acting White."[9] Teachers can shape instruction so that schooling, rather than presenting an either/or choice between literacy and students' values, renders the process of literacy acquisition a process that legitimizes students' cultures.

AFRICAN AMERICAN STUDENTS' LITERACIES

Throughout history, it has always been important to black people that they learn to read, and crucial that their children learn to read.[10] Black parents often prefer traditional schools for their children, even over schools boasting an Afrocentric curriculum,[11] perhaps because they see traditional schooling as a safer, more established route to acquiring literacy and do not want to take risks with their children's literacy acquisition by placing them in more alternative schools.

The way some traditional approaches are implemented can widen the gap between school culture and home culture. For example, low teacher expectations can lead to a self-fulfilling prophecy where teachers act on what they believe, and students, influenced by teachers' actions, fulfill teachers' expectations.[12] Teachers unfamiliar with students' backgrounds and home cultures might misinterpret students' performance in class as indicating low ability or low potential, and thus lower their expectations for students whose cultures they are unfamiliar with. In another vein, teachers unfamiliar with students' cultures might not be able to teach students literacy skills in ways that are meaningful—because they are unaware of what is meaningful in the everyday lives of their students.[13] For these reasons, contemporary scholars are giving greater attention to cultural relations between students and teachers, and to the implications of these relations for current teaching practices.

For example, Siddle Walker emphasized three commonly overlooked assumptions of process theory, all of which are embedded in the school-home culture gap.[14] Process theorists commonly assume that (1) students and teachers have the same goals for learning, (2) teachers' interactive styles with students are always positive, and (3) teachers never misinterpret their students' needs and backgrounds. The end result of these assumptions becomes a cultural mismatch between teachers' teaching and students' learning. That is, teachers using the process approach to teaching writing were not necessarily more able than other teachers to keep their students engaged. In fact, as Siddle Walker observed, African American students were just as likely to fall asleep.

In an opposite scenario, the teacher shares the same cultural background as her students.[15] In this scenario, black teachers lived in their students' neighborhoods and had a "Black Artful Style" in teaching. Foster argued that these teachers were effective in teaching reading to African American students because they communicated in a speech that was more familiar, and hence more direct, to students, and because they were members of their students' community. In addition, Foster suggested that teachers who understand the cultural background of their students were better able to gauge their students' abilities. Thus, a shared cultural background addressed at least two of Siddle Walker's concerns above: Teachers had better interactions with their students, and the shared background enabled them to avoid misinterpreting students' needs.

That teachers who share cultural ties with their students are less likely to misgauge, miscommunicate, and misinterpret their students seems reasonable. Yet statistical projections predict that more and more students and teachers—especially in urban schools—will come from differing cultural backgrounds.[16] In light of these projections, the need to prepare preservice teachers of all ethnic backgrounds to teach culturally diverse students is critical. Ladson-Billings' culturally relevant pedagogy[17] has become increasingly popular because it does not require that teachers belong to the same ethnic group as their students. Instead, it requires that teachers be "culturally immersed" in their students' cultures to facilitate the same understanding that Foster stressed was critical in the effective teaching of African American students.

Ladson-Billings' seminal study of eight culturally relevant teachers defined what culturally relevant pedagogy is and ought to be and what it looks like.[18] Examples of the culturally relevant literacy teaching of two

English teachers[19] included the following practical approaches to teaching reading:

1. validating student cultures by casting all texts initially from their cultural frame of reference;
2. dealing explicitly with race and culture; using physical contact to affirm students' presence; and
3. using standard English to speak and to teach, but also using black English in informal situations; and allowing students' home language to be spoken in the classroom while at the same time teaching students to switch between standard English and black English.

One example of an attempt to translate culturally relevant teaching from theory into practice is a culturally based cognitive apprenticeship model designed to teach skills in literary interpretation to "underachieving" African American high school seniors, with the dual goals of helping these students to improve their reading strategies and to appreciate literature by African American authors.[20] Lee reasoned that the more complex skills in reading that the students in her study had difficulty learning were implicit cognitive processes. An instructional model based on cognitive apprenticeship could allow students to explicitly construct these reading skills. Students explored a literary device that was similar to a conversational mode in the African American community: signifying.[21] "Signifying" is commonly known as a verbal play on words in which a speaker needles, insults, or pesters the listener; the listener, in turn, offers a clever rebuttal to top the speaker's insult. The tradition in African American communities dates back to slavery, in which older slaves would teach younger slaves how to withstand insults as a means of survival.

Lee's culturally relevant cognitive apprenticeship also provides an example of subject-specific representation.[22] Signifying becomes a means for teachers to reach students and to represent subject matter as containing possibilities for student affiliation, appreciation, and ownership. Students can know that their own cultural frame of reference holds a valid place in the academic, literary world. They can also know that signifying and other means of discourse are not simply transferences from speech to writing, but make up a whole genre replete with ironies and semiotics. These representations of subject matter present an accessible, viable, attractive, and critical choice for students—while at the same time helping them verbalize their own knowledge construction and improved reading strategies.

Researchers typically refer to literacy as a skill to gain, when, in fact, students already possess multiple literacies comprising what Obidah terms a "literate currency." With literate currency, students' home literacies and school literacies shape each other both within and outside of the school context.[23] Obidah suggested that all teachers, regardless of their cultural background, can come to know the literate currencies their students possess and learn how to develop them. Both Ladson-Billings[24] and Obidah stress the importance of using students' knowledges as teaching tools for empowering them to think and learn critically. In other words, teachers should learn collaboratively from students and allow students to inform them on what they need to know and want to learn.

Evidence from the past indicates that fundamental practices behind culturally relevant pedagogy are not a new phenomenon.[25] These culturally relevant reading pedagogies provide directions for the professional development and support of teachers who are teaching increasing numbers of African American students in urban settings. Taken together, they bespeak the significance of the kind of instruction received, rather than of the essential "methods" being used, for example, process theory, whole language, or phonics. These instructional methods provide a foundation for "good" teaching only if a cultural synchronization[26] is in place between a teacher's pedagogy and a student's learning.

In the present study, I focused on how one African American teacher's perspective was influenced not only by her ideas of what reading was and how to teach reading but also by the actual process of teaching and learning in the classroom. The purpose of the study was twofold. First, I traced the philosophy and pedagogy of an African American teacher in a Title I, urban classroom of African American eighth grade students. Second, I sought to delineate the teacher's praxis—the relationship between her philosophy of teaching reading and her pedagogical methods. "Philosophy" in this study refers to the teacher's stated principles about reading and teaching reading. "Pedagogy" refers to her acts of teaching in the classroom, as observed by me, including ways of interacting with students. "Praxis," defined by Freire as "action-reflection,"[27] brings together the philosophy (reflection) and the pedagogy (action) of the teacher, and embeds this action-reflection in the context of the teacher's classroom and school.

Patricia White (known as "Pat" for short) is an African American teacher who has been teaching reading for 30 years. I selected Pat for this study because she taught reading, as opposed to language arts or a more interdisciplinary subject. I also wanted to work with her because I found her to be inspirational in the CULTURES class, both in the way she demonstrated her style of teaching reading and in the way she spoke about the history of her school and community. She had also been named teacher of the year at her school.

PAT'S PHILOSOPHY

The first question for this study was, "What is Pat's stated perspective on reading and the teaching of reading?" Pat's philosophy of teaching reflected the following themes: (1) sparking an interest in reading; (2) listening; and (3) adapting.

Sparking an Interest in Reading

Pat told me that she hoped, above all, to "somehow spark an interest in just reading." She elaborated, "my goal is to inspire them to learn, to just light a spark, of something, a motivation to read, just to read." Lighting a spark and inspiring her African American students to learn are both concepts involving motivation. As such, Pat's philosophy of teaching students reading involved the desire to motivate them. She explained that she felt that an interest in reading would inspire students to learn because "reading helps a person by helping them to experience a lot of things— helps them to travel vicariously, increases vocabulary, makes them knowledgeable about a lot of different subjects—it informs, it entertains, it does it all! All through reading!" Pat believed that once the "spark" was lit, the act of reading provided enough rewards to keep the spark lit. The more students read, the more firmly their interest in reading would be grounded—eventually, reading would become a lifelong gift.

Pat believed that the key to maintaining students' interest in reading lay in gauging their reading abilities with the use of different levels of challenging reading materials. She reasoned that keeping students at a level where they "continue to do well" would encourage their confidence and thus promote their interest in reading. Because her African American students were "weak" in reading, she explained, they "naturally get turned off," so that sparking an interest in reading became a real challenge. Maintaining students' interest also meant keeping reading matter within their confidence levels and enjoyment.

Listening to Students

Pat stressed repeatedly in all five interviews over a time period of 16 weeks that an essential part of her approach to teaching her African American students was to simply listen to the students. Every Friday she used to hold a weekly discussion: "We just sat and talked. We talked, and they had some problems, and we just talked. Whatever they decided to talk about, that's what we did, we talked." The technique of "talking" was in itself a listening technique designed to encourage students to talk more. Pat explained, "I can sit down and talk with them. You know, we just talk. Let them talk, hear what they have to say."

For Pat, talking to students was essential to their academic progress because when students talked, they became more involved and interested in academic activities. Pat particularly felt that talking would help her African American students, whose confidence was low: "These kids, maybe because they're so low, their confidence is a little shaky. They won't talk as much. They try to shy away. So . . . [I] get them to do little things . . . to get them to go way out and just . . . get them to think about talking." She thus attended to why students would talk, not just to what they had to say.

Another reason Pat gave for encouraging her African American students to talk was because she herself learned a lot about her students when she listened to them. She explained that learning about them meant seeing more than the persona students would normally take on in the classroom: "I like it when I can sit down and talk one on one with them. And just talk. So I can see the other side of them." Listening reflected a genuine interest in the students themselves, an interest in knowing students beyond their participation in class.

Such attentiveness to students was not confined to what they were saying verbally. Students' drawings, papers, and even Pat's own "gut feeling" guided her attention to students, not only to the issues in question ("deep things"—guns and drugs), but to the reason for students' expression of these "deep things:" "I think when they talk about deep things like that, they want you to know." Pat was sensitive to students' privacy and confidentiality, respecting what they might be protective of or sensitive to. Even so, if she felt the need, she would use the general topic as a "springboard for discussion" without naming students, or she would speak with them individually.

In short, a large part of Pat's philosophy of teaching students embodied the simple act of listening. Listening involved talking because conversation encouraged students to say more and be more comfortable and confident in class. Listening also meant being sensitive to students beyond their verbal speech; it was a means of knowing "the other side" of students, of understanding what they did and did not want to say, and providing the atmosphere in which they felt free to say what they wanted to say. Listening meant responding to students, giving students the feeling that she had heard them; essentially, that she cared. Lastly, listening meant being careful how she responded, being particular to each situation and dealing with "deep things" in ways she felt was needed or wanted.

Adapting to Students

Asked her general philosophy of teaching, Pat replied, "My philosophy of teaching is a teacher must be flexible. And must adapt to her students. See, sometimes, we're so busy trying to get students to adapt to our way. I think sometimes we must adapt to theirs." For Pat, adaptation in teaching meant tinkering with her teaching constantly in the classroom. "I think it's the small things, actually," she said. "Because once you adapt to them, and they set the tone, then you in turn will be able to get more out of them, you see what I'm saying? Because you're not trying to get them to do it your way, so to speak, you know. And then they'll feel a little more comfortable." Pat also addressed students' reading weaknesses in ways that suggested an adaptive approach. These approaches included finding out students' weaknesses in reading, or their grade level for reading, allowing students to select their own books, and having them read aloud.

Indeed, the two themes of Pat's philosophy just presented, sparking an interest and listening, are also *adaptive* approaches to teaching. In summary, adapting included creating a safe classroom environment (setting the tone) and finding content material students could enjoy. The goals behind both strategies, and for adaptation in general, were to involve students and increase their comfort level in her classroom. Adapting was also academic in nature, because she believed she should assess students' capabilities and appeal to their interests (self-selection of books and reading aloud).

The three key tenets in Pat's philosophy consisted of sparking African American students' interest in reading, listening to them, and adapting her teaching style as much as possible to their needs. These three tenets overlap and influence each other. Sparking, listening, and adapting became different approaches toward reaching the same common goal: to motivate students into learning. Notice that the question, "What is the teacher's stated perspective of reading and the teaching of reading?" was really, for Pat, a question of the problem of general teaching and learning for students she felt entered the classroom already "turned off" to school, in general.

All three approaches also reflected an affective concern with teaching students, and they each involved "knowing the students." Sparking an interest required the teacher to know, in the first place, what students were interested in. Listening was the means of learning to know students. Finally, adapting to students—that is, teaching students "the students' way"—required knowing what "the students' way" was. Thus the three approaches shown in Figure 6.1 rest fundamentally on the assumption of knowing who her Title I students were. "These students, because they're so low," echoed like a refrain. Pat explained that her students had entered a cycle where difficulty in reading discouraged them from enjoying it. Their subsequent lack of motivation to read prevented them from practicing reading and gaining the fluency of their peers, so that by the eighth grade they lagged far below grade level on standardized tests in reading. The demonstrated "weakness" in reading, in turn, further lowered students' confidence and motivation, preserving a cycle of failure.

Pat's goals in all three approaches, as shown in Figure 6.1, consequently rested on attempts to push students into an altogether opposite cycle, in which a combination of intervening strategies were designed to interest and involve students to the extent that they became self-motivated to read and confident enough to take the risks required to improve their reading. Their subsequent successes, she hoped, would generate a more productive cycle, in which a desire to read led to improvement and success.

PAT'S PEDAGOGY

Analysis of the field notes revealed the following major strategies in Pat's teaching: (1) high interest, low level; (2) establishing rapport; and (3) adapting to students. My presence as observer allowed me to see Pat's teaching in action, to situate her teaching life within context, and to flesh

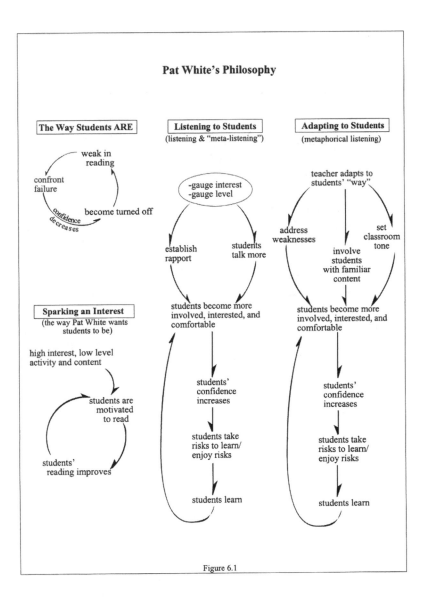

Figure 6.1

out consistencies and inconsistencies between her perspective, as told in interviews, and her practice, as observed by me. Nonetheless, to preserve her perspective and ensure that her voice is in the story told here, Pat's pedagogy, as observed by me, will be stated as much as possible in terms of her own words and the way she described what she was trying to do.

High Interest on a Low Level

Almost every teaching strategy employed by Pat seemed driven by her philosophy to teach students "on a low level, but [with] high interest so they won't know it." Pat respected students' maturity by engaging them at their age-level interests while using academic material lower than grade level. Examples of these high interest, low level activities were word games and puzzles, interactive games, various forms of reading aloud, and verbal presentations.

Word games included rebuses and brainteasers. Many of these word games and puzzles were used as class starters, activities waiting for students on their desks when they walked in the door. Interactive games included minute mystery, wheel of fortune, and pyramid 2000. Minute mysteries in particular were used frequently by Pat, and were very popular with the students on most occasions. Pat would split students up into three or four groups and provide each group with a set of laminated clues. The objective was for students to find the weapon, time, motive, place, murderer, and victim based on the set of clues she had given them. Typically Pat would give them thirty to forty-five minutes to work together in groups. Students within each group would discuss the possible answers, sometimes even arguing with each other. Pat would then have the whole class stop and volunteer answers, and discussion often became heated as students argued across groups. Pat would then reveal each correct answer, dramatically, and groups that had gotten individual answers right would celebrate, often exclaiming, "Yes!"

The high interest appeal of the minute mysteries and other interactive games was apparent from the excitement of the students themselves. Less clear was whether these minute mysteries really were "low level," because I did not get to see the clues myself. However, if the clues did represent low level content, they at least seemed to challenge students. Students argued back and forth, indicating that the answers were not obvious and easy for them to immediately find. Additionally, no group got all of the answers right on any occasion, showing that even as students were engaged, the process was still challenging for them. Most often word games and interactive games took place on what Pat called, "Thinking Thursday": the focus of every Thursday was for students to think. Students soon learned that the focus of every Thursday was also for them to have fun. "Low level" content, then, as Pat actually implemented the term, might be considered material that provided a challenge for students but remained within their capability range to facilitate enjoyment in the process of thinking. Pat explained that "low level" did not necessarily mean that she gave them material at or below the grade level they had actually tested on: "Because if I gave them the material that they really—at the level, you know, that they really worked on—some of them, you know, that would really, that would be too embarrassing, I think." Her choice was to give students more challenging material than they had tested on, or to interest students to the extent that "they won't know" the content level is lower than eighth grade.

One representative example of a high interest, low level activity was the use of the "Three Little Pigs." In the field notes, the story of the three little pigs unfolds as follows:

> Pat asks, "Who wants to start the story of the three little pigs?" Brent volunteers to start the story. She tells him, "Brent, stand."
>
> He protests, "Awww," but stands. He tells the story of the three little pigs: " . . . and there was this bad, bad wolf. . . ."
>
> Students laugh at his enactment of the bad wolf blowing houses down (he takes deep, dramatic breaths in and out).
>
> " . . . So the pig told him, 'hey man, you went and blew my house down.' . . . The wolf goes to the other two houses and says, 'Look, you two pigs gotta let me in your house or I'm gonna blow your house down.' And the pig goes, 'Naw, man, you can't come in here' and tells the other pig to shut the door. . . . So all three of them is in the brick house. So the wolf got to the door (Brent puffs himself up to take a breath), 'If you all don't let me in I'm gonna blow your house down.' And the pigs [say], "Naw, man, that ain't no fair . . . ' The wolf says, 'I'm comin right through this house,' and the pig [goes], 'All right, you do that.' And he turned the lights out. . . . But when [the wolf] hit the house, the [house] fell apart. . . . So [the pig] was out in the hood with no stove. He was cold. So, they just beat him up. . . ."

Students laugh, and Pat laughs with them. She thanks Brent, retells the traditional ending of the story, and then says, "I like that, Brent. That was a different version of the 'Three Little Pigs.'" She introduces the next exercise, where students will write, draw, or tape record their own versions of the "Three Little Pigs."

The scene shows that, besides encouraging verbal literacy, the storytelling resulted in students' engagement with the learning activity that was to follow. Pat capitalized on Brent's surprise ending by encouraging the other students to render their own creative versions of the "Three Little Pigs." Pat's request for a storyteller, as well as her own retelling of the traditional ending, ensured that students had a common knowledge base for referring to the story (in case there were students who were not familiar with the nursery tale or had not heard it in a long time). The scene also demonstrates a comfortable classroom environment; students clearly enjoyed the storytelling, and Brent seemed at ease to embellish the story as he told it.

The kind of "high interest" activities Pat provided necessarily qualifies the term "low level," because in her attempts to find material students would be interested in, she sought to stimulate thinking. Low level activity was also designed to bridge students between what they were already capable of doing and what they currently had some difficulty doing. "Low level" actually meant "designed to encourage a higher level" of thinking. Each classroom exercise required students to remember details and make guesses or predictions based on those details. Pat explained that the emphasis on details, guesses, and predictions was designed to address an overall "weakness in comprehension." Her practices seemed to reflect her belief that students' weakness in reading was comprehension, and that the solution for addressing this weakness was to have them think.

Establishing Rapport

Pat established rapport with her African American students by encouraging them, talking to them, and giving them a sense of ownership. Encouraging students meant repeating or affirming student responses, evaluating students' participation, and expressing pleasure with their work and progress. Talking to students involved discussing and "preaching." Pat frequently talked to students as a group to deal with peer perceptions of their Title I class and problems with other teachers. She also habitually initiated discussions based on her personal interest in students (e.g., "What happened last night?"). Sometimes discussions were directed toward dealing with a specific problem, such as their stress about taking the Iowa Test of Basic Skills, or the lack of cooperation among a particular group in the class.

Talking to students also involved occasional outbursts of "preaching," in which Pat passionately lectured to students about why they should help themselves more, or why they should improve in a particular area. One day, for example, after students had made impromptu speeches, Pat summarized their speeches and then jump-started them in a discussion as follows:

> Pat says, "You know what I heard each one of you say?" Sue: "We don't like coming to school." Sue, Murray, and Ryan talk very loudly at the same time about a teacher they all have that puts them down. . . . Pat sits and simply listens to them talking for about two minutes, and then says calmly, "All right, children." They stop. Pat: "What I'm hearing you say is you don't like school so much because the teacher influenced you and made you negative." She then tells them, "It's not the teacher's view, but yours," referring to the negative attitudes they claim the other teacher inspires. Ryan protests, and Murray argues, telling him they should ignore that teacher: "Don't pay her no attention. Just be quiet, (small laugh) and let them do all the talking." Pat asks them for their input, telling them she will share this with other teachers. "What should I say, that we as teachers need to do what?" . . . Ryan says, "She treats us like, 'Be quiet and sit down!'" . . . Pat says, "I hear you, and for those children coming in next year I will try to do something, but you also need to cooperate. If you don't have an education, knowledge here," (she points to her head with both fingers), "you're going to be left behind. You're going to have to do the work and the things you have to do."

In this episode, students felt comfortable complaining about another teacher. Pat expressed empathy for African American students' situation but also admonished them not to use their frustration as an excuse for not doing work. She "preached" that they should continue to work hard despite any degrading insults a teacher might make. Her preaching both summarized what students felt and drew more thoughts from them. These personal lessons formed a frequent part of Pat's teaching, showing her concern for both their academic and personal progress. In fact, she seemed to believe that students' academic progress depended on their personal outlook on life. Pat's role as teacher thus often became a role as "preacher."

Giving ownership, a third form of establishing rapport, involved soliciting help or appealing to students' expertise. Pat regularly asked students to help or assist her in the classroom, implying that they had capabilities she found helpful. For example, when her reading glasses broke, she asked for help. Three students immediately volunteered to read, as if forgetting they were supposed to be weak readers. Pat also often asked students to look up a word in the dictionary or give her the correct spelling if they knew.

Appealing to students' expertise was another way Pat found to give students a sense of ownership in the classroom. For example, when a student explained how water moved into the air and through the atmosphere and the earth, Pat expressed fascination with his explanation and encouraged him to continue sharing his knowledge of water. These on-the-spot tactics illustrate small ways Pat found to encourage a sense that students were a productive part of how the class came together.

Adapting to Students

Both the high interest, low level strategy and the approaches to establishing rapport represent ways of adapting to students. These strategies likewise resonated most strongly with Pat's philosophy of adapting to students. Another aspect of Pat's adaptation was her daily classroom structure. Each day, Pat allotted a special time at the end of the one and a half hour class in which students were given control to choose from various activities in the room: a library center, where students could select various magazines and books to read; a listening center, where students could either work with an electronic pronunciation machine or listen to tapes of books, or simply record themselves reading; a writing center, with binding materials; a "game" center, where two students could play checkers; and a "computer center," where students played various trivia, mystery, and word games on the computer.

Table 6.1: Adapting to Students as a Major Theme

Philosophy	Pedagogy	Praxis
Sparking an Interest in Reading	High Interest on a Low Level	Adapting to Students
Listening to Students	Establishing Rapport	Adapting to Students
Adapting to Students	Adapting to Students	Adapting to Students

In Pat's school, Title I students took both her class and the regular grade 8 language arts class. Therefore, instead of taking their "fun" exploratory class (such as drama or chorus), students had to take Pat's Title I class; all of their classes were strictly academic in nature, and students were given no free time during the school day. Thus Pat adapted to the constraints placed on her African American students by respecting their need for some time during the day that they could call "their own." At the end of each class period, she consistently gave them freedom to choose what they would like to do and incorporated this element of choice with literacy activities.

PAT'S PRAXIS

The final question for the study was, "In what ways does the teacher's perspective intersect with her pedagogy in the classroom?" The three major themes of Pat's overall praxis became (1) adapting to students, (2) teacher burnout, and (3) teacher hope.

Adapting

The theme that resonated most strongly was Pat's overriding philosophy and practice of always taking her cue from the students: The six pattern codes for both the field notes and the interviews merged together into a major theme of Pat's continual adaptation to students (see Table 6.1). Sparking an interest, for example, required adapting to students—that is, Pat had to know first what kind of reading material (content, form, etc.) her African American middle schoolers might already be interested in. Then, she needed to know which activities and ways of reading (such as reading aloud, storytelling, performing, etc.) students might enjoy. Likewise, the pedagogy Pat employed to spark their interest was chiefly a "high interest on a low level" strategy; her pedagogy rested on assumptions not only of what material and activities would engage students, but also on who students were: "low" level readers, with uncertain confidence, and students who were turned off to reading not necessarily because they did not like it but more because they were not good at it.

Listening to students was also a means of adapting to students because it directly required tuning in to students and taking cues from them to encourage them to talk and express themselves more. Establishing rapport was perhaps the most adaptive strategy, and at the same time seemed to be

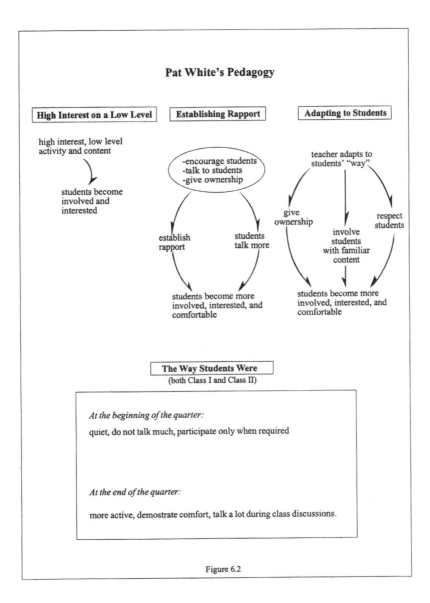

Pat White's Pedagogy

High Interest on a Low Level   **Establishing Rapport**   **Adapting to Students**

high interest, low level
activity and content

students become
involved and
interested

-encourage students
-talk to students
-give ownership

teacher adapts to
students' "way"

give
ownership

establish
rapport

students
talk more

involve
students
with familiar
content

respect
students

students become more
involved, interested, and
comfortable

students become more
involved, interested, and
comfortable

The Way Students Were
(both Class I and Class II)

At the beginning of the quarter:

quiet, do not talk much, participate only when required

At the end of the quarter:

more active, demostrate comfort, talk a lot during class discussions.

Figure 6.2

a goal of adaptation in actual practice. Comparison of Figure 6.2, Pat's Pedagogy, with Figure 6.1, Pat's Philosophy, shows that establishing rapport (getting students to feel more comfortable) was the observable endpoint of Pat's pedagogy, whereas in her philosophy, she hoped it would also generate a positive cycle of students' motivation leading to academic achievement and greater confidence.

Pat's adaptive approach to teaching matched general guidelines available in prevailing research about what urban students of color need from good teachers, particularly in the research on culturally responsive pedagogy. Whenever possible, Pat availed herself of students' prior knowledge and experience to increase their confidence and interest in reading and to empower them by giving them a sense of ownership in the classroom. Pat focused on establishing rapport as a foundation from which to teach. Her philosophy and pedagogy of "high interest, low level" strategies in adapting curriculum to students' needs did not mean "dumbing down" the curriculum, because these "low level" activities and material were actually difficult for students. Pat transformed "low level" from a label connoting student deficiency into a challenge for herself as a teacher who recognizes that, by the eighth grade, her students have not acquired the skills they should have acquired.

Context

When I first arrived in Pat's classroom, pen and notebook in hand, I was in no way prepared for the unexpected obvious: the context in which a teacher teaches profoundly influences not just her pedagogy, but also her philosophy, and not just her philosophy and pedagogy, but also her praxis. The answer to my third research question, "In what ways does the teacher's perspective intersect with her pedagogy?" cannot be answered without presenting context. I had originally intended to situate Pat's story within the context of her surroundings, but found context to persist as a theme in and of itself, mainly because it led to Pat becoming what she herself termed as "burned out." This context, more specifically, involved her perceptions of (1) lack of support, (2) change in the community, school, and students over time, and (3) students' struggles to learn. Pat cited lack of support from sectors of the educational community both within and outside her reach as the primary source of her personal "burnout."

The structure of Pat's school unintentionally undermined her efforts to teach students who tested several grade levels below their grade level. Each grade in her school was tracked into "teams" of students belonging to Teams A, B, and C. Students knew who belonged to which teams; further, they knew that Team A was the "smartest" team and Team C was "dumb." Worse, anyone in the only Title I class in the school (Pat's) was de facto labeled "SPED" (special education). Before Pat could even begin to teach, she first had to work to dispel myths, establish trust, and increase students' comfort in her class.

In the classroom, I observed that students grew more comfortable and active over the nine weeks of class they had with Pat. Pat thought she would be able to keep her students the entire semester. School administrators, however, decided that because she was a good teacher, more students should receive her instruction. In addition, state course requirements prevented students from being able to continue in Title I all semester. Consequently, Pat was given a new class for the fourth quarter. Instead of having students a whole year, much less a semester, she had only nine weeks to break down walls and teach. In other words, because her African American students were students who had trouble reading, they were also the same students who had confronted years of failure and years of expecting to fail. When they entered Pat's class, they expected to fail and showed no excitement or enthusiasm for learning. Therefore, Pat had to spend additional time simply connecting with students, finding out what their interests were, sparking their interest in reading materials, and designing thinking games to motivate their involvement before she could begin to give them more academic material that would facilitate their learning, progress, and improvement in reading.

The last quarter of the year, too, was particularly skewed by an inordinate number of surprise assemblies, last-minute student activities, end-of-the-year field trips, and graduation practice, all of which served to interrupt and consume time needed for instruction. Nevertheless, I observed that fourth-quarter students, like third-quarter students, demonstrated greater ease and comfort with time, speaking more freely and engaging more actively over time. Even so, Pat was confident that if she were given more time with her students (at least one semester, although in the past she had had them for a year), she would see more evidence of their progress.

Other elements in and around the school posed barriers for Pat. Other teachers threatened students with "special education" if they did not do well on the ITBS tests. The tests themselves consumed much of the focus of the third quarter class, and even a trip to the library was reprimanded by the principal because Pat "should have been practicing skills."

Pat felt she also needed support from parents, the community, and students. She said, "I don't see the parent involvement or parent support now. It used to be everybody looked after the child, and the teacher was like, way on the pedestal. But that's not so now." Students, too, were in some ways blamed, if only for their attitudes toward school: "The children, they'll come in less motivated, with less experiences to bring into the classroom, which makes it more difficult for them to assimilate any information, or to talk about things. Because they have such very limited experiences."

Pat may have especially noticed this lack of support in contrast to the amount and kind of support she had received in past years. In other words, she perceived change over the years in administrative policies—mainly the addition of more and more constraints on her teaching. She was also used to parents being deeply involved in their children's schooling, and she was used to having students be "highly motivated." Most of all, perhaps, she was used to seeing herself as a successful teacher, and over time this perception, too, had changed: "Over the years, I don't have that drive, that enthusiasm, maybe I'm a little bit burned out, I don't know what it is. . . . I've been more frustrated this year than I have in awhile. Because I'm not seeing that real spark from the students. I know they get bored. They don't want to have a teacher talk all of the time. I know that, but maybe I'm frustrated because I feel like I'm not being effective with them. Something I'm doing is not reaching the group that I have." Burnout was related, then, both to a sense of failure as a teacher and to a decreasing of care (see Figure 6.3). In fact, Pat said to me on my last day of observation, "I wish you could have seen what I used to be like. . . . I care, but I don't care." Class was beginning and I did not probe further, but her statement remained— clearly she still cared, because if she did not care at all she would not be frustrated with her perceived ineffectiveness; yet she also did not care, in the sense that she had lost some of her energy for teaching.

In the face of these odds, Pat still employed an adaptive teaching strategy that resonated with currently recommended guidelines for culturally responsive teaching: listen to the students, have them think critically, make them aware of their futures, and have them reflect on themselves, the environment around them, and the world beyond. Indeed, Pat's adaptive abilities as a teacher met the demands of both the children and the

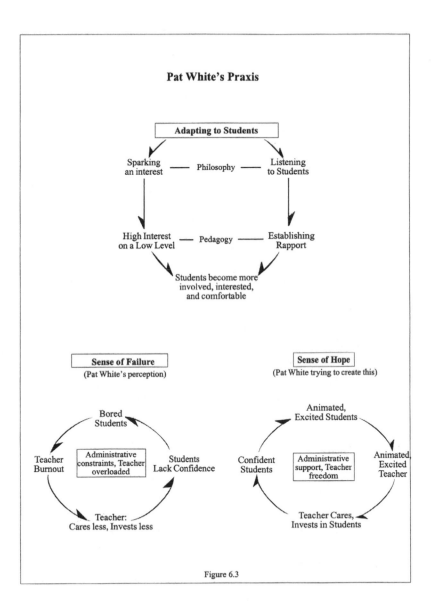

Figure 6.3

administration, as she conducted last-minute bookmakings, obediently lined her children up for surprise assemblies sure to interrupt her plan of action for learning, and worked within the school structure to diplomatically advise principals and assistant principals of her opinions, as a senior teacher, as to what school policies would work best for her students.

Despite her efforts, she sustained burnout, confessing not being able to wait for spring break, or, even better, for the kids to be out of school for the summer. Her five days at a reading conference gathering more resources and supplies for better teaching were likewise a "break" for her from teaching, one she admitted she had looked forward to as much as the conference itself.

Summary of Pat's Praxis: Chasing Hope

Pat's philosophy about how her students might learn better (see Fig. 6.1) also serves to explain how she sees her own teaching improve (see Fig. 6.3). When she is supported and confident about her teaching, she cares more and thus invests more, and then sees better results from her students. As she said, "when they're bored, quiet, it's boring for me. I can't get up with that. If they're getting more into the lesson, I get more into the lesson. It's just an exchange between us. Just seeing them succeed, Maria . . . [is] basically what makes me happy. I don't think I could ask for anything else."

Other hints of hope lay in the apparent rejuvenation Pat experienced with professional development opportunities, specifically the CULTURES workshop and the International Reading Association conference. Pat also talked about retiring and then starting her own dream school with a nursery, describing how she would have the nursery school set up and how she would like to have a swimming pool because so many of her African American students had never been to a pool. Clearly Pat loved children and still wanted to work with them in some capacity. For her own personal sake, however, she felt that she needed change. She wanted support, excitement, and fun to be part of her everyday work. Part of this excitement should include having the creative freedom to do what she deemed best for students. Most clear was that she wanted to be employed in ways that she could be successful, that she would help children the most if she was successful, that she would be more confident if she was more successful, and this would translate into her continued efforts as the master teacher that she is.

The following passage from the end of our last interview together sums Pat's burnout both with her sense of failure and her sense of hope:

MARIA: Do you see yourself teaching more than one more year?

PAT: I feel, you know what, if next year goes good, I will. Plus actually, with all is said and done, even with all my griping, and I'm so tired, and I'm burned out, and all this other stuff, I really do love children. I really do. And I do like my job. I really do. But you know it's just so frustrating when you can't reach them and you know the importance of it, and they cannot do it. It's very frustrating. It's even more frustrating when you've been accustomed to having classes where they're you know, smooth, there's rapport, the children focus—not that they are just like—they're lost, you know, the same as some of these other kids, but they come, and they're focused, you know, as to what they're gonna [do]—but this year, I can't get some of these kids to stay focused, like what you say. I'm just at my wit's end, and I get so frustrated, Maria. One day I just felt like crying, I really did. And I know I should not allow myself to get to that point. But it was only because I wanted to say, "Hey, listen, this isn't a game here. We're not playing. You need this. Now you need it. It's a hard core world out there. Nobody's gonna to baby you. You can't come back to the eighth grade ever again. Ever." You may go to remedial classes as an adult, but not in the eighth grade at their age. So it's just kind of frustrating, Maria. When I talk to some of my colleagues, they feel the same way. You know, they're—sometimes you think, what is wrong with me? (she points to herself)—You know, because I'll do that. And then I'll talk to someone and they'll say, "Oh, no, don't beat yourself up, it's not you, this is happening to me." Then I'll feel better. And I can imagine that's how the children kinda feel too sometimes, you know. "I thought it was only me. Unh-unh. Nope, it's not you."

The deep frustration in Pat's voice is saddening, particularly as she intones that she is not the only teacher this is happening to, and her students are not the only students. Her sense of failure stems exactly from the urgent needs she knows her students have—a need she felt unable to address, because she could not reach them, and they were, she felt, unable to reach her. Knowing that she used to be able to reach students, and teach students, only heightened her frustration. The hope in her last words is equally poignant: her love of children, and her love of teaching might, just might, keep her teaching one more year. What is chilling—knowing that she is not the only teacher—is also heartening, that she can still reach out to find her own kind of support within the school: "I thought it was only me. Unh-unh. Nope, it's not you."

CONCLUSION

If Pat's teaching follows most of the recent guidelines for literacy teaching of African American students, what are these guidelines missing? In other words, what can explain Pat's own perception of "failure"? Is it simply that in this situation at this time, she has reached the point where, as one teacher, she can only do so much within the general context of her school, students, and society? Pat provided the key herself: lack of support. This lack of support may help to explain why, if Pat's teaching looks like culturally responsive pedagogy, she still experiences "failure."

Pat was careful, in her description of lack of support, to explain that she perceived this lack of support not just from administrators but from policymakers outside the school, from other teachers in the school, from parents, and from the students themselves. In doing so, she named virtually everyone involved in schooling, suggesting that the holistic community in which she was teaching essentially lacked "community." In facing the odds, she found herself fighting against more than one wall at the same time.

Even her students, Pat felt, should be held accountable for taking charge of their own learning. She was quick to explain that not doing so was not, from the beginning, their fault, since their attitudes toward schooling were partly shaped by the experiences schooling had given them. In other words, schooling had given her students great cause to be disillusioned with the game of learning. All the same, she wished to hold them responsible for trying, preaching to them that "it's a two-way street."

Pat did not include the community around her school as a place where she felt a lack of support. Yet even her fond description of the actual neighborhood around the school revealed a disturbing sense of growing disconnection with the residents who lived close to the school. These residents, who were once very involved in the school, were now older, and very few of them still had children attending the school. Thus Pat's disconnection to parents, students, teachers, administrators—the "community-at-large" and the "community-within-school"—was mirrored in the physical geographical community around the school.

A culturally responsive philosophy and pedagogy, in tandem with unsupportive contextual forces, appear not to be enough, at least in one teacher's eyes. A successful culturally responsive *praxis,* which includes context, would include a good support structure as part of that context. In the end, the greatest message Pat and other master teachers in similar situations give is the need for continual support of teachers regardless of level of expertise or years of experience.

Chapter 7

AFRICAN AMERICAN TEACHERS' CULTURALLY SPECIFIC PEDAGOGY

The Collective Stories

Jacqueline Jordan Irvine

My work with African American teachers in CULTURES has led me to conclude that these teachers' views of their roles are based on unique cultural and historical perspectives. African American teachers look introspectively at how their ethnic identity, classroom practices, and their beliefs are related to the achievement of their African American students. The African American teachers in CULTURES often talked about how their own cultural notions of teaching guided them in their practice. These cultural views were often different from what they had been taught in their teacher preparation programs. In fact, some of these teachers had to "unlearn" and modify what they have been taught in the academy in order to address the specific learning needs of their African American students.

Here are a few stories African American teachers in CULTURES have shared with me:

1. A beginning African American teacher said: "I never thought that I had to convince my principal that my students labeled 'at risk' or 'low level' or some other insulting term could truly be successful if we all held high expectations. Just because they *aren't* learning doesn't mean they *can't*."

2. A 30-year veteran African American teacher said she never looks at the test profile of her students from central office. She said, "I just put them in the drawer."

3. Another teacher, commenting on what she learned in instructional methods courses, said: "I tried a lot of teaching methods that I learned in college—cooperative learning, whole language, centers. But, you know, when I work with my kids I found out how much they like to perform on a program. You know—like church, like an Easter speech."

4. Yet another teacher confronted her colleagues who had been taught that a good measure of parental involvement is the frequency with which parents attended school conferences. In an interview she said, "I heard a teacher say that African American parents didn't care about their kids because they don't come to school. My parents didn't come to school meetings but I know they cared about us. So I said something to her about that."

5. Finally, another shared this comment: "You know, I can tackle and teach the worst child and make a difference. I can see some good in anybody and that includes the worst child in this building. . . . Our job as the adult and as the educator is to try to help that child find the good within himself and to identify the good in us. I can't think of any child that I would just like to shove off on somebody else— and that's the truth!"

AFRICAN AMERICAN TEACHERS' PERSPECTIVES

This chapter will describe the culturally specific pedagogy of African American teachers and how they situate themselves professionally and personally to address the needs of their African American students. Researchers often ignore or devalue the culturally specific pedagogy and teaching beliefs of African American teachers; that is, the culturally specific ways in which African American teachers see themselves, not as part of the problem of black students' failure to achieve in school, but, rather, as part of the solution. This oversight in the research is a serious issue because it leaves the perspectives and voices of African American teachers and the African American community silenced, marginalized, and invisible.

The African American teachers in CULTURES verbalized strong beliefs about their ability to "make a difference" in the personal and school lives of their students. The typical CULTURES teacher was an African American female teacher from an elementary school in the Atlanta public schools with over sixteen years of teaching experience. These experienced African American teachers were competent and masterful pedagogues. The average participant had a masters degree and 16 years of teaching experience. These teachers had studied the micro and cultural explanations of African American students' school failure in their degree and certification programs, but thought that the researchers' explanations were less powerful and convincing than their sense of teaching efficacy and mission. Their efficacy and mission were revealed in the ways in which they described their practice, beliefs, and students, and the communities in which they worked. The African American teachers, in my research, not only viewed teaching as telling, guiding, and facilitating mastery of mandated content standards, but they also defined teaching as: "other mothering" and a calling, and as caring, believing, demanding the best, and disciplining.

Teaching Is Caring

Teaching is about caring relationships, and the teachers in this research understood the power of care. As Jane Roland Martin said, they turn schoolhouses into school homes where the three Cs (care, concern, and connection) are as important as the three Rs.[1] Researchers, like the ones in an impressive 18-month ethnographic study of four multiethnic schools, concluded that the most consistent and powerful finding related to school achievement for diverse students was this issue of care.[2] Students said they liked school and did their best when they thought that teachers cared about them or did special things for them. Students said teachers cared when they laughed with them, trusted and respected them, and recognized them as individuals. Students were not saying that they liked teachers who let them have their way: just the opposite. Students defined caring teachers as those who set limits, provided structure, had high expectations, and pushed them to achieve. Franita Ware's synthesis of the research illustrates that the "ethic of caring" continues to be a critical part of African American teachers' pedagogy.

Vanessa Siddle Walker explains that African American teachers have a different view of caring than the view described in the research literature.[3] She charges that conceptions of caring in African American schools have been excluded from published research and that this omission has been "tragic" given the high failure rate of African American students. She specifically states that African American teachers:

1. Focused on caring in all aspects of a child's life rather than in narrow interpersonal ways;
2. Cared for students by providing an honest and truthful feedback to students about their performance;
3. Cared for their students but never relinquished their authority or attempted to be friends of their students; and
4. Demonstrated that their caring is representative of a history of African American, culturally specific teaching behaviors.

In addition to seeing their teaching as caring, the African American teachers in my work saw teaching as "other mothering."

Teaching Is Other Mothering

Black teachers in my work, mostly women, felt a sense of personal attachment and kinship to the low-income African American children they taught. Patricia Hills Collins called these adults the "other mothers"—teachers who emotionally adopt hundreds of students each school year.[4] One CULTURES teacher told me about a rather interesting naming ritual with her students on the first day of school. Mrs. Jones said: "The kids call me mama. You know, I take ownership of these kids. I tell them on the first day to attach my last name to their name."

Mrs. Jones described how, at the beginning of the school year, she gives every child a new hyphenated name. For example, if a child's name is James Smith, Mrs. Jones tells him his new name is James Smith-Jones. When asked why she insists on this re-naming ritual, she stated that she wanted the children to know that "You now belong to me and how you act and what you do reflects me."

"Other mothering" is different from researchers' description of teacher identification and surrogate parenting. These African American teachers were attached both to the individual child as well as the race. Their willingness to "adopt" was *not* solely because of their desire to help a child but also to advance the entire race. These "other mothers" had strong beliefs about their students' ability to achieve despite widely publicized data, such as the black-white achievement gap, that could have convinced them otherwise.

Franita Ware's chapter provides additional examples of these "other mothering" behaviors in the works of Michele Foster, Pauline Lipman, and Annette Henry.

Teaching Is Believing

Teachers' beliefs about their teaching and their ability to influence the achievement of their African American students are critically important.[5] Teachers who have confidence about their practice are persistent and resilient in the face of obstacles and seemingly overwhelming odds against them. The African American teachers I have worked with in CULTURES had confidence in their ability to teach and they believe their students could learn.

Gloria Lee's work suggests that highly efficacious teachers use more challenging and creative instructional techniques, are more persistent with failing students, remain in the profession longer, and receive higher evaluations than their less efficacious colleagues.[6] In addition, teacher efficacy has been linked to student achievement as well as students' attitudes about school.

Unlike their white counterparts, who expressed beliefs about their African American students such as the often-touted phrase, "All children can learn," these African American teachers acted on these beliefs and demanded that their African American students perform. "Demanding the Best," the next category, illustrates this belief.

Teaching Is Demanding the Best

Teachers are significant others in the lives of their African American students, and their expectations about their students seem to be related to achievement.[7] One teacher summarized this research by asserting, "If you expect nothing, you get nothing!" Another teacher said, "I expect an awful lot, but I refuse to settle for less."

Professor Michael Eric Dyson, in an interesting essay called, "Shakespeare and Smokey Robinson"[8] describes his fifth-grade black teacher, Mrs. James, who would not let them "skate through school without studying hard, " without mastering high standards, and without appreciating their black culture. He wrote: "Mrs. James was extraordinarily demanding and insisted that our oral and written work aspire to consistently high levels of expression. . . . She taught us the importance of Roland Hayes and

Bessie Smith. . . . She provided a means of appreciating the popular culture that shaped our lives as well as extending the quest for literacy by more traditional means. Thus we never viewed The Temptations and Smokey Robinson as the antithesis to cultured life. . . . Thus the postmodern came crushing in on me before I gained insight of it in Derrida and Foucault."[9]

These teachers' unrelenting and "no excuses" expectations are consistent and logical if you understand that they believed that teaching is not just a career or profession but a calling.

Teaching Is a Calling

Historically, teachers in the African American community were held in high esteem and saw teaching as a moral act reminiscent of the "lifting as we climb" philosophy of late-nineteenth-and-early-twentieth-century black women educators like Lucy Laney, Charlotte Hawkins Brown, Fanny Jackson Coppin, and Ana J. Cooper.[10] In my research with CULTURES teachers, I found that African American teachers have a strong and apparent sense of spirituality, and they use phrases like "special Godly anointing" and "sacred calling" to describe their work. The interviews of these teachers are replete with references to words like "blessings" and "mission."

In the tradition of the religious conception of a calling, these teachers saw their work as having religious and spiritual purpose. This spirituality—evident in their teaching behaviors, values, and beliefs—often bore themes of transcendence and transformation. These teachers served as spiritual mentors and advisors for African American students. Sometimes their teaching became preaching when these teachers thought it necessary to bolster these children with sermonettes about hard work, achievement, hope, appropriate behavior, and respect. One teacher told me she does not *just* teach her subject matter. She said, "I teach life." When I asked an African American teacher to name her greatest asset, she quickly responded, "My faith."

Angela Rickford's work illustrates how one black teacher used black church rituals in his disciplinary and classroom management strategies, and in spite of the fact that not all the children were regular churchgoers, they were familiar with these church-based rituals.[11] For example, the student who was assigned the role of class monitor assumed the role as if it was comparable to that of church usher. The student's hand signals directed the group's sitting, standing, and exiting. Rickford writes, "These classroom seating procedures represent direct borrowings from the black Church where assigned ushers formally welcome members and visitors on Sunday morning, and escort them to their seats. . . . In effect, Mr. Peters (the African American teacher) transported the familiar concept of church into the classroom."[12]

Similar findings about the influence of spirituality and religion on African American teachers can be found in the works of Lipman[13] and Siddle Walker.[14]

Teaching Is Disciplining

It is not surprising that these mission-driven, spiritually grounded African American teachers also tended to be strong yet compassionate disciplinarians who were admired, not resented, by their pupils. One student wrote the following about one of the CULTURES teachers: "This woman is my favorite teacher because she's always on my back making me do better. I don't mind though because some days I need that extra push."

Vasquez called these no-nonsense teachers "warm demanders"—committed, respectful, dedicated, and competent educators who are not afraid, resentful, or hostile toward their pupils.[15] According to Patricia Cooper, these African American warm demanders stand in contrast with their white colleagues who were "less willing to exercise authority directly when teaching." [16]These African American teachers also stand in contrast to researchers' prescriptions that teachers acts as facilitators and joint constructors of knowledge.

CONCLUSION

The African American teachers, in my research, demonstrated culturally specific teaching styles and beliefs. They viewed teaching as telling, guiding, and facilitating mastery of mandated content standards, but they also defined teaching as: "other mothering" and a calling, and as caring, believing, demanding the best, and disciplining. These behaviors are related, I believe, to the success and achievement of the African American students they teach.

There are startling data that suggest, however, that African American teachers will soon become an "endangered species" in education. Ironically, as the number of African American students increases in urban schools, the number of African American teachers, like the ones referred to in this chapter, is dramatically decreasing. Teaching has historically attracted a disproportionate number of persons of color who entered the profession as a vehicle for upper mobility. This is particularly true for African American college graduates. It has been estimated that in 1950 one-half of all black professionals in the United States were teachers.[17] Desegregation brought about dramatic changes in the existing social order. Ethridge[18] estimated that between 1954 and 1972 there were at least 39,386 documented cases of African American teachers who lost their jobs in 17 southern states.

Education is now facing a second, somewhat different, crisis related to black teachers. The issue today is not the callous, insensitive firing of black teachers that followed desegregation, but the present inability of the profession to recruit and retain such teachers. The chapters of Ware and Cooper provide convincing arguments that the pedagogy and beliefs of African American teachers are different from those of white teachers and that their presence in the profession is needed and should be valued. In addition, high stakes testing that devalues the culturally specific effective classroom behaviors of these African American teachers should be re-evaluated.

Anthropological, sociological, and pedagogical research is clear and convincing that teaching and learning (like most human behaviors) are influenced by one's cultural framework, beliefs, and worldview. Hence effective teaching is related to context—teachers' and students' ethnic and cultural experiences, as well as their needs and motivation. Newly implemented standards aimed to increase teacher quality and accountability have ignored the cultural pedagogical style and beliefs that African American teachers bring to their classrooms. Although culture is learned and hence can be unlearned, and although culture is not deterministic nor predictive of behavior, researchers must begin to acknowledge how culture and context influences teachers and their interactions with their students.

Chapter 8

RESPONSES FROM THE TEACHERS

Comments from Beverley Cockerham, Vivian Stephens, and Patricia White

BEVERLEY COCKERHAM

I wrestled with the question Gloria Lee asked me: Do you think of yourself as a teacher who happens to be African American or an African American teacher? The question, I believe, presents a false distinction. I am not going to minimize my professional identity as a teacher, but I am an African American teacher. I am first an African American, and I happen to be a teacher. I could be a doctor or a lawyer, or whatever, but I am an African American first and a teacher. Being an African American, as a matter of fact, has enhanced my teaching. I bring my experiences, my prior socialization, and my background to my classroom. I share these experiences with my students.

With my African American students, I ask them to think of their heritage. "What would your grandmother say about this?" "What about your grandfather?" I tell my African American students that they must represent our race well. They must represent their family with excellence. For some reason, my teaching always comes back to the family.

I think of myself as a culturally responsive teacher and make cultural connections with my students with whom I share common interests. I give my students a questionnaire at the beginning of the school year to determine what they enjoy doing and encourage them to plan with me. A culturally responsive teacher, I think, promotes real-life lessons for her students. However, a culturally responsive teacher goes beyond these classroom activities. I always involve the parents and the community through phone calls, classroom visits, home visits, and attendance at church services in the community. Being a culturally responsive teacher means being aware of my students, maintaining their dignity, and being positive. You have to recognize your students' strengths and their weaknesses and try to work with them. I believe that my personal relationship with them helps a great deal. I also permit my students to see me as a learner. I am always reading something. If I attend a workshop or a seminar, my students know about it.

The CULTURES professional development assisted me in becoming a more culturally responsive teacher by encouraging me to incorporate more books and stories about African American culture and more community involvement into my teaching. I can think of two examples. I taught one student who was very interested in a book that we read, which subsequently inspired her to find out more about her family history. She interviewed her family in Tuskegee, Alabama, took photographs, and shared the information with the class. As a result of this student's interest and enthusiasm, the class made a heritage wall and brought in pictures of their family members. Another student, a special education student, was very interested in football so I invited a football player to come to my class and mentor him. As a result, the student began to read the sports pages of the newspaper and books about football. Consequently, I try to find activities that match my students' interests and incorporate these elements into writing, reading, and mathematics classroom activities.

Finally, I felt honored to participate in this book project because I felt I might gain some experience and learn something about myself as a teacher. This particular type of research about professional development is important because it allows teachers to reflect and because it gives us a voice in expressing our opinions and our feelings on education. I must admit that initially I wondered if this writing project would result in extra work for me, but it didn't. Gloria Lee accurately described the events in my classroom and I felt nothing essential was omitted from her chapter.

VIVIAN STEPHENS

I think of myself more and more as an African American teacher than I have in recent years. In the past I thought of myself as a teacher who just happened to be African American because I received a lot of respect from my school system and my school for being just a teacher.

I am not sure if race influences my teaching or if it is a combination of race and culture. These two factors are intertwined so completely that it is difficult to distinguish between the two. However, the CULTURES experience helped me to deal with issues of race and culture by freeing me to share my background and culture with my students. Before CULTURES I considered my race, ethnic background, and experiences to be private areas. I was even somewhat ashamed of the cultural differences between my mostly white students and me until CULTURES taught me to cherish these cultural differences in myself, my students of African American descent, as well as all other students.

Acknowledging my race and culture through the CULTURES program has changed my relationship with my students, particularly my African American students. Unlike my previous teaching philosophy, I am not trying to assimilate my African American students into the mainstream white culture. Since CULTURES I feel more responsible for the African American students in the school. Through community circles, group work, and daily reflections in my classroom, I encourage all of my students to share their unique differences. I even share my obsessions as well as my strengths, which often leaves me vulnerable in front of my students. However, my reflections on my race and ethnicity invite my students to share their unique cultural attributes and promote their self-esteem and desire to learn about each other and from each other.

My transformation into a culturally responsive teacher could not have been possible without the unique relationship I have with my principal. She believes in my abilities and me even when I do not believe in myself. I also think there were several influences in my childhood socialization that helped me to reclaim culturally responsive teaching. First, my mother was a teacher in the segregated South, and she instilled in me the importance of education and the value of learning. My parents were my greatest teachers. My daddy was forced to drop out of school in the ninth grade in order to support the family, but he never allowed any of his nine children to consider this option—no matter how destitute the family might have been. Second, one of my teachers in the segregated schools I attended, Mr. James, selected me as his assistant and made learning fun and interesting. He taught social studies, and his dramatic teaching made history come alive for me. I am not sure when I realized his influence on my teaching except I always, like Mr. James, try to help introverted students feel good about themselves. My segregated school experiences motivated me to encourage all students to always do their best. I particularly want my African American students to appreciate the fact that they do not have hand-me-down books, a dilapidated school, and that they can attend any school they wish.

Finally, I agreed to participate in this project because of the relationship I have with my chapter's author, Kim Archung. However, I am not a writer and I had serious reservations about participating in this part of the project. I did not want to be in yet another intimidating situation, but knowing that Kim and the other writers believed in me was enough to get a commitment from me. I also agreed to participate in the project for the future of education and the vast numbers of children who have yet to pass through our educational system.

I think it is imperative that teachers lend their voices to this kind of research. There are other voices making decisions about education that are not grounded in real classroom experiences. Others are writing new policies and laws based on their own views and not the views and experiences of teachers who could shed light on so many issues. If only their voices could be heard.

PAT WHITE

The question, do you think of yourself as a teacher who happens to be African American or as an African American teacher, was really a thought-provoking one. I wrestled with this question, and I cannot tell you how many times I vacillated between yes, I am a teacher who happens to be African American, and no, I am an African American teacher. So many people think of the term "African American teacher" as having a negative connotation. Initially I thought of myself as a teacher who happens to be African American, but I later changed my perspective and now think of myself as an African American teacher because that is what I am. Ideally a teacher should be skilled in teaching students from all racial/cultural backgrounds, without any regard to race; however, in reality this is not always the case. I am an African American teacher and I am proud to be one.

When I reflect on my past teaching experiences, my race did not influence my teaching. Before the CULTURES experience, I never thought of myself as an African American teacher—just a teacher. The CULTURES class helped me see some areas of insensitivity toward other cultural groups. This professional development experience changed me. I thought that I treated all my students with respect regardless of their race. I have taught white students and Hispanic students and I never had any problems. The only difference that I am aware of is the different interactions with the Hispanic students, primarily because there was a language barrier. In order to make my Hispanic students feel comfortable, I learned some Spanish words to win their respect, to make them feel comfortable, and to establish rapport. As far as my African American and white students were concerned, I treated them the same, although occasionally I used slang and dialect with my African American students. Most of my teaching experience has been with African American students who were at risk. I learned early in my career to listen to them, to talk to them as individuals, and let them talk to me about their feelings, goals, and fears. This strategy helped me to see the real person behind the exterior persona that the students often presented in class.

After the CULTURES class, I became a more culturally responsive teacher. I have tried to enhance my African American students' knowledge of their heritage and culture and expand their reading skills. My students came to me unmotivated, reading two to three grade levels below their grade and with no interest in reading. I felt that in order to motivate them to read, I had to first spark their interest in reading. I decided to provide a variety of activities that they could relate to and get excited about that would validate their ability to read. For example, we viewed the video *The Learning Tree*, by Gordon Parks, and compared and contrasted segregation in American society currently and in the past. This discussion surprised me because what the students were sharing verbally was far beyond their reading levels as measured by standardized tests. Often my students and I would transform the setting, events, and plot of a book based on their own cultural experiences.

I retired in June 1999 because I had become so frustrated with the administration and the demands that they placed on teachers that I felt I could not teach anymore. Teachers had no voice. I also tried to be a voice for the students. I tried to be a voice for teachers who felt as I do, but that voice fell on deaf ears. I was just maintaining the status quo. The emphasis was always on raising standardized test scores. I just felt that teaching had become too overwhelming and I couldn't take that anymore. I do not regret choosing teaching as a career. Teaching has been good to me with rewards and fun memories. I can't think of anything else that I would have done and enjoyed.

I gave no thought to the idea of participating in this project when Maria asked me to. The one reservation that I had was that Maria's presence might be distracting for the students. But once we settled in the process and began our work, I enjoyed having her in my class. It is important for teachers to participate in research like this for several reasons: (1) to provide glimpse of various teaching strategies that may or may not be culturally responsive to the African American student and; (2) to note teachers' concerns that affect the instruction of African American students. I was actually amazed at the accuracy of Maria's observations and notes. As I read her notes, I commented to her, "You got it just right." However, there is one statement in Maria's chapter that needs further clarification. Maria reported that I said, "I care, but I don't care." I really care about my students and felt responsible for them. The frustration from all of the administrative demands was just so overwhelming that I often threw my hands up and said, "You can't fight the system. You can't do it." That's what I meant. It didn't mean I did not care for the students I taught.

NOTES

INTRODUCTION

1. Villegas, A. M. (1991). *Culturally responsive pedagogy for the 1990s.* Princeton, NJ: Educational Testing Service.
2. Westheimer, J., and Kahne, J. (1993). Building school communities: An experience-based model. *Phi Delta Kappan* 75: 324–328.
3. Schon, D. (1987). *Educating the reflective practitioner. Toward a new design of teaching and learning professionals.* San Francisco, CA: Jossey-Bass, Inc.
4. Pollard, A., and Tann, S. (1987). *Reflective teaching in the primary school.* London: Cassell Education Limited.
5. Shulman, L. S. (1987). Knowledge and teaching: Foundations of the new reform. *Harvard Educational Review.* 57: 1–22.
6. Ibid., p. 8.
7. Brophy, J. E. (1985). Teacher-student interactions. In J. B. Dusek, ed., *Teacher expectations* (pp. 303–328). Hillsdale, NJ: Lawrence Erlbaum; Jussim, L. (1986). Self-fulfilling prophecies: A theoretical and integrative review. *Psychological Review* 93: 429–445; Rios, F. A. (1996). *Teacher thinking in cultural contexts.* Albany, NY: State University of New York Press.
8. Foster, M. (1997). *Black teachers on teaching* (p. XLIX). New York: The New Press.
9. Bennett, C. I. (1999). *Comprehensive multicultural education.* Boston: MA: Allyn and Bacon; and Banks, J. A. (2001). *Cultural diversity and education.* Boston, MA: Allyn and Bacon.

CHAPTER 1

1. Carter, R. T., and Goodwin, A. L. (1994). Racial identity and education. In L. Darling-Hammond, ed., *Review of Research in Education* Vol. 20 (pp. 291–336). Washington, D.C.: American Education Research Association, p. 307.
2. Bennett, M. J. (1986). A developmental approach to training for intercultural sensitivity. *International Journal of Intercultural Relations* 10: 179–195.
3. Banks, J. (1994). *Multiethnic education: Theory and practice.* Needham Heights, MA: Allyn and Bacon; and Hollins, E. R. (1996). *Culture in school learning: Revealing the deep meaning.* Mahwah, NJ: Lawrence Erlbaum.
4. McAllister, G. (1999). *Urban teachers' beliefs about culture and the relationship of those beliefs to their practice.* Ph.D. diss., Emory University, Atlanta.

5. Foster, M. (1995). African American teachers and culturally relevant pedagogy. In J. Banks and C. Banks, eds., *Handbook of research on multicultural education* (pp. 570–581). New York: Macmillan; Foster, M. (1997). *Black teachers on teaching.* New York: New Press; Siddle Walker, V. S. (1996). *Their highest potential: An African American school community in the segregated south.* Chapel Hill: University of North Carolina.

6. Foster, African American teachers and culturally relevant pedagogy; and Siddle Walker, *Their highest potential.*

7. Foster, *Black teachers on teaching;* and Walker, V. S., *Their highest potential.*

8. McAllister, *Urban teachers' beliefs about culture and the relationship of those beliefs to their practice.*

9. Ponterotto, J. G. (1988). Racial consciousness development among white counselor trainees: A stage model. *Journal of Multicultural Counseling and Development* 16: 146–156.

10. Lawrence, S. M., and Tatum, B. D. (1997a). Teachers in transition: The impact of anti-racist professional development on classroom practice. *Teachers College Record* 99: 162–178; and Lawrence, S. M., and Tatum, B. D. (1997b). White educators as allies: Moving from awareness to action. In M. Fine, L. Weiss, L. Powell, and M. Wong, eds., *Off white: Critical perspectives on race* (pp. 332–342). New York: Routledge.

11. Bennett, M. J. (1993). Towards ethnorelativism: A developmental model of intercultural sensitivity. In M. Paige, ed., *Education for the intercultural experience* (pp. 21–72). Yarmouth, ME: Intercultural Press.

12. Banks, *Multiethnic education;* and Hollins, E. R. (1999). Relating ethnic and racial identity development to teaching. In R. H. Sheets and E. R. Hollins, eds., *Racial and ethnic identity in school practices* (pp. 183–194). Mahwah, NJ: Lawrence Erlbaum.

13. Bennett, 1993, Towards ethnorelativism.

14. Banks, *Multiethnic education;* Gillette, M., and Boyle-Baise, M. (April 1995). *Multicultural education at the graduate level: Assisting teachers in developing multicultural perspectives.* Paper presented at the annual meeting of the American Education Research Association, San Francisco, CA.; and Nieto, S., and Rolon, C. (November 1995). *The preparation and professional development of teachers: A perspective from two Latinas.* Paper presented at the invitational conference on Defining the Knowledge Base for Urban Teacher Education, Emory University, Atlanta, GA.

15. Banks, *Multiethnic education;* Gillette and Boyle-Baise, *Multicultural education at the graduate level;* Nieto and Rolon, *The preparation and professional development of teachers;* Sleeter, C. (1992). *Keepers of the American dream: A study of staff development and multicultural education.* Washington, D.C.: Falmer; Villegas, A. M. (1991). Culturally responsive pedagogy for the 1990s and beyond. *Trends and Issues Paper No. 6.* Washington D.C.: ERIC Clearinghouse on Teacher Education.

16. Hollins, Relating ethnic and racial identity development to teaching; McAllister, *Urban teachers' beliefs about culture and the relationship of those beliefs to their practice.*

17. Ladson-Billings, G. (1992). Reading between the lines and beyond the pages: A culturally relevant approach to literacy teaching. *Theory into Practice* 31: 312–20, p. 314.

18. Irvine, J. J. (1990). *Black students and school failure: Policies, practices, and prescriptions.* New York: Greenwood Press, p. 49.
19. Gay, G. (1999). Ethnic identity development and multicultural education. In R. H. Sheets and E. R. Hollins, eds., *Racial and ethnic identity in school practices* (pp. 195–212). Mahwah, NJ: Lawrence Erlbaum, p. 201.
20. Tatum, B. D. (1997). *Why are all the black kids sitting together in the cafeteria?: And other conversations about race.* New York: Basic Books.
21. Irvine, *Black students and school failure;* Oakes, J. (1986). Keeping track, part 2: Curriculum inequality and school reform. *Phi Delta Kappan* 68: 148–151; Rist, R. C. (1970). Student social class and teacher expectations: The self-fulfilling prophecy and ghetto education. *Harvard Educational Review:* 411–451.
22. Hollins, Relating ethnic and racial identity development to teaching.
23. Tatum, *Why are all the black kids sitting together in the cafeteria?*
24. Hollins, Relating ethnic and racial identity development to teaching; Lawrence and Tatum, Teachers in transition; and Lawrence and Tatum, White educators as allies.
25. Ibid.
26. Cross, W. E., Strauss, L., and Fhagen-Smith, P. (1999). African American identity development across the life span: Educational implications. In R. H. Sheets and E. R. Hollins, eds., *Racial and ethnic identity in school practices* (pp. 29–48). Mahwah, NJ: Lawrence Erlbaum.
27. Tomlinson, L. M. (1996a). *Applying Banks' typology of ethnic identity development and curriculum goals to story content: Classroom discussion, and the ecology of classroom and community: Phase one, instructional resource, no. 24.* University of Georgia, National Reading Research Center; Tomlinson, L. M. (1996b). *Teachers' applications of Banks' typology of ethnic identity development and curriculum goals to story context and classroom discussion: Phase two, instructional resource no. 35.* University of Georgia, National Reading Research Center.
28. McAllister, G. and Irvine, J. J. (2000). Cross cultural competency and multicultural teacher education. *Review of Educational Research* 70: 3–24.
29. Cochran-Smith, M. (November 1995). *Knowledge, skills, and experiences for teaching culturally diverse learners: A perspective for practicing teachers.* Paper presented at the Invitational conference on Defining the Knowledge Base for Urban Teacher Education, Emory University, Atlanta, GA.
30. Abell, P. K. (1999). Recognizing and valuing differences: Process considerations. In E. R. Hollins and E. I. Oliver, eds., *Pathways to success in school: Culturally responsive teaching* (pp. 175–196). Mahwah, NJ: Lawrence Erlbaum; Banks, *Multiethnic education;* Lawrence and Tatum, Teachers in transition.
31. Grant, C., and Secada, W. G. (1990). Preparing teachers for diversity. In W. R. Houston, ed., *Handbook of research on teacher education* (pp. 403–422). New York: Macmillan; York, D. E. (1994). *Cross-cultural training programs.* Westport, CN: Bergin and Garvey.
32. Helms, J. E., ed., (1990). *Black and white racial identity: Theory, research, and practice.* New York: Greenwood.
33. Bennett, J. (1993). Cultural marginality: Identity issues in training. In M. Paige ed., *Cross-cultural orientation* (pp. 109–136). Lanham, MD: University Press of

America; Helms, *Black and white racial identity;* and Widick, C., Knefelkamp, and Parker, C. A. (1975). The counselor as a developmental instructor. *Counselor Education and Supervision* 14: 286–296.

34. Banks, *Multiethnic education;* Cadray, J. P. (1995). Enhancing multiculturalism in a teacher preparation program: A reflective analysis of a practitioner's intervention. *Dissertation Abstracts International* 57(8). University Microfilms No. 9701563.
35. Helms, *Black and white racial identity;* Taylor, T. Y. (1994). *A study of the effectiveness of a cognitive-developmental program to promote cross-cultural sensitivity among employees.* Ph.D. diss., North Carolina State University, Asheville, NC.
36. Greeley, A. T., Garcia, V. L., Kessler, B. L., and Gilchrest, G. (1992). Training effective multicultural group counselors: Issues for a group training course. *The Journal for Specialists in Group Work* 17: 196–209.
37. Cochran-Smith, M., and Lytle, S. L. (1995). *Inside/outside: Teacher research and knowledge.* New York: Teachers College.
38. Taylor, T. Y. (1994). *A study of the effectiveness of a cognitive-developmental program to promote cross-cultural sensitivity among employees.* Ph.D. diss., North Carolina State University, Asheville, N.C.
39. Bennett, Cultural marginality; Carney, C. G., and Kahn, K. B. (1984). Building competencies for effective cross-cultural counseling. *The Counseling Psychologist* 12: 111–119; Widick, Knefelcamp, and Parker, The counselor as a developmental instructor.
40. Taylor, A study of the effectiveness of a cognitive-developmental program to promote cross-cultural sensitivity among employees.
41. For example, Helms, J. E. (1994). The conceptualization of racial identity and other "racial" constructs. In E. Trickett, R. Watts, and D. Birman, eds., *Human diversity: Perspectives on people in context* (pp. 285–311). San Francisco: Jossey-Bass.
42. Mezirow, J. (1978). Perspective transformation. *Adult Education* 28: 100–110.
43. Ibid., p. 106.
44. Parham, T. A. (1989). Cycles of psychological nigrescence. *The Counseling Psychologist* 17(2): 187–226.
45. Bennett, Towards ethnorelativism.
46. Jones, W. T. (1990). Perspectives on ethnicity. In L. Moore, ed., *Evolving theoretical perspectives on students* (pp. 59–72). San Francisco: Jossey-Bass.
47. Meyers, L. J., Speight, S. L., Highlen, P. S., Chickaco, I. C., Reynolds, A. L., Adams, E. M., and Hanley, C. P. (1991). Identity development and worldview: Toward an optimal conceptualization. *Journal of Counseling and Development* 70: 54–63.
48. Jones, Perspectives on ethnicity; Phinney, J. S. (1990). Ethnic identity in adolescents and adults: Review of research. *Psychological Bulletin* 108: 499–514; and Taylor, *A study of the effectiveness of a cognitive-developmental program to promote cross-cultural sensitivity among employees.*
49. Helms, *Black and white racial identity.*
50. Meyers et al., Identity development and worldview.
51. Carter and Goodwin, Racial identity and education; and Tatum, B. D. (1992). Talking about race, learning about racism: The application of racial identity development theory in the classroom. *Harvard Educational Review* 62: 1–24.

52. Carter and Goodwin, Racial identity and education; and Lawrence and Tatum, Teachers in transition.

53. Kailin, J. (1994). Anti-racist staff development for teachers: Considerations of race, class, and gender. *Teaching and Teacher Education* 10(2): 169–184; Lawrence and Tatum, Teachers in transition; and Sleeter, *Keepers of the American dream.*

54. Sleeter, *Keepers of the American dream;* Villegas, A. M. (1991). Culturally responsive pedagogy for the 1990s and beyond. *Trends and Issues Paper No. 6.* Washington D.C.: ERIC Clearinghouse on Teacher Education.

55. Helms, *Black and white racial identity,* p. 3.

56. Ibid., p. 4.

57. Sue, D. W. (1981). *Counseling the Culturally Different.* Canada: John Wiley and Sons.

58. Cross, W. E. (1978). The Thomas and Cross models of psychological nigrescence: A review. *Journal of Black Psychology* 5: 13–31; Helms, Towards a theoretical explanation of the effects of race on counseling.

59. Cross, The Thomas and Cross models of psychological nigrescence; and Helms, Toward a theoretical explanation of the effects of race on counseling.

60. Atkinson, D., Morten, G., and Sue, D. (1983). *Counseling American minorities: A cross-cultural perspective.* Dubuque, IA: William C. Brown.

61. Root, M. P (2000). Rethinking racial identity development. In P. Spickard and W. J. Burroughs, eds., *We are a people: Narrative and multiplicity in constructing ethnic identity* (pp. 205–220). Philadelphia: Temple University.

62. Helms, *Black and white racial identity.*

63. Cross, The Thomas and Cross models of psychological nigrescence; and Cross, W. E. (1995). In search of blackness and Afrocentricity: The psychology of black identity. In H.W. Herbert, J. C. Blue, and E. E. H. Griffeth, eds., *Racial and ethnic identity: Psychological development and creative expression* (pp. 53–72). New York: Routledge.

64. Cross, Strauss, and Fhagen-Smith, African American identity development across the life span.

65. Hollins, Relating ethnic and racial identity development to teaching.

66. Cross, In search of blackness and Afrocentricity, p. 67.

67. Hollins, E. R. (1996). *Culture in school learning: Revealing the deep meaning.* Mahwah, NJ: Lawrence Erlbaum.

68. Cross, W. E. (presenter), and Oldershaw, B. (producer). (1993). *Shades of black : Diversity in African American identity* [videorecording]. North Amherst, MA: Microtraining Associates, Inc.

69. Hollins, Culture in school learning.

70. Hollins, Relating ethnic and racial identity development to teaching.

71. Taylor, *A study of the effectiveness of a cognitive-developmental program to promote cross-cultural sensitivity among employees.*

72. Brown, S. P., Parham, T. A., and Yonker, R. A. (1996). Influence of a cross-cultural training course on racial identity attitudes of white women and men: Preliminary perspectives. *Journal of Counseling and Development* 74: 510–516; Helms, *Black and white racial identity;* Neville, H. A., Heppner, J. J., Louie, C. E., and Thompson,

C. I. (1996). The impact of multicultural training on white racial identity attitudes and therapy competencies. *Professional Psychology: Research and Practice* 27: 83–89; and Ottavi, T. M., Pope-Davis, D. B., and Dings, J. G. (1994). Relationship between white racial identity attitudes and self-reported multicultural counseling competencies. *Journal of Counseling Psychology* 41:149–154.

73. Taylor, *A study of the effectiveness of a cognitive-developmental program to promote cross-cultural sensitivity among employees.*

74. Ibid.

75. Brown, Parham, and Yonker, Influence of a cross-cultural training course; Helms, *Black and white racial identity;* Neville et al., The impact of multicultural training; Ottavi, Pope-Davis, and Dings, Relationship between white racial identity attitudes and self-reported multicultural counseling competencies.

76. Lawrence, S. M., and Tatum, B.D. (1997a). Teachers in transition: The impact of anti-racist professional development on classroom practice. *Teachers College Record* 99: 162–178. Lawrence, S. M., and Tatum, B.D. (1997b). White educators as allies: Moving from awareness to action. In M. Fine, L. Weiss, L. Powell, and M. Wong, eds., *Off white: Critical perspectives on race* (pp. 332–342). New York: Routledge.

77. Sleeter, *Keepers of the American dream.*

78. Banks, *Multiethnic education.*

79. Ibid.

80. Ibid., p. 223.

81. Ibid., p. 227.

82. Ibid., p. 227.

83. Ibid., p. 225.

84. Ibid.

85. Banks, *Multiethnic education;* Martin, H. J., and Atwater, M. M. (1992). *The stages of ethnicity of preservice teachers and in-service personnel involved in multicultural education experiences.* ERIC Document Reproduction Services No. ED 397 203; Smith, A. J. (1983). *The relationship of teachers' preparedness in multicultural education to levels of ethnic awareness and multicultural exposure among elementary school certificated personnel.* Ph.D. diss., University of Washington, Pullman, WA.

86. Smith, *The relationship of teachers preparedness in multicultural education to levels of ethnic awareness and multicultural exposure among elementary school certificated personnel.*

87. Martin and Atwater, *The stages of ethnicity of preservice teachers and in-service personnel involved in multicultural education experiences.*

88. Tomlinson, *Applying Banks' typology;* Tomlinson, *Teachers' application of Banks' typology.*

89. Bennett, Cultural marginality.

90. Bennett, A developmental approach to training for intercultural sensitivity, p. 25.

91. Ibid., p. 187.

92. Ibid.

93. Ibid.

94. Ibid.

95. Adler, P. (1977). Beyond cultural identity: Reflections upon cultural and multicultural man. In R. W. Brislin, ed., *Culture learning: Concepts, applications, and research* (pp. 22–41). Honolulu: University of Hawaii Press. p. 26.

NOTES **159**

96. Villegas, A. M. (1991). Culturally responsive pedagogy for the 1990s and beyond. *Trends and Issues Paper No. 6*. Washington D.C.: ERIC Clearinghouse on Teacher Education.
97. Ibid.
98. Paige, M. (1993). On the nature of intercultural experiences and intercultural education. In M. Paige, ed., *Cross-cultural orientation* (pp. 1–21). Lanham, MD: University Press of America.
99. Turner, D. (1990). *Assessing intercultural sensitivity of American expatriates in Kuwait*. Masters thesis, Portland State University, Portland, OR.
100. Cox, B. B. (1982). *A research study focusing on Banks' stages of ethnicity typology as related to elementary teachers' multicultural experiences*. Ph.D. diss., University of Houston, Houston, Texas; Helms, *Black and white racial identity;* Martin and Atwater, *The stages of ethnicity of preservice teachers and in-service personnel;* and Turner, *Assessing intercultural sensitivity.*
101. Neville et al., The impact of multicultural training; and Ottavi et al., Relationship between white racial identity attitudes and self-reported multicultural counseling competencies.
102. Lawrence and Tatum, Teachers in transition; Lawrence and Tatum, White educators as allies.
103. Lawrence and Tatum, White educators as allies; and Taylor, *A study of the effectiveness of a cognitive-developmental program to promote cross-cultural sensitivity among employees.*
104. Cox, *A research study focusing on Banks' stages of ethnicity typology;* Ottavi et al., Relationship between white racial identity attitudes and self-reported multicultural counseling competencies; Smith, *The relationship of teachers preparedness in multicultural education;* and Turner, *Assessing intercultural sensitivity.*
105. Cross, The Thomas and Cross models of psychological nigrescence; Cross, In search of Blackness and Afrocentricity; Helms, *Black and white racial identity;* and Sabnani, H. B., Ponterotto, J. G., and Borodovsky. (1991). White racial identity development and cross-cultural counselor training: A stage model. *The Counseling Psychologist* 19: 76–102.
106. Bennett, Towards ethnorelativism.
107. Banks, *Multiethnic education.*
108. McAllister and Irvine, Cross cultural competency and multicultural teacher education. Taylor, A study of the effectiveness of a cognitive-developmental program to promote cross-cultural sensitivity among employees.
109. Bennett, Towards ethnorelativism.
110. For example, Lawrence and Tatum, Teachers in transition.
111. Brown, S. P., Parham, T. A., and Yonker, R. A. (1996). Influence of a cross-cultural training course on racial identity attitudes of white women and men: Preliminary perspectives. *Journal of Counseling and Development* 74: 510–516; Sabnani, Ponterotto, and Borodovsky, White racial identity development; and York, *Cross-cultural training programs.*
112. Martin, R. (1995). *Practicing what we preach: Confronting diversity in teacher education*. Albany, NY: State University of New York; and Paige, On the nature of intercultural experiences and intercultural education.

113. Taylor, *A study of the effectiveness of a cognitive-developmental program to promote cross-cultural sensitivity among employees.*

114. Bennett, Towards ethnorelativism; and Helms, *Black and white racial identity.*

115. Brown, Parham, and Yonker, Influence of a cross-cultural training course; Helms, *Black and white racial identity development;* Ottavi et al., Relationship between white racial identity attitudes; Neville et al., The impact of multicultural training; Sleeter, *Keepers of the American dream.*

116. Bennett, Towards ethnorelativism.

117. Grant and Secada, Preparing teachers for diversity, p. 429.

CHAPTER 2

1. Irvine, J. (1989). Beyond role models: An examination of cultural influences on the pedagogical perspectives of black teachers. *Peabody Journal of Education* 66(4): 51–63.

2. King, S. H. (1993). The limited presence of African American teachers. *Review of Educational Research* 63(2): 115–149.

3. Ibid., p. 117.

4. Meier, K. J., Stewart, J., and England, R. E. (1989). *Race, class and education: The politics of second generation discrimination.* Madison, WI: University of Wisconsin Press.

5. Toliver, K. (1993). The Kay Toliver mathematics program. *Journal of Negro Education* 62: 35–46, p. 35.

6. Ibid., p. 36.

7. Foster, M. (1993a). Educating for competence in community and culture: Exploring the views of exemplary African American teachers. *Urban Education* 27: 370–394, p. 376.

8. Cochran-Smith, M. (1997). Knowledge, skills, and experiences for teaching culturally diverse learners: A perspective for practicing teachers. In J. Irvine, ed., *Critical knowledge for diverse teachers and learners* (pp. 27–87). Washington, DC: The American Association of Colleges for Teacher Education; Ladson-Billings, G. (1994a). *The dreamkeepers.* San Francisco: Jossey-Bass; and Collins, P. (1991). *Black feminist thought: Knowledge, consciousness, and the politics of empowerment.* New York: Routledge, Chapman and Hall.

9. Collins, *Black feminist thought.*

10. Ibid., p. 149.

11. Lipman, P. (1995). "Bringing out the best in them": The contribution of culturally relevant teachers to educational reform. *Theory Into Practice* 34(3): 202–208.

12. Toliver, The Kay Toliver mathematics program.

13. Foster, M. (1990). The politics of race: Through the eyes of African American teachers. *Journal of Education* 172(3): 123–141; Foster, M. (1991). "Just got to find a way": Case studies of the lives and practice of exemplary black high school teachers. In M. Foster, ed., *Qualitative investigations into schools and schooling* (pp. 273–309). New York: Aims Press; Foster, M. Educating for competence in community and culture; Foster, M. (1993b). Resisting racism: Personal testimonies of African American teachers. In L. Weiss and M. Fine, eds., *Silenced voices: Race and gender in today's schools.* Albany, NY: State University of New York Press; and Fos-

ter, M. (1993c). Urban African American teachers' views of organizational change: Speculations on the experiences of exemplary teachers. *Equity and Excellence in Education* 26(2): 16–24.

14. Foster, M. (1997). *Black teachers on teaching.* New York: The New Press, p. 9.
15. Collins, *Black feminist thought,* p. 149; Foster, "Just got to find a way," p. 274; and Toliver, The Kay Toliver mathematics program.
16. Collins, *Black feminist thought.*
17. Foster, *Black teachers on teaching.*
18. Ibid., p. 31.
19. Henry, A. (1992). African Canadian women teachers' activism: Recreating communities of caring and resistance. *Journal of Negro Education* 61: 392–404; and Lipman, P. (1998). *Race, class, and power in school restructuring.* Albany: State University of New York Press.
20. Henry, African Canadian women teachers' activism.
21. Foster, "Just got to find a way;" and Foster, Urban African American teachers' views of organizational change.
22. Foster, M. (1993d). *Resisting racism: Personal testimonies of African American teachers* (p. 3). State University of New York, Albany: State University of New York Press.
23. Foster, *Black teachers on teaching,* p. 35.
24. Baker, S. (December 1982). *Characteristics of effective urban language arts teachers: An ethnographic study of retired teachers.* Paper presented at the meeting of the American Reading Forum, Sarasota, FL.
25. Ibid., p. 19.
26. Stanford, G. (1998). African-American teachers' knowledge of teaching: Understanding the influence of their remembered teachers. *The Urban Review* 30(3): 229–243.
27. Foster, Educating for competence in community and culture; and Foster, *Black teachers on teaching.*
28. Foster, *Black teachers on teaching;* Ladson-Billings, *The dreamkeepers;* Stanford, G. (April 1995). *African American pedagogy: Needed perspectives for urban education.* Paper presented at the annual meeting of American Educational Research Association, San Francisco, CA; and Toliver, The Kay Toliver mathematics program.
29. King, J. (1991). Unfinished business: Black students' alienation and black teacher's emancipatory pedagogy. In M. Foster, ed., *Qualitative investigations into schools and schooling* (pp. 245–271). New York: AMS Press.
30. Foster, *Black teachers on teaching;* and King, Unfinished business.
31. Foster, *Black teachers on teaching.*
32. King, Unfinished business; and Ladson-Billings, *The dreamkeepers.*
33. Foster, *Black teachers on teaching,* p. 173.
34. Foster, *Black teachers on teaching;* Ladson-Billings, *The dreamkeepers.*
35. Tolliver, The Kay Toliver mathematics program.
36. Henry, African Canadian women teachers' activism; Lipman, "Bringing out the best in them"; Toliver, The Kay Toliver mathematics program; and Walker, V. S. (1996). *Their highest potential.* Chapel Hill, NC: North Carolina Press.
37. Ladson-Billings, *The dreamkeepers.*

38. Irvine, R., and Irvine J. (1983). The impact of the desegregation process on the education of black students: Key variables. *Journal of Negro Education* 52: 410–422; and Walker, *Their highest potential.*
39. Ladson-Billings, *The dreamkeepers.*
40. Walker, *Their highest potential.*
41. Ibid., p. 71
42. Foster, *Black teachers on teaching;* Toliver, The Kay Toliver mathematics program.
43. Toliver, The Kay Toliver mathematics program.
44. Ladson-Billings, *The dreamkeepers;* Toliver, The Kay Toliver mathematics program.
45. Foster, *Black teachers on teaching.*
46. Hollins, R. (1989). The Marva Collins story revisited: Implications for regular classroom instruction. In B. J. Shade, ed., *Culture, style, and the education proven* (pp. 321–329). Springfield, IL: Charles C. Thomas.
47. Slavin, R. (1995). Cooperative learning and intergroup relations. In Banks, J., and Banks, C., eds., *Handbook of research on multicultural education* (pp. 628–634). New York: MacMillan.
48. Ladson-Billings, *The dreamkeepers;* Foster, *Black teachers on teaching.*
49. Foster, *Black teachers on teaching;* Henry, A. (1994). The empty shelf and other curricular challenges of teaching children of African descent: Implications for teacher practice. *Urban Education* 29(3): 298–319; King, Unfinished business; and Stanford, *African American pedagogy.*
50. Stanford, *African American pedagogy,* p. 11.
51. King, Unfinished business.
52. Ibid., p. 253.
53. Ibid., p. 254.
54. Noblit, G. (1993). Power and caring. *American Educational Research Journal* 30: 23–38; Toliver, The Kay Toliver mathematics program.
55. Toliver, The Kay Toliver mathematics program.
56. Ibid., p. 44.
57. Noblit, Power and caring.
58. Ibid., p. 33.
59. Baker, *Characteristics of effective urban language arts teachers;* Hollins, The Marva Collins story revisited; Ladson-Billings, *The dreamkeepers;* Lipman, "Bringing out the best in them."
60. Hollins, The Marva Collins story revisited.
61. Ibid., p. 324.
62. Lipman, "Bringing out the best in them."
63. Ibid., p. 204.
64. Ladson-Billings, *The dreamkeepers,* p. 82.
65. Irvine, J. J. (1990). *Black students and school failure: Policies, practices, and prescription.* New York: Greenwood Press, p. 30.
66. Noblit, Power and caring; Toliver, The Kay Toliver mathematics program.
67. Ladson-Billings, G. (1989). *A tale of two teachers: Exemplars of successful pedagogy of black students.* Paper presented at the Educational Equality Project Colloquium "Celebrating Diversity: Knowledge, Teachers, and Teaching," New York.

68. Baker, *Characteristics of effective urban language arts teachers.*
69. Hollins, The Marva Collins story revisited, p. 325.
70. Ibid., p. 325.

CHAPTER 3

1. National Education Association (1996). NEA today: *Status of the American public school teacher 1995–1996.* West Haven, CT: NEA Professional Library.
2. Foster, M. (1997). *Black teachers on teaching.* New York: New Press; Grant, C. (1990). Urban teachers: Their new colleagues and the curriculum. *Phi Delta Kappan* 70(10): 764–770; and Irvine, J. J. (1990). *Black students and school failure: Policies, practices, and prescriptions.* New York: Greenwood Press.
3. Anyon, J. (1997). *Ghetto schooling: A political economy of urban educational reform.* New York: Teachers College Press.
4. Zimpher, N. L. and Ashburn, E. A. (1992). Countering parochialism in teacher candidates. In M. E. Dilworth, ed., *Diversity in teacher education: New expectations* (pp. 40–62). San Francisco: Jossey-Bass.
5. Brooks, C. K. (1987). Teachers: Potent learning forces in the learning lives of black children. In Strickland, D. S. and Cooper, E. J., eds., *Educating black children: America's challenge.* Washington, D.C.: Bureau of Educational Research; Foster, *Black teachers on teaching;* Irvine, *Black students and school failure;* King, S. H. (1993). The limited presence of African-American teachers. *Review of Educational Research* 63(2): 115–149; Ladson-Billings, G. (1994a). *The dreamkeepers: Successful teachers of African American children.* San Francisco: Jossey-Bass; and Lipman, P. (1998). *Race, class, and power in school restructuring.* Albany, NY: SUNY Press.
6. McIntyre, A. (1997). *Making meaning out of whiteness: Exploring racial identity with white teachers.* Albany, NY: SUNY Press.
7. King, The limited presence of African-American teachers.
8. Irvine, *Black students and school failure;* and Irvine, J. and Foster, M., ed., (1995). *Growing up African American in Catholic schools.* New York: Teachers College Press.
9. Irvine, *Black students and school failure.*
10. Ibid., p. xix.
11. Ibid., p. xix.
12. Irvine, J. J. (April 1988). *Teacher race as a factor in black students' achievement.* Paper presented at the meeting of the American Educational Research Association, New Orleans.
13. Irvine and Foster, *Growing up African American in Catholic schools;* and Hilliard, A. G. (1994). Teachers and cultural styles in a pluralist society. In B. Bigelow, L. Christensen, S. Karp, B. Miner, and B. Peterson, eds., *Rethinking our classrooms: Teaching for equity and justice* (pp. 127). Milwaukee, WI: Rethinking Schools.
14. Bryk, T., Lee, V., and Holland. (1993). *Catholic schools and the common good.* Boston: Harvard University Press.
15. York, D. E. (1995). The academic achievement of African Americans in Catholic schools: A review of the literature. In Irvine and Foster, *Growing up African American in Catholic schools.*

16. King, J. E. (1994). The purpose of schooling for African-American children. In Hollins, King, and Hayman, eds., *Teaching diverse populations* (pp. 25–56). Albany, NY: SUNY Press.

17. Delpit, L. (1995). *Other people's children: Cultural conflict in the classroom.* New York: The New Press.

18. Irvine and Foster, *Growing up African American in Catholic schools.*

19. Banks, J. A. (1988). *Multiethnic education: Theory and practice.* 2nd ed. Boston: Allyn and Bacon; and Irvine, *Black students and school failure.*

20. Ladson-Billings, *The dreamkeepers.*

21. Walker, V. S. (1996). *Their highest potential: An African American school community in the segregated South.* Chapel Hill, NC: University of North Carolina Press.

22. Banks, *Multiethnic education;* Boykin, A. W. (1992). The triple quandary and the schooling of Afro-American children. In U. Neisser, *The school achievement of minority children: New perspectives* (pp. 59–70). Hillsdale, NJ: Lawrence Erlbaum; Delpit, L. (1988). The silenced dialogue: Power and pedagogy in educating other people's children. *Harvard Educational Review* 58(3): 280–298; Delpit, *Other people's children;* Dyson, A. H. (1992). The case of the singing scientist: A performance perspective on the "stages" of school literacy. *Written Communication* 9(1): 3–47; Dyson, A. H. (1995). The courage to write: Child meaning making in a contested world. *Language Arts* 72: 324–333; Foster, M. (1994). Effective black teachers: A literature review. In E. Hollins, J. King, and W. Hayman, eds., *Teaching diverse populations: Formulating a knowledge base* (pp. 207–25). Albany: SUNY Press; Irvine, *Black students and school failure;* Ladson-Billings, *The dreamkeepers;* Ladson-Billings, G. (1994b). Who will teach our children?: Preparing teachers to successfully teach African American students. In E. Hollins, J. King, and W. Hayman, eds., *Teaching diverse populations.* Albany, NY: SUNY Press, 106–129; and Walker, *Their highest potential.*

23. Walker, *Their highest potential.*

24. Ladson-Billings, *The dreamkeepers;* Foster, M. (1993). Self-portraits of black teachers: Narratives of individual and collective struggle against racism. In D. McLaughlin and W. G. Tierney, eds., *Many silenced lives: Personal narratives on the process of educational change* (pp. 155–175). New York: Routledge; and Foster, *Black teachers on teaching.*

25. Ladson-Billings, *The dreamkeepers,* p. 18.

26. Ibid.

27. Foster, Effective black teachers; Foster, *Black teachers on teaching.*

28. Stanford, G. C. (1995). *African American pedagogy: Needed perspectives for urban education.* Paper presented at the American Educational Research Association, San Francisco, CA.

29. Foster, Self-portraits of black teachers; Foster, *Black teachers on teaching;* and Ladson-Billings, *The dreamkeepers.*

30. Lipman, *Race, class, and power.*

31. Noblit, G. W. (1993). Power and caring. *American Education Research Journal* 30(1): 23–38.

32. Noddings, N. (1984). *Caring: A feminine approach to ethics and moral education.* Los Angeles: University of California Press.

33. Walker, *Their highest potential.*
34. Foster, Effective black teachers.
35. Banks, *Multiethnic education;* Boykin, The triple quandary; Darder, A. (1991). *Culture and power in the classroom.* Westport, CT: Bergin and Garvey; and Scheurich, J. J. (1993). Toward a white discourse on white racism. *Educational Researcher* 24(8): 5–16.
36. Ayers, W. (1993). *To teach: The journey of a teacher.* New York: Teachers College Press; Ayers, W. (1995). *To become a teacher.* New York: Teachers College Press; Banks, *Multiethnic education;* Delpit, *Other people's children;* Greene, M. (1986). In search of critical pedagogy for democratic alternatives. *Harvard Educational Review* 56: 427–441; Greene, M. (1993). The passions of pluralism: Multiculturalism and the expanding community. *Educational Researcher* 22(1): 13–18; Hilliard, Teachers and cultural styles in a pluralist society; Horton, M. (1998). *The long haul: An autobiography.* New York: Teachers College Press; Irvine and Foster, *Growing up African American in Catholic Schools;* Krater, J., Zeni, J., and Cason, N. D. (1994). *Mirror images: Teaching writing in black and white.* Portsmouth, NH: Heinemann; Ladson-Billings, *The dreamkeepers;* Ladson-Billings, Who will teach our children?; Noddings, N. (1992). *The challenge to care in schools: An alternative approach to education.* New York: Teachers College Press; Paley, V. G. (1979). *White teacher.* Cambridge, MA: Harvard University Press; Paley, V. G. (1995). *Kwanzaa and me: A teacher's story.* Cambridge, MA: Harvard University Press; Paley, V. G. (1997). *The girl with the brown crayon.* Cambridge, MA: Harvard University Press; Sleeter, C. E. (1993). How white teachers construct race. In C. McCarthy and W. Crichlow, eds., *Race, identity, and representation in education* (pp. 157–171). New York: Routledge; and Webster, L. (1997). *Looking back and thinking forward: Reexaminations of teaching and schooling.* New York: Teachers College Press.
37. Au, K. H. and Kawakami, A. J. (1994). Cultural congruence in instruction. In E. Hollins, J. King, and W. Hayman, eds., *Teaching diverse populations* (pp. 5–23). Albany, NY: SUNY Press; Banks, *Multiethnic education;* Cochran-Smith, M. (1995). Uncertain allies: Understanding the boundaries of race and teaching. *Harvard Educational Review* 65(4): 541–570; Hollins, E. R., King, J. E., and Hayman, W. C. (1994). *Teaching diverse populations: Formulating a knowledge base.* Albany, NY: SUNY Press; Sleeter, How white teachers construct race; and Williams, B., ed. (1996). *Closing the achievement gap: A vision for changing beliefs and practices.* Alexandria, VA: ASCD.
38. Hilliard, Teachers and cultural styles in a pluralist society.
39. Rist, R. (1970). Student social class and teacher expectations: The self-fulfilling prophecy in ghetto education. *Harvard Educational Review* 40(3): 411–451.
40. Kleinfeld, J., McDiarmid, G. W., Grubis, S., and Parrett, W. (1983). Doing research on effective cross-cultural teaching: The teacher tale. *Peabody Journal of Education* 61(1): 86–108.
41. Delpit, *Other people's children.*
42. Cochran-Smith, Uncertain allies; McIntyre, *Making meaning out of whiteness.*
43. Burdell. P. and Swadener, B. B. (1999). Critical personal narrative and autoethnography in education: Reflections on a genre. *Educational Researcher* 28(6): 21–26.

44. Freedman, S. G. (1998). A century of art on a blackboard canvas. *New York Times,* 17 May 1998.
45. Ayers, *To teach*; Ayers, *To become a teacher*; Hoffman, M. (1996). *Chasing hellhounds: A teacher learns from his students.* Minneapolis, MN: Milkweed Editions; Kohl, H. (1967). *36 children.* New York: New American Library; Kohl, H. (1998). *The discipline of hope.* New York: Simon and Schuster; Kozol, J. (1967). *Death at an early age.* New York: Plume; Meier, D. (1995). *The power of their ideas: Lessons from a small school in Harlem.* Boston: Beacon Press; O'Connor, S. (1996). *Will my name be shouted out?: Reaching inner city students through writing.* New York: Simon and Schuster; Paley *White Teacher;* and Paley, *Kwanzaa and me.*
46. Foster, Self-portraits of black teachers; Foster, *Black teachers on teaching.*
47. Ladson-Billings, *The dreamkeepers.*
48. Haberman, M. (1995). *Star teachers of children in poverty.* West Lafayette, IN: Kappa Delta Pi.
49. Ladson-Billings, *The dreamkeepers,* p. 13.
50. Foster, *Black teachers on teaching.*
51. Baldwin, J. (1963). A talk to teachers. In W. Ayers and P. Ford, eds., *City kids, city teachers* (pp. 219–227). New York: New Press.
52. Delpit, *Other people's children.*
53. See, for example, Wilson, Catherine. (2000). *Telling a different story: Teaching and literacy in an urban preschool.* New York: Teachers College Press, p. 23.
54. Ayers, To teach; Ayers, To become a teacher; Hoffman, *Chasing hellhounds;* Meier, *The power of their ideas;* O'Connor, *Will my name be shouted out?;* Paley, *White teacher;* Paley, *Kwanzaa and me;* Paley, *The girl with the brown crayon.*
55. Ayers, *To teach*; Ayers, *To become a teacher;* Kohl, *36 children;* Kohl, *The discipline of hope;* Kozol, *Death at an early age;* and O'Connor, *Will my name be shouted out?*
56. King, The purpose of schooling for African American children, pp. 25–56.
57. Hoffman, *Chasing hellhounds;* Paley, *White teacher;* and Paley, *Kwanzaa and me;* and Paley, *The girl with the brown crayon.*
58. Hoffman, *Chasing hellhounds;* Meier, *The power of their ideas.*
59. Kohl, *36 children,* and Kozol, *Death at an early age.*
60. Kohl, *The discipline of hope,* p. 108.
61. Hoffman, *Chasing hellhounds,* p. 23.
62. Paley, *White teacher,* p. 114.
63. Meier, *The power of their ideas,* p. 3.
64. Ayers, *To teach,* p. 115.
65. Kohl, *36 children*, p. 176.
66. Ayers, *To teach,* p. 88.
67. O'Connor, *Will my name be shouted out?*
68. Hoffman, *Chasing hellhounds.*
69. Paley, *Kwanzaa and me.*
70. Kohl, *36 children,* p. x.
71. Ayers, *To teach,* p. 16.
72. Kohl, *36 children.*
73. Paley, *White teacher.*

74. Ibid., p. 12.
75. Ayers, *To teach*, p. 39.
76. Kohl, *36 children;* Meier, *The power of their ideas;* and Ayers, *To teach.*
77. Kohl, *36 children*, p. 15.
78. Hoffman, *Chasing hellhounds*, p. 3.
79. Kohl, *The discipline of hope*, p. 49.
80. Paley, *White teacher*, p. xv.
81. Paley, *Kwanzaa and me*, p. 9.
82. O'Connor, *Will my name be shouted out?*
83. Meier, *The power of their ideas*, p. 52.
84. Lipman, *Race, class, and power in school restructuring.*
85. Delpit, *Other people's children;* and Miner, B. (1997). "Embracing Ebonics and teaching standard English." In Delpit, L. and Perry, T., eds., *Rethinking schools: The real Ebonics debate.* Milwaukee, WI: Rethinking Schools Limited, pp. 18–34.
86. Ladson-Billings, *The dreamkeepers;* and Foster, *Black teachers on teaching.*
87. Kohl, *36 children.*
88. Paley, *White teacher;* and Paley, *Kwanzaa and me.*
89. Meier, *The power of their ideas.*
90. Irvine, J. and Fraser, J. (13 May 1998). Warm demanders: Do national certification standards leave room for the culturally responsive pedagogy of African-American teachers? *Education Week:* 42.
91. Foster, 1995; Irvine and Fraser, Warm demanders; Noblit, Power and caring; Noddings, N. (1992). *The challenge to care in schools: An alternative approach to education.* New York: Teachers College Press; and Walker, *Their highest potential.*
92. Whitehead, A. N. (1929). *The aims of education and other essays.* New York: Macmillan.
93. Kohl, *36 children.*
94. Paley, *White teacher;* and Paley, *Kwanzaa and me.*
95. Ayers, *To teach.*
96. Delpit, *Other people's children*, p. 24.
97. Lipman, *Race, class, and power in school restructuring.*
98. Paley, *Kwanzaa and me.*
99. Foster, *Black teachers on teaching*, p. 61.
100. Foster, *Black teachers on teaching*, p. 48.
101. Foster, *Black teachers on teaching*, p. 34.
102. Ladson-Billings, *The dreamkeepers.*

CHAPTER 4

1. Sparks, D. (April 1997). Student success requires caring, standards, beliefs in student abilities. *The Developer:* 2.
2. Benz, C. R., Bradley, L., Alderman, M. K., and Flowers, M. A. (1992). Personal teaching efficacy: Developmental relationships in education. *Journal of Educational Research* 85: 274–285; Gibson, S., and Dembo, M. (1984). Teacher efficacy: A construct validation. *Journal of Educational Psychology* 36: 569–582; and Pajares, F.

(1992). Teachers' beliefs and educational research: Cleaning up a messy construct. *Review of Educational Research* 62: 307–332.

3. Kagan, D. M. (1992). Implications of research on teacher belief. *Educational Psychologist* 27: 65–90, p. 85.

4. Tschannen-Moran, M., Woolfolk Hoy, A., and Hoy, W. K. (1998). Teacher efficacy: Its meaning and measure. *Review of Educational Research* 68: 202–248, p. 233.

5. Ashton, P. T. (1985). Motivation and the teacher's sense of efficacy. In C. Ames and R. Ames, eds., *Research on motivation in education: Vol. 2: The classroom milieu* (pp. 141–171). Orlando, FL: Academic Press; Dembo, M. H., and Gibson, S. (1985). Teachers' sense of efficacy: An important factor in school improvement. *The Elementary School Journal* 86: 173–184; and Ross, J. A. (June 1994). *Beliefs that make a difference: The origins and impacts of teacher efficacy.* Paper presented at the annual meeting of the Canadian Association for Curriculum Studies, Calgary, Alberta, Canada.

6. Bandura, A. (1997). *Self-efficacy: The exercise of control.* New York: Freeman; and Pajares, F. (1997). Current directions in self-efficacy research. In P. R. Pintrich and M. Maehr, eds., *Advances in motivation and achievement.* Vol. 10 (pp.1–49). Greenwich, CT: JAI.

7. Bandura, A. (1977). Self-efficacy: Toward a unifying theory of behavioral change. *Psychological Review* 84: 191–215; Bandura, A. (1986). *Social foundations of thought and action: A social cognitive theory.* Englewood Cliffs, NJ: Prentice Hall; and Bandura, *Self-efficacy: The exercise of control.*

8. Bandura, *Social foundations of thought and action;* and Bandura, *Self-efficacy: The exercise of control.*

9. Bandura, *Self-efficacy: The exercise of control.*

10. Schunk, D. H. (1989). Self-efficacy and cognitive skill learning. In C. Ames and R. Ames, eds., *Research on motivation in education: Vol. 3. Goals and cognitions* (pp. 13–44). San Diego, CA: Academic Press.

11. Bandura, *Self-efficacy: The exercise of control.*

12. Tschannen-Moran et al., Teacher efficacy.

13. Bandura, *Self-efficacy: The exercise of control;* and Zeldin, A. L., and Pajares, F. (2000). Against the odds: Self-efficacy beliefs of women in mathematical, scientific, and technological careers. *American Educational Research Journal* 37:215–246.

14. Bandura, *Self-efficacy: The exercise of control.*

15. Tschannen-Moran et al., Teacher efficacy.

16. Bandura, Self-efficacy: Toward a unifying theory of behavioral change; Bandura, *Social foundations of thought and action;* and Bandura, *Self-efficacy: The exercise of control.*

17. Armor, D. J., Conry-Oseguera, P., Cox, M. A., King, N., McDonnell, L. M., Pascal, A. H., Pauly, E., Zellman (1976). *Analysis of the school preferred reading program in selected Los Angeles minority schools.* Report R-2007-LAUSD. Santa Monica, CA: Rand.

18. Midgley, C., Feldlaufer, H., and Eccles, J. S. (1989). Change in teacher efficacy and student self-and task-related beliefs in mathematics during the transition to junior high school. *Journal of Educational Psychology* 81: 247–258.

19. Behar-Horenstein, L. S., Pajares, F., and George, P. S. (1996). The effect of teachers' beliefs on students' academic performance during curriculum innovation. *The High School Journal* 79: 324–332; Berman, P., McLaughlin, M. W., Bass, G., Pauly, E., and Zellman, G. (1977). *Federal programs supporting educational change: Vol. VII: Factors affecting implementation and continuation*. Report R-1589/7-HEW. Santa Monica, CA: Rand; and Guskey, T. R. (1988). Teacher efficacy, self-concept, and attitudes toward the implementation of instructional innovation. *Teaching and Teacher Education* 4: 63–69.

20. Trentham, L., Silvern, S., and Brogdon, R. (1985). Teacher efficacy and teacher competency ratings. *Psychology in the Schools* 22: 343–352.

21. Ashton, P. T., and Webb, R. B. (1986). *Making a difference: Teachers' sense of efficacy and student achievement*. New York: Longman; Woolfolk, A. E., and Hoy, W. K. (1990). Prospective teachers' sense of efficacy and beliefs about control. *Journal of Educational Psychology* 82: 81–91; Woolfolk, A. E., Rosoff, B., and Hoy, W. K. (1990). Teachers' sense of efficacy and their beliefs about managing students. *Teacher and Teacher Education* 6: 137–148.

22. Rich, Y., Lev, S., and Rischer, S. (1996). Extending the concept and assessment of teacher efficacy. *Educational and Psychological Measurement* 56: 1015–1025.

23. Bandura, *Self-efficacy: The exercise of control*.

24. Saklofske, D. H., Michaluk, J. O., and Randhawa, B. S. (1988). Teachers' efficacy and teaching behaviors. *Psychological Report* 63: 407–414.

25. Hoover-Dempsey, K. V., Bassler, O. C., and Brissie, J. S. (1992). Explorations in parent-school relations. *Journal of Educational Research* 85: 287–294.

26. Bandura, *Self-efficacy: The exercise of control*.

27. Guskey, Teacher efficacy, self-concept, and attitudes toward the implementation of instructional innovation.

28. Allinder, R. M. (1994). The relationship between efficacy and the instructional practices of special education teachers and consultants. *Teacher Education and Special Education* 17: 86–95.

29. Podell, D. M., and Soodak, L. C. (1993). Teacher efficacy and bias in special education referrals. *Journal of Educational Research* 96: 247–253.

30. Guskey, T. R. (1984). The influence of change in instructional effectiveness upon the affective characteristics of teachers. *American Educational Research Journal* 21: 245–259.

31. Trentham et al., Teacher efficacy and teacher competency ratings.

32. Glickman, C., and Tamashiro, R. (1982). A comparison of first-year, fifth-year, and former teachers on efficacy, ego development, and problem solving. *Psychology in Schools* 19: 558–562.

33. Anderson, R., Greene, M., and Loewen, P. (1981). Relationships among teachers' and students' thinking skills, sense of efficacy, and student achievement. *Alberta Journal of Educational Research* 34(2): 148–165; Ross, J. A. (1992). Teacher efficacy and the effect of coaching on student achievement. *Canadian Journal of Education* 17: 51–56; Ross, J. A., and Cousins, J. B. (1993). Enhancing secondary school students' acquisition of correlational reasoning skills. *Research in Science and Technological Education* 11(3): 191–206.

34. Ashton and Webb, *Making a difference: Teachers' sense of efficacy and student achievement.*
35. Miskel, C., McDonald, D., and Bloom, S. (1983). Structural and expectancy linkages within schools and organizational effectiveness. *Educational Administration Quarterly* 19(1): 49–82.
36. Midgley et al., Change in teacher efficacy and student self- and task-related beliefs in mathematics during the transition to junior high school.
37. Rose, J. S., and Medway, F. J. (1981). Measurement of teachers' beliefs in their control over student outcome, *Journal of Educational Research,* 74: 185–190.
38. Bandura, *Self-efficacy: The exercise of control.*
39. Bandura, *Self-efficacy: The exercise of control.*
40. Pajares, Current directions in self-efficacy research.
41. Pajares, F. (1996). Self-efficacy beliefs in academic settings. *Review of Educational Research* 66: 543–578; Tschannen-Moran et al., Teacher efficacy.
42. Bandura, *Self-efficacy: The exercise of control;* and Tschannen-Moran et al., Teacher efficacy.
43. Coladarci, T. (1992). Teachers' sense of efficacy and commitment to teaching. *Journal of Experimental Education* 60: 323–337.
44. Moore, W. and Esselman, M. (April 1992). *Teacher efficacy, power, school climate and achievement: A desegregating district's experience.* Paper presented at the Annual Meeting of the American Educational Research Association, San Francisco.
45. Lee, V., Dedick, R., and Smith, J. (1991). The effect of the social organization of schools on teachers' efficacy and satisfaction. *Sociology of Education* 64: 190–208.
46. Chester, M. D., and Beaudin, B. Q. (1996). Efficacy beliefs of newly hired teachers in urban schools. *American Educational Research Journal* 33: 233–257.
47. Ashton and Webb, *Making a difference: Teachers' sense of efficacy and student achievement.*
48. Tschannen-Moran et al., Teacher efficacy.
49. Pajares, Current directions in self-efficacy research.

CHAPTER 5

1. Anderson, R., and Mitchener, C. (1989). Teachers' perspective: Developing and implementing and STS curriculum. *Journal of Research in Science Teaching,* 26(4): 351–369; Gallagher, J. J. (1989). Research on secondary school science teachers' practices, knowledge and beliefs: A basis for restructuring. In Matayas, M., Tobin, K. and Fraser, B., eds., *Looking into windows: Qualitative research in science education* (pp. 43–57). Washington, DC: American Association for the Advancement of Science; and Kelble, E. S. (1994). Enhancing physical science instruction for gifted elementary students: Developing teacher confidence and skills. *Roeper Review* 16(3): 162–166.
2. Allexsaht-Snider, M. (1996). Windows into diverse worlds: The telling and sharing of teachers' life histories. *Education and Urban Society* 29(1): 103–119; Jaworski, B. (1991). Develop your teaching. *Mathematics in School* 20(1): 18–21; and Sherman, H. and Thomas, J. (1995). Professional development: Teachers' communication

NOTES 171

and collaboration—keys to student achievement. *Mathematics Teaching in the Middle School* 1(6): 30–32.

3. French, M. P. (1985). An inservice plan for teaching reading in kindergarten: A description. *Reading Horizons* 25(4): 264–267.

4. Banks, J. A. and Banks, C. A. (1995). Multicultural education: Historical development, dimensions, and practice. In J. A. Banks and C. A. Banks, eds., *Handbook of research on multicultural education* (pp. 3–24). New York: Macmillan; Banks, J. A., and Banks, C. A. (1997). Reforming schools in a democratic pluralistic society. *Educational Policy* 11(2): 183–193; Bennett, C. (1995). Preparing teachers for cultural diversity and national standards of academic excellence. *Journal of Teacher Education* 46: 259–266; Cadray, J. P. (1995). *Enhancing multiculturalism in a teacher preparation program: A reflective analysis of a practitioner's intervention.* Ph.D. diss., University of New Orleans, New Orleans, LA; Cochran-Smith, M. (1997). Knowledge, skills, and experiences for teaching culturally diverse learners: A perspective for practicing teachers. In J. J. Irvine, ed., *Critical knowledge for diverse teachers and learners* (pp. 27–88). Washington, D.C.: American Association of Colleges for Teacher Education; Gomez, M. L. (1996). Prospective teachers' perspectives on teaching "other people's children." In Zeichner, K., Melnick, S. and Gomez, M. L., eds., *Currents of reform in preservice teacher education* (pp. 109–131). New York: Teachers College, Columbia University; Ladson-Billings, *The dreamkeepers;* Nelson, R. F. (1997). *Teaching student teachers how to promote cultural awareness in urban and suburban schools.* Paper presented at the annual meeting of the American Association of Colleges for Teacher Education, Phoenix, AZ; and Oakes, J. (1996). Making the rhetoric real. *Multicultural Education* 4(2): 4–10.

5. Gomez, Prospective teachers' perspectives on teaching "other people's children"; and Zeichner, K. and Melnick, S. (1996). The role of community field experiences in preparing teachers for cultural diversity. In Zeichner, Melnick, and Gomez, *Currents of reform in preservice teacher education.*

6. Solomon, R. P. (1995). Beyond prescriptive pedagogy: Teacher inservice education for cultural diversity. *Journal of Teacher Education* 46(4): 251–258.

7. Ball, S. J. and Goodson, I. F. (1985). *Teachers' lives and careers.* Philadelphia: Falmer Press; Goodson, I. F., ed., (1992). *Studying teachers' lives.* London: Routledge; Goodson, I. F. and Hargreaves, A., eds., (1996). *Teachers' professional lives.* Washington, D.C.: Falmer Press.

8. Olson, L. (2000). Finding and keeping competent teachers. *Education Week* 19(18): 12–18.

9. Huberman, M. (1995). Professional careers and professional development: Some intersections. In T. R. Guskey and M. Huberman, eds., *Professional development in education: New paradigms and practices* (pp. 193–224). New York: Teachers College, Columbia University.

10. Fessler, R. (1995). Dynamics of teacher career stages. In T. R. Guskey and M. Huberman, eds., *Professional development in education: New paradigms and practices* (pp. 171–192). New York: Teachers College; Huberman, Professional careers and professional development; and Vonk as cited in Fessler, Dynamics of teacher career stages.

172   NOTES

11. Fessler, Dynamics of teacher career stages.
12. Ibid., p. 185.
13. Ibid.
14. Huberman, Professional careers and professional development.
15. Fessler, Dynamics of teacher career stages, p. 174; Gregorc, A. F. (1973). Developing plans for professional growth. *NASSP Bulletin* 57: 1–8; Katz, L. G. (1972). Development stages of preschool teachers. *Elementary School Journal* 3: 50–54; Unruh, A., and Turner, H. E. (1970). *Supervision for change and innovation.* Boston: Houghton Mifflin.
16. Fessler, Dynamics of teacher career stages, p. 174.
17. 1Burke, P., Fessler, R., and Christensen, J. (1994). *Teacher career stages: Implications for staff development.* Bloomington, IN: Phi Delta Kappa; Fessler, Dynamics of teacher career stages; Huberman, M. (1989). *La vie des enseignants* [The lives of teachers]. Switzerland: Delachaux and Niestle SA; and Huberman, Professional careers and professional development.
18. Fessler, Dynamics of teacher career stages.
19. Ibid., p. 188.
20. Ibid., p. 181.
21. Speck, M. (1996). Best practice in professional development for sustained educational change. *ERS Spectrum* 4(2): p. 38.
22. Cole, D. B., and Ormond, J. E. (1995). Effectiveness of teaching pedagogical content knowledge through summer geography institutes. *Journal of Geography* 94: 427–433; Lawrentz, F. (1985). Impact of a five-week energy education program on teacher beliefs and attitudes. *School Science and Mathematics* 85(1): 27–36; Tillema, H. H. (1994). Training and professional experience: Bridging the gap between new information and pre-existing beliefs of teachers. *Teaching and Teacher Education* 10(6): 601–615; Walsted, W. B. (1980). The impact of "trade-offs" and teacher training on economic understanding and attitudes. *Journal of Economic Education* 12(1): 41–48; and Wolfe, L. J. (1996). *The effectiveness of an inservice geography institute on participating teachers.* Unpublished paper presented at the meeting of the National Council for Geographic Education, Santa Barbara, CA.
23. Gomez, Prospective teachers' perspectives on teaching "other people's children"; and Zeichner and Melnick, The role of community field experiences in preparing teachers for cultural diversity.
24. Gomez, Prospective teachers' perspectives on teaching "other people's children," p. 109.
25. Irvine, J. J. (1990). *Black students and school failure: Policies, practices, and prescriptions.* New York: Greenwood Press; and Villegas, A. M. (1991). Culturally responsive pedagogy for the 1990s and beyond. *Trends and Issues Paper No. 6.* Washington, D.C.: ERIC Clearinghouse on Teacher Education.
26. Cochran-Smith, Knowledge, skills, and experiences for teaching culturally diverse learners.
27. Ibid., p. 32.
28. Ibid., p. 32.

29. Foster, M. (1995). African American teachers and culturally relevant pedagogy. In J. Banks and C. Banks, eds., *Handbook of research on multicultural education* (pp. 570–581). New York: McMillan; and Goodson, *Studying teachers' lives.*
30. McAllister, G., and Irvine, J. J. (2000). Cross cultural competency and multicultural teacher education. *Review of Educational Research* 70(1): 3–24.
31. Helms, J. E. 1990. *Black and white racial identity: Theory, research, and practice.* New York: Greenwood Publishing Group.
32. Jones, W. T. (1990). Perspectives on ethnicity. In L. Moore, ed., *Evolving theoretical perspectives on students* (pp. 59–72). San Francisco: Jossey Bass; Loevinger, J. (1976). *Ego development: Conceptions and theories.* San Francisco: Jossey Bass; Phinney, J. S. (1990). Ethnic identity in adolescents and adults: Review of research. *Psychological Bulletin* 108: 400–514; and Prosser, M. H. (1978). *The cultural dialogue: An introduction to intercultural communication.* Boston: Houghton Mifflin; and Taylor, T. Y. (1994). A study of the effectiveness of a cognitive-developmental program to promote cross-cultural sensitivity among employees. Ph.D. diss., North Carolina State University, Asheville, NC.
33. Cochran-Smith, Knowledge, skills, and experiences for teaching culturally diverse learners.
34. Goodson, *Studying teachers' lives;* Goodson and Hargreaves, *Teachers' professional lives;* and Huberman, *La vie des enseignants.*
35. Gore, G. W. (1940). *In-service professional improvement of Negro public school teachers in Tennessee.* New York: Teachers College, Columbia University; Holmes, M. and Weiss, B. J. (1995). *Lives of women public school teachers: Scenes from American educational history.* New York: Garland.
36. Henry, A. (1998). *Taking back control: African Canadian women teachers' lives and practice.* Albany: State University of New York Press.
37. Osler, A. (1997). *The education and careers of black teachers: Changing identities, changing lives.* Buckingham, England: Open University Press.
38. Foster, M. (1997). *Black teachers on teaching.* New York: New Press; Ladson-Billings, G. (1994a). *The dreamkeepers: Successful teachers of African American children.* San Francisco: Jossey-Bass; and Walker, V. S. (1996). *Their highest potential.* Chapel Hill: North Carolina Press.
39. Walker, *Their highest potential.*
40. Foster, *Black teachers on teaching.*
41. Ladson-Billings, *The dreamkeepers.*
42. Fessler, Dynamics of teacher career stages; Huberman, Professional careers and professional development; and Vonk as cited in Fessler, Dynamics of teacher career stages.
43. Stephens, V. (1996). Learning noise. In D. Udall, D, and A. Mednick, eds., *Journeys through our classrooms* (pp. 67–75). Dubuque, IA: Kendall Hunt, p. 67.
44. Walker, *Their highest potential.*
45. Stephens, Learning noise, p. 68.
46. Fessler, Dynamics of teacher career stages, p.185.
47. Vonk, as cited in Fessler, Dynamics of teacher career stages, p. 176.
48. Fessler, Dynamics of teacher career stages.

49. Stephens, Learning noise, p. 73.
50. Ladson-Billings, *The dreamkeepers*, p. 17.
51. Ibid., pp. 17–18.
52. Cochran-Smith, Knowledge, skills, and experiences for teaching culturally diverse learners, p. 32.
53. Stephens, Learning noise, p. 69.

CHAPTER 6

1. Chall, J. S. (1996). *Learning to read: The great debate.* 3d ed. Fort Worth, TX: Harcourt Brace.
2. Ladson-Billings, G. (1992). Reading between the lines and beyond the pages: a culturally relevant approach to literacy teaching. *Theory into Practice* 31: 312–320; Siddle Walker, E. V. (1992). Falling asleep and failure among African-American students: Rethinking assumptions about process teaching. *Theory into Practice* 31: 321–335.
3. Gadsden, V. L. (1992). Giving meaning to literacy: Intergenerational beliefs about access. *Theory into Practice* 31: 328–335.
4. Irvine, J. J. (1990). *Black students and school failure: Policies, practices, and prescriptions.* New York: Greenwood Press.
5. Fine, M. (1991). *Framing dropouts: Notes on the politics of an urban public high school.* Albany, NY: State University of New York Press.
6. Harris, V. J. (1992). African American conceptions of literacy: A historical perspective. *Theory into Practice* 31: 276–286.
7. Gadsden, V. L. (1995). Introduction: Literacy among African-American youth: Legacy and struggle. In V. L. Gadsden and D. A. Wagner, eds., *Literacy among African-American youth: Issues in learning, teaching, and schooling* (pp. 1–12). Creskill, NJ: Hampton Press.
8. Delpit, L. (1996). *Other people's children: Cultural conflict in the classroom.* New York: The New Press.
9. See Fordham, S., and Ogbu, J. U. (1986). Black students' school success: Coping with the "burden of 'acting white'." *Urban Review* 18: 176–206.
10. Anderson, J. D. (1988). *The education of blacks in the South, 1860–1935.* Chapel Hill: University of North Carolina Press; Gadsden, Giving meaning to literacy; and Harris, African American conceptions of literacy.
11. Irvine, *Black students and school failure.*
12. Ibid.
13. Delpit, *Other people's children.*
14. Siddle Walker, Falling asleep and failure among African-American students.
15. Foster, M. (1992). Social linguistics and the African American community: Implications for literacy. *Theory into Practice* 31: 303–311.
16. Zeichner, K., Melnick, S., Gomez, M., eds. (1996). *Currents of reform in preservice teacher education.* New York: Teachers College Press.
17. Ladson-Billings, G. (1995). Toward a theory of culturally relevant pedagogy. *American Educational Research Journal* 32: 465–491.

18. Ladson-Billings, G. (1994a). *The Dreamkeepers: Successful teachers of African American children.* San Francisco: Jossey-Bass.
19. Ladson-Billings, Reading between the lines and beyond the pages.
20. Lee, C. D. (1995). A culturally based cognitive apprenticeship: Teaching African American high school students skills in literary interpretation. *Reading Research Quarterly* 30: 608–630.
21. For example, playing the dozens; see also Gates, H. L. (1992). *Loose canons: Notes on the culture wars.* New York: Oxford University Group; and Smitherman, G. (1986). *Talkin and testifyin: The language of black America.* Detroit: Wayne State University Press.
22. McDiarmid, G. W. (1991). What teachers need to know about cultural diversity: Restoring subject matter to the picture. In M. M. Kennedy, ed., *Teaching academic subjects to diverse learners* (pp. 257–269). New York: Teachers College Press; McDiarmid, G. W., Ball, D. L., and Anderson, C. W. (1989). Why staying one chapter ahead doesn't really work: Subject-specific pedagogy. In M. C. Reynolds, ed., *Knowledge base for the beginning teacher* (pp. 193–205). Oxford, England: Pergamon Press.
23. Obidah, J. E. (1998). Black-Mystory: Literate currency in everyday schooling. In D. Alverman, ed., *Reconceptualizing the literacies in adolescents' lives* (pp. 51–71). Prentice-Hall, NJ: Erlbaum.
24. Ladson-Billings, Reading between the lines and beyond the pages; and Ladson-Billings, Toward a theory of culturally relevant pedagogy.
25. Foster, M. (1997). *Black teachers on teaching.* New York: The New Press; Walker, V. S. (1996). *Their highest potential: An African American school community in the segregated South.* Chapel Hill, NC: University of North Carolina Press.
26. Irvine, *Black students and school failure.*
27. Freire, P. (1993). *Pedagogy of the oppressed.* New York: Continuum.

CHAPTER 7

1. Martin, J. R. (1995). A philosophy of education for the year 2000. *Phi Delta Kappan* 76(5): 355–359.
2. Institute for Education in Transformation. (1992). *Voices from the Inside.* (Claremont, CA: Claremont Graduate School.
3. Walker, V.S. (in press). Caring in a past time: Southern segregated schooling for African American children. In V. S. Walker and J. Snarey, eds., *Racing moral formation.* New York: Teachers College Press.
4. Collins, P. H. (1991). *Black feminist thought: Knowledge, consciousness, and the politics of empowerment.* New York: Routledge and Kegan Paul.
5. Pajares, M. F. (1992). Teachers' beliefs and educational research: Cleaning up a messy construct. *Review of Educational Research* 66(3): 543–578.
6. Lee, G. H. (1997). *Teacher efficacy: A research review.* Unpublished comprehensive review qualifying paper, Emory University, Division of Educational Studies, Atlanta, GA.
7. Johnson, S. T., and Prom-Jackson, S. The memorable teacher: Implications for teacher selection. *Journal of Negro Education* 55: 272–283.

8. Dyson, M. E. (1996). *Between god and gansta rap: Bearing witness to black culture.* New York: Oxford University Press.
9. Ibid., p. 128.
10. Irvine, J. J., and Hill, L. B. (1990). From plantation to school house: The rise and decline of black women teachers. *Humanity and Society* 14(3): 244–256.
11. Rickford, A. (1999). *I can fly.* Lanham, MD: University Press of America.
12. Ibid., p. 54.
13. Lipman, P. (1998). *Race, class, and power in school restructuring.* Albany, NY: State University of New York Press.
14. Walker, V. S. (1996). *Their highest potential.* Chapel Hill, NC: The University of North Carolina Press.
15. Vasquez, J. A., (1988). Contexts of learning for minority students. *Educational Forum* 56: 6–11.
16. Cooper, P. M. (2000). *Does race matter?* Unpublished comprehensive review qualifying paper, Emory University, Division of Educational Studies, Atlanta, GA.
17. Cole, B. P. (1986). The black educator: An endangered species. *Journal of Negro Education* 55: 326–334.
18. Ethridge, S. B. (1979). The impact of the 1954 Brown vs. Topeka Board of Education decision on black educators. *The Negro Educational Review* 30: 217–232.

BIBLIOGRAPHY

Abell, P. K. (1999). Recognizing and valuing differences: Process considerations. In E. R. Hollins and E. I. Oliver, eds., *Pathways to success in school: Culturally responsive teaching* (pp. 175–196). Mahwah, NJ: Lawrence Erlbaum.

Adler, P. (1977). Beyond cultural identity: Reflections upon cultural and multicultural man. In R. W. Brislin, ed., *Culture learning: Concepts, applications, and research* (pp. 22–41). Honolulu: University of Hawaii Press.

Allexsaht-Snider, M. (1996). Windows into diverse worlds: The telling and sharing of teachers' life histories. *Education and Urban Society* 29(1): 103–119.

Allinder, R. M. (1994). The relationship between efficacy and the instructional practices of special education teachers and consultants. *Teacher Education and Special Education* 17: 86–95.

Anderson, R., and Mitchener, C. (1989). Teachers' perspectives: Developing and implementing an STS curriculum. *Journal of Research in Science Teaching* 26(4): 351–369.

Anderson, J. D. (1988). *The education of blacks in the South, 1860–1935.* Chapel Hill: University of North Carolina Press.

Anderson, R., Greene, M., and Loewen, P. (1981). Relationships among teachers' and students' thinking skills, sense of efficacy, and student achievement. *Alberta Journal of Educational Research* 34(2): 148–165.

Anyon, J. (1997). *Ghetto schooling: A political economy of urban educational reform.* New York: Teachers College Press.

Armor, D. J., Conry-Oseguera, P., Cox, M. A., King, N., McDonnell, L. M., Pascal, A. H., Pauly, E., Zellman (1976). *Analysis of the school preferred reading program in selected Los Angeles minority schools.* Report R-2007-LAUSD. Santa Monica, CA: Rand.

Ashton, P. T. (1985). Motivation and the teacher's sense of efficacy. In C. Ames and R. Ames, eds., *Research on motivation in education: Vol. 2. The classroom milieu* (pp. 141–171). Orlando, FL: Academic Press.

Ashton, P. T., and Webb, R. B. (1986). *Making a difference: Teachers' sense of efficacy and student achievement.* New York: Longman.

Atkinson, D., Morten, G., and Sue, D. (1983). *Counseling American minorities: A cross-cultural perspective.* Dubuque, IA: William C. Brown.

Au, K. H. and Kawakami, A. J. (1994). Cultural congruence in instruction. In E. Hollins, J. King, and W. Hayman, eds., *Teaching diverse populations* (pp. 5–23). Albany, NY: SUNY Press.

Ayers, W. (1993). *To teach: The journey of a teacher.* New York: Teachers College Press.

Ayers, W. (1995). *To become a teacher.* New York: Teachers College Press.

Baker, S. (December 1982). *Characteristics of effective urban language arts teachers: An ethnographic study of retired teachers.* Paper presented at the meeting of the American Reading Forum, Sarasota, FL.

Baldwin, J. (1963). A talk to teachers. In W. Ayers and P. Ford, eds., *City kids, city teachers* (pp. 219–227). New York: New Press.

Ball, S. J. and Goodson, I. F. (1985). *Teachers' lives and careers.* Philadelphia: Falmer Press.

Bandura, A. (1977). Self-efficacy: Toward a unifying theory of behavioral change. *Psychological Review* 84: 191–215.

Bandura, A. (1986). *Social foundations of thought and action: A social cognitive theory.* Englewood Cliffs, NJ: Prentice Hall.

Bandura, A. (1997). *Self-efficacy: The exercise of control.* New York: Freeman.

Banks, J. A., and Banks, C. A. (1997). Reforming schools in a democratic pluralistic society. *Educational Policy* 11(2): 183–193.

Banks, J. A. (1994). *Multiethnic education: Theory and practice.* Needham Heights, MA: Allyn and Bacon.

Banks, J. A. and Banks, C. A. (1995) Multicultural education: Historical development, dimensions, and practice. In J. A. Banks and C. A. Banks, eds., *Handbook of research on multicultural education* (pp. 3–24). New York: Macmillan.

Banks, J. A. (1988). *Multiethnic education: Theory and practice.* 2d ed. Boston: Allyn and Bacon.

Banks, J. A. (2001). *Cultural diversity and education.* Boston, MA: Allyn and Bacon.

Behar-Horenstein, L. S., Pajares, F., and George, P. S. (1996). The effect of teachers' beliefs on students' academic performance during curriculum innovation. *The High School Journal* 79: 324–332.

Bennett, C. (1995). Preparing teachers for cultural diversity and national standards of academic excellence. *Journal of Teacher Education* 46: 259–266.

Bennett, C.I. (1999). *Comprehensive multicultural education.* Boston, MA: Allyn and Bacon.

Bennett, M. J. (1993). Towards ethnorelativism: A developmental model of intercultural sensitivity. In M. Paige, ed., *Education for the intercultural experience* (p. 56). Yarmouth, ME: Intercultural Press.

Bennett, J. (1993). Cultural marginality: Identity issues in training. In M. Paige, ed., *Cross-cultural orientation* (pp. 109–136). Lanham, MD: University Press of America.

Bennett, M. J. (1986). A developmental approach to training for intercultural sensitivity. *International Journal of Intercultural Relations* 10: 179–195.

Bennett, M. J. (1993). Towards ethnorelativism: A developmental model of intercultural sensitivity. In M. Paige, ed., *Education for the intercultural experience* (pp. 21–72). Yarmouth, ME: Intercultural Press.

Benz, C. R., Bradley, L., Alderman, M. K., and Flowers, M. A. (1992). Personal teaching efficacy: Developmental relationships in education. *Journal of Educational Research* 85: 274–285.

Berman, P., McLaughlin, M. W., Bass, G., Pauly, E., and Zellman, G. (1977). *Federal programs supporting educational change: Vol. VII, Factors affecting implementation and continuation.* Report R-1589/7-HEW. Santa Monica, CA: Rand.

Boykin, A. W. (1992). The triple quandary and the schooling of Afro-American children. In U. Neisser, *The school achievement of minority children: New perspectives* (pp. 59–70). Hillsdale, NJ: Lawrence Erlbaum.

Brooks, C. K. (1987). Teachers: Potent learning forces in the learning lives of black children. In Strickland, D. S. and Cooper, E. J., eds., *Educating black children: America's challenge.* Washington, D. C.: Bureau of Educational Research.

Brophy, J. E. (1985). Teacher-student interactions. In J. B. Dusek, ed. *Teacher expectations* (pp. 303–328). Hillsdale, NJ: Lawrence Erlbaum.

Brown, S. P., Parham, T. A., and Yonker, R. A. (1996). Influence of a cross-cultural training course on racial identity attitudes of white women and men: Preliminary perspectives. *Journal of Counseling and Development* 74: 510–516.

Bryk, T., Lee, V., and Holland. (1993). *Catholic schools and the common good.* Boston: Harvard University Press.

Burdell. P. and Swadener, B. B. (1999). Critical personal narrative and autoethnography in education: Reflections on a genre. *Educational Researcher* 28(6): 21–26.

Burke, P., Fessler, R., and Christensen, J. (1994). *Teacher career stages: Implications for staff development.* Bloomington, IN: Phi Delta Kappa.

Cadray, J. P. (1995). Enhancing multiculturalism in a teacher preparation program: A reflective analysis of a practitioner's intervention. *Dissertation Abstracts International,* 57(8): University Microfilms no. 9701563.

Cadray, J. P. (1995). *Enhancing multiculturalism in a teacher preparation program: A reflective analysis of a practitioner's intervention.* Ph.D. diss., University of New Orleans, New Orleans, LA.

Carney, C. G., and Kahn, K. B. (1984). Building competencies for effective cross-cultural counseling. *The Counseling Psychologist* 12: 111–119.

Carter, R. T., and Goodwin, A. L. (1994). Racial identity and education. In L. Darling-Hammond, ed., *Review of Research in Education, Vol. 20* (pp. 291–336). Washington, D.C.: American Education Research Association.

Chall, J. S. (1996). *Learning to read: The great debate.* 3d ed. Fort Worth, TX: Harcourt Brace.

Chester, M. D., and Beaudin, B. Q. (1996). Efficacy beliefs of newly hired teachers in urban schools. *American Educational Research Journal* 33: 233–257.

Cochran-Smith, M. (1995). Uncertain allies: Understanding the boundaries of race and teaching. *Harvard Educational Review* 65(4): 541–570.

Cochran-Smith, M. (November 1995). *Knowledge, skills, and experiences for teaching culturally diverse learners: A perspective for practicing teachers.* Paper presented at the Invitational conference on Defining the Knowledge Base for Urban Teacher Education, Emory University, Atlanta, GA.

Cochran-Smith, M. (1997). Knowledge, skills, and experiences for teaching culturally diverse learners: A perspective for practicing teachers. In J. J. Irvine, ed., *Critical knowledge for diverse teachers and learners* (pp. 27–87). Washington, D.C.: The American Association of Colleges for Teacher Education.

Cochran-Smith, M., and Lytle, S. L. (1995). *Inside/outside: Teacher research and knowledge.* New York: Teachers College.

Coladarci, T. (1992). Teachers' sense of efficacy and commitment to teaching. *Journal of Experimental Education* 60: 323–337.

Cole, D. B., and Ormond, J. E. (1995). Effectiveness of teaching pedagogical content knowledge through summer geography institutes. *Journal of Geography* 94: 427–433.

Cole, B. P. (1986). The black educator: An endangered species. *Journal of Negro Education* 55: 326–334.

Collins, P. H. (1991). *Black feminist thought: Knowledge, consciousness, and the politics of empowerment.* New York: Routledge and Kegan Paul.

Cooper. P. M. (2000). *Does race matter?* Unpublished comprehensive review qualifying paper, Emory University, Division of Educational Studies, Atlanta, GA.

Cox, B. B. (1982). *A research study focusing on Banks' stages of ethnicity typology as related to elementary teachers' multicultural experiences.* Ph.D. diss., University of Houston, Houston, TX.

Cross, W. E. (1978). The Thomas and Cross models of psychological nigrescence: A review. *Journal of Black Psychology* 5: 13–31.

Cross, W. E. (1995). In search of blackness and Afrocentricity: The psychology of black identity. In H. W. Herbert, J. C. Blue, and E. E. H. Griffeth, eds. *Racial and ethnic identity: Psychological development and creative expression* (pp. 53–72). New York: Routledge.

Cross, W. E., Strauss, L., and Fhagen-Smith, P. (1999). African American identity development across the life span: Educational implications. In R. H. Sheets and E. R. Hollins, eds. *Racial and ethnic identity in school practices* (pp. 29–48). Mahwah, NJ: Lawrence Erlbaum.

Cross, W.E. (presenter), and Oldershaw, B. (producer). (1993). *Shades of black : Diversity in African American identity* [videorecording]. North Amherst, MA : Microtraining Associates, Inc.

Darder, A. (1991). *Culture and power in the classroom.* Westport, CT: Bergin and Garvey.

Delpit, L. (1988). The silenced dialogue: Power and pedagogy in educating other people's children. *Harvard Educational Review* 58(3): 280–298.

Delpit, L. (1995). *Other people's children: cultural conflict in the classroom.* New York: The New Press.

Dembo, M. H., and Gibson, S. (1985). Teachers' sense of efficacy: An important factor in school improvement. *The Elementary School Journal* 86: 173–184.

Dyson, A. H. (1992). The case of the singing scientist: A performance perspective on the "stages" of school literacy. *Written Communication* 9(1): 3–47.

Dyson, A. H. (1995). The courage to write: Child meaning making in a contested world. *Language Arts* 72: 324–333.

Dyson, M. E. (1996) *Between god and gansta rap: Bearing witness to black culture.* New York: Oxford University Press.

Ethridge, S. B. (1979). The impact of the 1954 Brown vs. Topeka Board of Education decision on black educators. *The Negro Educational Review* 30: 217–232.

Fessler, R. (1995). Dynamics of teacher career stages. In T. R. Guskey and M., eds. *Professional development in education: New paradigms and practices* (pp. 171–192). New York: Teachers College.

Fessler, R. and Christensen, J. C. (1992). *The teacher career cycle: Understanding and guiding the professional development of teachers.* Boston: Allyn and Bacon.

Fine, M. (1991). *Framing dropouts: Notes on the politics of an urban public high school.* Albany, NY: State University of New York Press.

Fordham, S., and Ogbu, J. U. (1986). Black students' school success: Coping with the "burden of 'acting white.'" *Urban Review* 18: 176–206.

Foster, M. (1990). The politics of race: Through the eyes of African American teachers. *Journal of Education* 172(3): 123–141.

Foster, M. (1991). "Just got to find a way": Case studies of the lives and practice of exemplary black high school teachers. In M. Foster, ed., *Qualitative investigations into schools and schooling* (pp. 273–309). New York: Aims Press.

Foster, M. (1992). Social linguistics and the African American community: Implications for literacy. *Theory into Practice* 31: 303–311.

Foster, M. (1993). Self-portraits of black teachers: Narratives of individual and collective struggle against racism. In D. McLaughlin and W. G. Tierney, eds., *Many silenced lives: Personal narratives on the process of educational change* (pp. 155–175). New York: Routledge.

Foster, M. (1993a). Educating for competence in community and culture: Exploring the views of exemplary African American teachers. *Urban Education* 27: 370–394.

Foster, M. (1993b). Resisting racism: Personal testimonies of African American teachers. In L. Weiss and M. Fine, eds., *Silenced voices: Race and gender in today's schools.* Albany, NY: State University of New York Press.

Foster, M. (1993c). Urban African American teachers' views of organizational change: Speculations on the experiences of exemplary teachers. *Equity and Excellence in Education* 26(2): 16–24.

Foster, M. (1993d). *Resisting racism: Personal testimonies of African American teachers.* State University of New York, Albany: State University of New York Press.

Foster, M. (1994). Effective black teachers: A literature review. In E. Hollins, J. King, and W. Hayman, eds., *Teaching diverse populations: Formulating a knowledge base* (pp. 207–25). Albany: SUNY Press.

Foster, M. (1995). African American teachers and culturally relevant pedagogy. In J. Banks and C. Banks, eds., *Handbook of research on multicultural education* (pp. 570–581). New York: Macmillan.

Foster, M. (1997). *Black teachers on teaching.* New York: The New Press.

Freedman, S. G. (1998). A century of art on a blackboard canvas. *New York Times,* 17 May.

Freire, P. (1993). *Pedagogy of the oppressed.* New York: Continuum.

French, M. P. (1985). An inservice plan for teaching reading in kindergarten: A description. *Reading Horizons* 25(4): 264–267.

Gadsden, V. L. (1992). Giving meaning to literacy: Intergenerational beliefs about access. *Theory into Practice* 31: 328–335.

Gadsden, V. L. (1995). Introduction: Literacy among African-American youth: Legacy and struggle. In V. L. Gadsden and D. A. Wagner, eds., *Literacy among African-American youth: Issues in learning, teaching, and schooling* (pp. 1–12). Creskill, NJ: Hampton Press.

Gallagher, J. J. (1989). Research on secondary school science teachers' practices, knowledge and beliefs: A basis for restructuring. In Matayas, M., Tobin, K. and Fraser, B., eds., *Looking into windows: Qualitative research in science education* (pp. 43–57). Washington, D.C.: American Association for the Advancement of Science.

Gates, H. L. (1992). *Loose canons: Notes on the culture wars.* New York: Oxford University Group.

Gay, G. (1999). Ethnic identity development and multicultural education. In R. H. Sheets and E. R. Hollins, eds. *Racial and ethnic identity in school practices* (pp. 195–212). Mahwah, NJ: Lawrence Erlbaum.

Gibson, S., and Dembo, M. (1984). Teacher efficacy: A construct validation. *Journal of Educational Psychology* 36: 569–582.

Gillette, M., and Boyle-Baise, M. (April 1995). *Multicultural education at the graduate level: Assisting teachers in developing multicultural perspectives.* Paper presented at the annual meeting of the American Education Research Association, San Francisco, CA.

Glickman, C., and Tamashiro, R. (1982). A comparison of first-year, fifth-year, and former teachers on efficacy, ego development, and problem solving. *Psychology in Schools* 19: 558–562.

Gomez, M. L. (1996). Prospective teachers' perspectives on teaching "other people's children." In Zeichner, K., Melnick, S. and Gomez, M. L., eds. *Currents of reform in preservice teacher education* (pp. 109–131). New York: Teachers College, Columbia University.

Goodson, I. F. and Hargreaves, A., eds. (1996). *Teachers' professional lives.* Washington, D.C.: Falmer Press.

Goodson, I. F., ed. (1992). *Studying teachers' lives.* London: Routledge.

Gore, G. W. (1940). *In-service professional improvement of Negro public school teachers in Tennessee.* New York: Teachers College, Columbia University.

Grant, C. (1990). Urban teachers: Their new colleagues and the curriculum. *Phi Delta Kappan* 70(10): 764–770.

Grant, C., and Secada, W. G. (1990). Preparing teachers for diversity. In W. R. Houston, ed., *Handbook of research on teacher education* (pp. 403–422). New York: Macmillan.

Greeley, A. T., Garcia, V. L., Kessler, B. L., and Gilchrest, G. (1992). Training effective multicultural group counselors: Issues for a group training course. *The Journal for Specialists in Group Work* 17: 196–209.

Greene, M. (1986). In search of critical pedagogy for democratic alternatives. *Harvard Educational Review* 56: 427–441.

Greene, M. (1993). The passions of pluralism: Multiculturalism and the expanding community. *Educational Researcher* 22(1): 13–18.

Gregorc, A. F. (1973). Developing plans for professional growth. *NASSP Bulletin* 57: 1–8.

Guskey, T. R. (1984). The influence of change in instructional effectiveness upon the affective characteristics of teachers. *American Educational Research Journal* 21: 245–259.

Guskey, T. R. (1988). Teacher efficacy, self-concept, and attitudes toward the implementation of instructional innovation. *Teaching and Teacher Education* 4: 63–69.

Haberman, M. (1995). *Star teachers of children in poverty.* West Lafayette, IN: Kappa Delta Pi.

Harris, V. J. (1992). African American conceptions of literacy: A historical perspective. *Theory into Practice* 31: 276–286.

Helms, J. E. (1990). *Black and white racial identity: Theory, research, and practice.* New York: Greenwood Publishing Group.

Helms, J. E. (1984). Toward a theoretical explanation of the effects of race on counseling: A black and white model. *Counseling Psychologist* 12: 153–165.

Helms, J. E. (1994). The conceptualization of racial identity and other "racial" constructs. In E. Trickett, R. Watts, and D. Birman, eds., *Human diversity: Perspectives on people in context* (pp. 285–311). San Francisco: Jossey-Bass.

Helms, J. E., ed. (1990). *Black and white racial identity: Theory, research, and practice.* New York: Greenwood.

Henry, A. (1992). African Canadian women teachers' activism: Recreating communities of caring and resistance. *Journal of Negro Education* 61: 392–404.

Henry, A. (1994). The empty shelf and other curricular challenges of teaching children of African descent: Implications for teacher practice. *Urban Education* 29(3): 298–319.

Henry, A. (1998). *Taking back control: African Canadian women teachers' lives and practice.* Albany: State University of New York Press.

Hilliard, A. G. (1994). Teachers and cultural styles in a pluralist society. In B. Bigelow, L. Christensen, S. Karp, B. Miner, and B. Peterson, eds., *Rethinking our classrooms: Teaching for equity and justice* (pp. 127). Milwaukee, WI: Rethinking School.

Hilliard, A. G. (1994). Teachers and cultural styles in a pluralist society. In B. Bigelow, L. Christensen, S. Karp, B. Miner, and B. Peterson, eds., *Rethinking our classrooms: Teaching for equity and justice* (pp. 127). Milwaukee, WI: Rethinking Schools.

Hoffman, M. (1996). *Chasing hellhounds: A teacher learns from his students.* Minneapolis, MN: Milkweed Editions.

Hollins, E. R. (1996). *Culture in school learning: Revealing the deep meaning.* Mahwah, NJ: Lawrence Erlbaum.

Hollins, E. R. (1999). Relating ethnic and racial identity development to teaching. In R. H. Sheets and E. R. Hollins, eds. *Racial and ethnic identity in school practices* (pp. 183–194). Mahwah, NJ: Lawrence Erlbaum.

Hollins, E. R., King, J. E., and Hayman, W. C. (1994). *Teaching diverse populations: Formulating a knowledge base.* Albany, NY: SUNY Press.

Hollins, R. (1989). The Marva Collins story revisited: Implications for regular classroom instruction. In B. J. Shade, ed., *Culture, style, and the education proven* (pp. 321–329). Springfield, IL: Charles C. Thomas.

Holmes, M. and Weiss, B. J. (1995). *Lives of women public school teachers: Scenes from American educational history.* New York: Garland.

Hoover-Dempsey, K. V., Bassler, O. C., and Brissie, J. S. (1992). Explorations in parent-school relations. *Journal of Educational Research* 85: 287–294.

Horton, M. (1998). *The long haul: An autobiography.* New York: Teachers College Press.

Huberman, M. (1989). *La vie des enseignants* [The lives of teachers]. Switzerland: Delachaux and Niestle SA.

Huberman, M. (1995). Professional careers and professional development: Some intersections. In T. R. Guskey and M. Huberman, eds., *Professional development in education: New paradigms and practices* (pp. 193–224). New York: Teachers College, Columbia University.

Institute for Education in Transformation. (1992). *Voices from the Inside.* Claremont, CA: Claremont Graduate School.

Irvine, J. and Fraser, J. (1998). Warm demanders: Do national certification standards leave room for the culturally responsive pedagogy of African-American teachers? *Education Week,* 13 May, p. 42.

Irvine, J. and Foster, M., eds. (1995). *Growing up African American in Catholic schools.* New York: Teachers College Press.

Irvine, J. (1989). Beyond role models: An examination of cultural influences on the pedagogical perspectives of black teachers. *Peabody Journal of Education* 66(4): 51–63.

Irvine, J. J. (April 1988). *Teacher race as a factor in black students' achievement.* Paper presented at the meeting of the American Educational Research Association, New Orleans.

Irvine, J. J. (1990). *Black students and school failure: Policies, practices, and prescriptions.* New York: Greenwood Press.

Irvine, J. J., and Hill, L. B. (1990) From plantation to school house: The rise and decline of black women teachers. *Humanity and Society* 14(3): 244–256.

Irvine, R., and Irvine J. (1983). The impact of the desegregation process on the education of black students: Key variables. *Journal of Negro Education* 52: 410–422.

Jaworski, B. (1991). Develop your teaching. *Mathematics in School* 20(1): 18–21.

Johnson, S. T., and Prom-Jackson, S. The memorable teacher: Implications for teacher selection. *Journal of Negro Education* 55: 272–283.

Jones, W. T. (1990). Perspectives on ethnicity. In L. Moore, ed., *Evolving theoretical perspectives on students* (pp. 59–72). San Francisco: Jossey-Bass.

Jussim, L. (1986). Self-fulfilling prophecies: A theoretical and integrative review. *Psychological Review* 93: 429–445.

Kagan, D. M. (1992). Implications of research on teacher belief. *Educational Psychologist* 27: 65–90.

Kailin, J. (1994). Anti-racist staff development for teachers: Considerations of race, class, and gender. *Teaching and Teacher Education* 10(2): 169–184.

Katz, L. G. (1972). Development stages of preschool teachers. *Elementary School Journal* 3: 50–54.

Kelble, E. S. (1994). Enhancing physical science instruction for gifted elementary students: Developing teacher confidence and skills. *Roeper Review* 16(3): 162–166.

King, J. (1991). Unfinished business: Black students' alienation and black teacher's emancipatory pedagogy. In M. Foster, ed., *Qualitative investigations into schools and schooling* (pp. 245–271). New York: AMS Press.

King, J. E. (1994). The purpose of schooling for African-American children. In Hollins, King, and Hayman, eds., *Teaching diverse populations* (pp. 25–56). Albany, NY: SUNY Press.

King, S. H. (1993). The limited presence of African-American teachers. *Review of Educational Research* 63(2): 115–149.

Kleinfeld, J., McDiarmid, G. W., Grubis, S., and Parrett, W. (1983). Doing research on effective cross-cultural teaching: The teacher tale. *Peabody Journal of Education* 61(1): 86–108.

Kohl, H. (1967). *36 children*. New York: New American Library.

Kohl, H. (1998). *The discipline of hope*. New York: Simon and Schuster.

Kozol, J. (1967). *Death at an early age*. New York: Plume.

Krater, J., Zeni, J., and Cason, N. D. (1994). *Mirror images: Teaching writing in black and white*. Portsmouth, NH: Heinemann.

Ladson-Billings, G. (1989). A tale of two teachers: Exemplars of successful pedagogy of black students. Paper presented at the Educational Equality Project Colloquium, "Celebrating Diversity: Knowledge, Teachers, and Teaching," New York.

Ladson-Billings, G. (1992). Reading between the lines and beyond the pages: A culturally relevant approach to literacy teaching. *Theory into Practice* 31: 312–320.

Ladson-Billings, G. (1994a). *The dreamkeepers: Successful teachers of African American children*. San Francisco: Jossey-Bass.

Ladson-Billings, G. (1994b). Who will teach our children?: Preparing teachers to successfully teach African American students. In E. Hollins, J. King, and W. Hayman, eds., *Teaching diverse populations*. Albany, NY: SUNY Press.

Ladson-Billings, G. (1995). Toward a theory of culturally relevant pedagogy. *American Educational Research Journal* 32: 465–491.

Lawrence, S. M., and Tatum, B.D. (1997a). Teachers in transition: The impact of anti-racist professional development on classroom practice. *Teachers College Record* 99: 162–178.

Lawrence, S. M., and Tatum, B.D. (1997b). White educators as allies: Moving from awareness to action. In M. Fine, L. Weiss, L. Powell, and M. Wong, eds., *Off white: Critical perspectives on race* (pp. 332–342). New York: Routledge.

Lawrentz, F. (1985). Impact of a five-week energy education program on teacher beliefs and attitudes. *School Science and Mathematics* 85(1): 27–36.

Lee, C. D. (1995). A culturally based cognitive apprenticeship: Teaching African American high school students skills in literary interpretation. *Reading Research Quarterly* 30: 608–630.

Lee, G. H. (1997). *Teacher efficacy: A research review.* Unpublished comprehensive review qualifying paper, Emory University, Division of Educational Studies, Atlanta, GA.

Lee, V., Dedick, R., and Smith, J. (1991). The effect of the social organization of schools on teachers' efficacy and satisfaction. *Sociology of Education* 64: 190–208.

Lipman, P. (1995). "Bringing out the best in them": The contribution of culturally relevant teachers to educational reform. *Theory Into Practice* 34(3): 202–208.

Lipman, P. (1998) *Race, class, and power in school restructuring.* Albany, NY: State University of New York Press.

Loevinger, J. (1976). *Ego development: Conceptions and theories.* San Francisco: Jossey Bass.

Martin, H. J., and Atwater, M. M. (1992). *The stages of ethnicity of preservice teachers and in-service personnel involved in multicultural education experiences.* ERIC Document Reproduction Services no. ED 397 203.

Martin, J. R. (1995). A philosophy of education for the year 2000. *Phi Delta Kappan* 76(5): 355–359.

Martin, R. (1995). *Practicing what we preach: Confronting diversity in teacher education.* Albany, NY: State University of New York Press.

McAllister, G. and Irvine, J. J. (2000). Cross cultural competency and multicultural teacher education. *Review of Educational Research* 70: 3–24.

McAllister, G. (1999). *Urban teachers' beliefs about culture and the relationship of those beliefs to their practice.* Ph.D. diss., Emory University, Atlanta.

McDiarmid, G. W. (1991). What teachers need to know about cultural diversity: Restoring subject matter to the picture. In M. M. Kennedy, ed., *Teaching academic subjects to diverse learners* (pp. 257–269). New York: Teachers College Press.

McDiarmid, G. W., Ball, D. L., and Anderson, C. W. (1989). Why staying one chapter ahead doesn't really work: Subject-specific pedagogy. In M. C. Reynolds, ed., *Knowledge base for the beginning teacher* (pp. 193–205). Oxford, England: Pergamon Press.

McIntyre, A. (1997). *Making meaning out of whiteness: Exploring racial identity with white teachers.* Albany, NY: SUNY Press.

Meier, D. (1995). *The power of their ideas: Lessons from a small school in Harlem.* Boston: Beacon Press.

Meier, K. J., Stewart, J., and England, R. E. (1989). *Race, class and education: The politics of second generation discrimination.* Madison, WI: University of Wisconsin Press.

Meyers, L. J., Speight, S. L., Highlen, P. S., Chickaco, I. C., Reynolds, A. L., Adams, E. M., and Hanley, C. P. (1991). Identity development and world view: Toward an optimal conceptualization. *Journal of Counseling and Development* 70: 54–63.

Mezirow, J. (1978). Perspective transformation. *Adult Education* 28: 100–110.

Midgley, C., Feldlaufer, H., and Eccles, J. S. (1989). Change in teacher efficacy and student self- and task-related beliefs in mathematics during the transition to junior high school. *Journal of Educational Psychology* 81: 247–258.

Miner, B. (1997). "Embracing Ebonics and teaching standard English." In Delpit, L. and Perry, T., eds., *Rethinking schools: The real Ebonics debate*. Milwaukee, WI: Rethinking Schools Limited.

Miskel, C., McDonald, D., and Bloom, S. (1983). Structural and expectancy linkages within schools and organizational effectiveness. *Educational Administration Quarterly* 19(1): 49–82.

Moore, W. and Esselman, M. (April 1992). *Teacher efficacy, power, school climate and achievement: A desegregating district's experience*. Paper presented at the Annual Meeting of the American Educational Research Association, San Francisco.

National Education Association. (1996). NEA today: *Status of the American public school teacher 1995–1996*. West Haven, CT: NEA Professional Library.

Nelson, R. F. (1997). *Teaching student teachers how to promote cultural awareness in urban and suburban schools*. Paper presented at the Annual Meeting of the American Association of Colleges for Teacher Education, Phoenix, AZ.

Neville, H. A., Heppner, J. J., Louie, C. E., and Thompson, C. I. (1996). The impact of multicultural training on white racial identity attitudes and therapy competencies. *Professional Psychology: Research and Practice* 27: 83–89.

Nieto, S., and Rolon, C. (November 1995). *The preparation and professional development of teachers: A perspective from two Latinas*. Paper presented at the invitational conference on Defining the Knowledge Base for Urban Teacher Education, Emory University, Atlanta, GA.

Noblit, G. W. (1993). Power and caring. *American Education Research Journal* 30: 23–38.

Noddings, N. (1984). *Caring: A feminine approach to ethics and moral education*. Los Angeles: University of California Press.

Noddings, N. (1992). *The challenge to care in schools: An alternative approach to education*. New York: Teachers College Press.

Oakes, J. (1986). Keeping track, part 2: Curriculum inequality and school reform. *Phi Delta Kappan* 68: 148–151.

Oakes, J. (1996). Making the rhetoric real. *Multicultural Education* 4(2): 4–10.

Obidah, J. E. (1998). Black-Mystory: Literate currency in everyday schooling. In D. Alverman, ed., *Reconceptualizing the literacies in adolescents' lives* (pp. 51–71). Prentice-Hall, NJ: Erlbaum.

O'Connor, S. (1996). *Will my name be shouted out?: Reaching inner city students through writing*. New York: Simon and Schuster.

Olson, L. (2000). Finding and keeping competent teachers. *Education Week* 19(18): 12–18.

Osler, A. (1997). *The education and careers of black teachers: Changing identities, changing lives*. Buckingham, England: Open University Press.

Ottavi, T. M., Pope-Davis, D. B., and Dings, J. G. (1994). Relationship between white racial identity attitudes and self-reported multicultural counseling competencies. *Journal of Counseling Psychology* 41: 149–154.

Paige, M. (1993). On the nature of intercultural experiences and intercultural education. In M. Paige, ed., *Cross-cultural orientation* (pp. 1–21). Lanham, MD: University Press of America.

Pajares, F. (1992). Teachers' beliefs and educational research: Cleaning up a messy construct. *Review of Educational Research* 62: 307–332.

Pajares, F. (1996). Self-efficacy beliefs in academic settings. *Review of Educational Research* 66: 543–578.

Pajares, F. (1997). Current directions in self-efficacy research. In P. R. Pintrich and M. Maehr, eds., *Advances in motivation and achievement*. Vol. 10 (pp.1–49). Greenwich, CT: JAI.

Paley, V. G. (1979). *White teacher*. Cambridge, MA: Harvard University Press.

Paley, V. G. (1995). *Kwanzaa and me: A teacher's story*. Cambridge, MA: Harvard University Press.

Paley, V. G. (1997). *The girl with the brown crayon*. Cambridge, MA: Harvard University Press.

Parham, T. A. (1989). Cycles of psychological nigrescence. *The Counseling Psychologist* 17(2): 187–226.

Pascal, A. H., Pauly, E., Zellman. (1976). *Analysis of the school preferred reading program in selected Los Angeles minority schools*. Report R-2007-LAUSD. Santa Monica, CA: Rand.

Phinney, J. S. (1990). Ethnic identity in adolescents and adults: Review of research. *Psychological Bulletin* 108: 499–514.

Podell, D. M., and Soodak, L. C. (1993). Teacher efficacy and bias in special education referrals. *Journal of Educational Research* 96: 247–253.

Pollard, A., and Tann, S. (1987). *Reflective teaching in the primary school*. London: Cassell Education Limited.

Ponterotto, J. G. (1988). Racial consciousness development among white counselor trainees: A stage model. *Journal of Multicultural Counseling and Development* 16: 146–156.

Prosser, M. H. (1978). *The cultural dialogue: An introduction to intercultural communication*. Boston: Houghton Mifflin.

Rich, Y., Lev, S., and Rischer, S. (1996). Extending the concept and assessment of teacher efficacy. *Educational and Psychological Measurement* 56: 1015–1025.

Rickford, A. (1999). *I can fly*. Lanham, MD: University Press of America.

Rios, F. A. (1996). *Teacher thinking in cultural contexts*. Albany, NY: State University of New York Press.

Rist, R. C. (1970). Student social class and teacher expectations: The self-fulfilling prophecy in ghetto education. *Harvard Educational Review* 40(3): 411–451.

Root, M. P. (2000). Rethinking racial identity development. In P. Spickard and W. J. Burroughs, eds., *We are a people: Narrative and multiplicity in constructing ethnic identity* (pp. 205–220). Philadelphia: Temple University.

Rose, J. S., and Medway, F. J. (1981). Measurement of teachers' beliefs in their control over student outcome. *Journal of Educational Research* 74: 185–190.

Ross, J. A. (1992). Teacher efficacy and the effect of coaching on student achievement. *Canadian Journal of Education* 17: 51–56.

Ross, J. A. (June 1994). *Beliefs that make a difference: The origins and impacts of teacher efficacy.* Paper presented at the annual meeting of the Canadian Association for Curriculum Studies, Calgary, Alberta, Canada.

Ross, J. A., and Cousins, J. B. (1993). Enhancing secondary school students' acquisition of correlational reasoning skills. *Research in Science and Technological Education* 11(3): 191–206.

Sabnani, H. B., Ponterotto, J. G., and Borodovsky. (1991). White racial identity development and cross-cultural counselor training: A stage model. *The Counseling Psychologist* 19: 76–102.

Saklofske, D. H., Michaluk, J. O., and Randhawa, B. S. (1988). Teachers' efficacy and teaching behaviors. *Psychological Report* 63: 407–414.

Scheurich, J. J. (1993) Toward a white discourse on white racism. *Educational Researcher* 24(8): 5–16.

Schon, D. (1987). *Educating the reflective practitioner: Toward a new design of teaching and learning professionals.* San Francisco, CA: Jossey-Bass.

Schunk, D. H. (1989). Self-efficacy and cognitive skill learning. In C. Ames and R. Ames, eds., *Research on motivation in education: Vol. 3: Goals and cognitions* (pp. 13–44). San Diego, CA: Academic Press.

Sherman, H. and Thomas, J. (1995). Professional development: Teachers' communication and collaboration—keys to student achievement. *Mathematics Teaching in the Middle School* 1(6): 30–32.

Shulman, L. S. (1987). Knowledge and teaching: Foundations of the new reform. *Harvard Educational Review* 57: 1–22.

Siddle Walker, E. V. (1992). Falling asleep and failure among African-American students: Rethinking assumptions about process teaching. *Theory into Practice* 31: 321–335.

Slavin, R. (1995). Cooperative learning and intergroup relations. In Banks, J., and Banks, C., eds., *Handbook of research on multicultural education* (pp. 628–634). New York: MacMillan.

Sleeter, C. (1992). *Keepers of the American dream: A study of staff development and multicultural education.* Washington, D.C.: Falmer.

Sleeter, C. E. (1993). How white teachers construct race. In C. McCarthy and W. Crichlow, eds., *Race, identity, and representation in education* (pp. 157–171). New York: Routledge.

Smith, A. J. (1983). *The relationship of teachers' preparedness in multicultural education to levels of ethnic awareness and multicultural exposure among elementary school certificated personnel.* Ph.D. diss., University of Washington, Pullman, WA.

Smitherman, G. (1986). *Talkin and testifyin: The language of black America.* Detroit: Wayne State University Press.

Solomon, R. P. (1995). Beyond prescriptive pedagogy: Teacher inservice education for cultural diversity. *Journal of Teacher Education* 46(4): 251–258.

Sparks, D. (April 1997). Student success requires caring, standards, beliefs in student abilities. *The Developer: 2.*

Speck, M. (1996). Best practice in professional development for sustained educational change. *ERS Spectrum* 4(2): 38.

Stanford, G. C. (April 1995). *African American pedagogy: Needed perspectives for urban education.* Paper presented at the annual meeting of American Educational Research Association, San Francisco, CA.

Stanford, G. (1998). African-American teachers' knowledge of teaching: Understanding the influence of their remembered teachers. *The Urban Review* 30(3): 229–243.

Stevens, V. (1996). Learning noise. In D. Udall, D, and A. Mednick, eds., *Journeys through our classrooms* (pp. 67–75). Dubuque, IA: Kendall Hunt.

Tatum, B. D. (1992). Talking about race, learning about racism: The application of racial identity development theory in the classroom. *Harvard Educational Review* 62: 1–24.

Tatum, B. D. (1997). *Why are all the black kids sitting together in the cafeteria?: And other conversations about race.* New York: Basic Books.

Taylor, T. Y. (1994). *A study of the effectiveness of a cognitive-developmental program to promote cross-cultural sensitivity among employees.* Ph.D. diss., North Carolina State University, Asheville, NC.

Tillema, H. H. (1994). Training and professional experience: Bridging the gap between new information and pre-existing beliefs of teachers. *Teaching and Teacher Education* 10(6): 601–615.

Toliver, K. (1993). The Kay Toliver mathematics program. *Journal of Negro Education* 62: 35–46.

Tomlinson, L. M. (1996a). *Applying Banks' typology of ethnic identity development and curriculum goals to story content: Classroom discussion, and the ecology of classroom and community: Phase one, instructional resource no. 24.* University of Georgia, National Reading Research Center.

Tomlinson, L. M. (1996b). *Teachers' applications of Banks' typology of ethnic identity development and curriculum goals to story context and classroom discussion: Phase two, instructional resource no. 35.* University of Georgia, National Reading Research Center.

Trentham, L., Silvern, S., and Brogdon, R. (1985). Teacher efficacy and teacher competency ratings. *Psychology in the Schools* 22: 343–352.

Tschannen-Moran, M., Woolfolk Hoy, A., and Hoy, W. K. (1998). Teacher efficacy: Its meaning and measure. *Review of Educational Research* 68: 202–248.

Turner, D. (1990). *Assessing intercultural sensitivity of American expatriates in Kuwait.* Masters thesis, Portland State University, Portland, OR.

Unruh, A., and Turner, H. E. (1970). *Supervision for change and innovation.* Boston: Houghton Mifflin.

Vasquez, J. A. (1988). Contexts of learning for minority students. *Educational Forum* 56: 6–11.

Villegas, A. M. (1991). Culturally responsive pedagogy for the 1990s and beyond. *Trends and Issues Paper No. 6.* Washington D.C.: ERIC Clearinghouse on Teacher Education.

Villegas, A. M. (1991). *Culturally responsive pedagogy for the 1990s.* Princeton, NJ: Educational Testing Service.

Walker, V. S. (1996). *Their highest potential: An African American school community in the segregated South.* Chapel Hill, NC: University of North Carolina Press.

Walker, V. S. (In press). Caring in a past time: Southern segregated schooling for African American children. In V. S. Walker and J. Snarey, eds., *Racing moral formation.* New York: Teachers College Press.

Walsted, W. B. (1980). The impact of "trade-offs" and teacher training on economic understanding and attitudes. *Journal of Economic Education* 12(1): 41–48.

Webster, L. (1997). *Looking back and thinking forward: Reexaminations of teaching and schooling.* New York: Teachers College Press.

Westheimer, J., and Kahne, J. (1993). Building school communities: An experience-based model. *Phi Delta Kappan* 75: 324–328.

Whitehead, A. N. (1929). *The aims of education and other essays.* New York: Macmillan.

Widick, C., Knefelkamp, and Parker, C. A. (1975). The counselor as a developmental instructor. *Counselor Education and Supervision* 14: 286–296.

Williams, B., ed. (1996). *Closing the achievement gap: A vision for changing beliefs and practices.* Alexandria, VA: ASCD.

Wilson, Catherine. (2000). *Telling a different story: Teaching and literacy in an urban preschool.* New York: Teachers College Press.

Wolfe, L. J. (1996). *The effectiveness of an inservice geography institute on participating teachers.* Unpublished paper presented at the meeting of the National Council for Geographic Education, Santa Barbara, CA.

Woolfolk, A. E., and Hoy, W. K. (1990). Prospective teachers' sense of efficacy and beliefs about control. *Journal of Educational Psychology* 82: 81–91.

Woolfolk, A. E., Rosoff, B., and Hoy, W. K. (1990). Teachers' sense of efficacy and their beliefs about managing students. *Teacher and Teacher Education* 6: 137–148.

York, D. E. (1994). *Cross-cultural training programs.* Westport, CN: Bergin and Garvey.

York, D. E. (1995). The academic achievement of African Americans in Catholic schools: A review of the literature. In J. Irvine and M. Foster, eds., *Growing up African American in Catholic schools* (pp. 11–46). New York: Teachers College Press.

Zeichner, K. and Melnick, S. (1996). The role of community field experiences in preparing teachers for cultural diversity. In Zeichner, K., Melnick, S. and Gomez, M. L., eds., *Currents of reform in preservice teacher education* (pp. 176–195). New York: Teachers College Press.

Zeichner, K., Melnick, S., Gomez, M., eds. (1996). *Currents of reform in preservice teacher education.* New York: Teachers College Press.

Zeldin, A. L., and Pajares, F. (2000). Against the odds: Self-efficacy beliefs of women in mathematical, scientific, and technological careers. *American Educational Research Journal* 37: 215–246.

Zimpher, N. L. and Ashburn, E. A. (1992). Countering parochialism in teacher candidates. In M. E. Dilworth, ed., *Diversity in teacher education: New expectations* (pp. 40–62). San Francisco: Jossey-Bass.

NOTES ON CONTRIBUTORS

KIM NESTA ARCHUNG, doctoral candidate at Emory University, is a co-founder and a former teacher at Paige Academy, an independent African-centered school in Boston. Her experiences include teacher professional development in both national and international settings. Kim's research specialty is culturally responsive/multicultural professional development of teachers.

BEVERLEY COCKERHAM is a teacher and former principal in the Decatur City Schools (GA). She received her undergraduate and graduate degrees from City College of New York.

PATRICIA M. COOPER, Emory University graduate, is an assistant professor of Language Arts at Hofstra University. Her research focus is the intersection of schooling, early literacy, and home culture. She is also the founder and former director of the Rice University School Literacy and Culture Project in Houston, and a former preschool and elementary school teacher.

JAMES FRASER is the dean of the School of Education at Northeastern University in Boston and professor of History and Education. His books include *Freedom's Plow: Teaching in Multicultural Classrooms* (with Theresa Perry), *Reading Writing, and Justice,* and *Between Church and State.*

JACQUELINE JORDAN IRVINE is the Charles Howard Candler Professor of Urban Education in the Division of Educational Studies at Emory University. She received the Outstanding Writing Award from the American Association of Colleges of Teacher Education, Distinguished Career Award from the Black Special Interest Group of the American Education Research Association, an award from the Association for Supervision and Curriculum Development for exemplary contributions to the education of African American children, and the 2000 Dewitt-Wallace/American Educational Research Association Lecture Award.

MARIA LEONORA LOCKABY KARUNUÑGAN, former high school teacher, is a doctoral candidate and teaching fellow at Emory University specializing in comparative and multicultural education. Her area of specialization is the civic and cultural identity development of Filipino American youth.

GLORIA HARPER LEE, principal of Winnona Park Elementary School in Decatur, Georgia, is a graduate of Emory University. She is a former teacher and central office administrator.

GRETCHEN MCALLISTER, a former middle school educator, is a graduate of Emory University. Currently an assistant professor at Northern Arizona University, she teaches elementary education methods and bilingual education courses. Her areas of specialization include multicultural teacher education and the role of empathy in developing democratic citizens.

VIVIAN STEPHENS retired from the City Schools of Decatur. She is a graduate of Spelman College and received a Masters in Elementary Education from Georgia State University. In 1990, Vivian was awarded the National Milliken Educator Award. Currently she works as a teacher-mentor at Georgia State University.

FRANITA WARE is a lecturer at Spelman College and a doctoral candidate at Emory University. She is a former elementary teacher and professional development consultant. Her research focus investigates African American teachers as culturally responsive pedagogists.

PATRICIA WHITE is a retired Title 1 teacher in the Atlanta Public Schools. She is a graduate of Clark Atlanta University and Georgia State University.